Modern Fly-Tying Materials

Modern Fly-Tying Materials

by
Dick Talleur

LYONS & BURFORD, PUBLISHERS

Printed in the United States of America

Design by M.R.P.

Color insert photographs by Tim Savard.

10 9 8 7 6 5 4 3 2 1

Library of Congress Cataloging-in-Publication Data
Talleur, Richard W.
   Modern fly-tying materials / by Dick Talleur.
   p.   cm.
   Includes bibliographical references and index.
   ISBN 1-55821-344-9
   1. Fly-tying—Equipment and supplies.   I. Title.
   SH451.T2915   1995
   688.7'912—dc20   94-44660
                                            CIP

To everyone in fly fishing—
manufacturer, distributor, retailer,
guide, publisher, writer, fly tyer, or simply angler.
You make it possible for me to earn a living
doing something I love, and for this
I sincerely thank you.

Contents

Introduction

I began tying flies around 1959, for two reasons: to save money (flies cost 20 to 30 cents apiece, big bucks!) and to enhance my supply and its quality. Never did I dream that from these simple beginnings would evolve a life style and, at least in part, a way of making a living!

The first year or two, my entire kit, vise and all, would have fit into a couple of shoe boxes. Then a few desk drawers. Then the whole desk. Thirty years down the road, I spent over $5,000 on special cabinetry, just to hold and properly organize all my stuff—and it's *still* not enough. What's next? A fly-tyer's house, perhaps?

Hardly a week goes by that I'm not introduced to some new material or component. When I'm on the road at consumer and trade shows, I see an ever-growing array of stuff—some innovative, some improved, some simply "me-too's." There are many newly developed items that make tying easier, encourage innovation, contribute to strength and structure and represent significant improvements. Others are of more limited value. There is an enormous amount of duplication and redundancy or at least there's a ton of stuff that is very much alike in appearance. But is it really the same, from a tying and fishing standpoint? A good question.

Yes, things have gotten very complicated. For several years I've been hearing moans and groans, some of which have emanated from me. But essentially, the themes are the same: What is this stuff? What's it good for? How does it stack up against similar stuff? How do I use it? What problems does it solve and/or create? What are its positive and negative attributes? And last, but hardly least, Will the fish like it?

Which brings me to what I perceive as a serious problem with fly-tying materials in general and, in particular, with new and novel materials. Like life itself, they often come without instructions. On my scavenger hunts in fly shops and at various shows, I've found all sorts of stuff with seductive names and enticing appearances, but no information on usage or application. The average tyer has problems enough working to master technique, and getting his or her flies to come out as hoped. Trying to decipher the hyperbole on packages of materials and figure out what the contents might be used for can be a nightmare.

Even worse than no information is inaccurate information. In several cases, I tried out materials that had instructions for executing various procedures. The trouble was, they didn't work. I have to wonder if the materials and applications described were subjected to the acid tests of tying, casting, and fishing prior to being put on the market.

I would urge suppliers to include detailed, accurate instructions with their materials. Not only would this help the tyers, it would help sell the products. I couldn't begin to guess how many times I've watched a tyer staring in utter shock at a display of materials. Soon, eyes glaze over and the person walks to the next rack and buys a bag of hare's ear dubbing, or something that at least gives a feeling of comfort and certainty.

Catchy names are fine. I have no problem with them. But that's *all* they are, catchy! Seldom do they convey any meaningful information, or provide assistance and guidance to the tyer. And talk about redundant! I wish I had a dollar for every time I read the word "super" while working on this book.

This book attempts to deal with these sorts of questions, and seeks to clear up as much confusion as can be addressed in a single volume. Does it cover absolutely everything? No, that's an impossibility. But it does try to cover the most critical points, and to help the tyer develop a rationale for selecting materials. There are now some specialized books—for example, Phil Camera's *Fly Tying with Synthetics*—that go into great depth on their particular subjects. I have used such books for research, and rather than repeat what they have described, I'll refer my readers to them as appropriate.

While writing this book, I had to keep certain things in mind, and while reading it, so must you. The fly-fishing/fly-tying business is, for those who make a living in it, exactly that—a business. It is subject to the same dynamics as any modern business: constant change, short product life cycles, unannounced competition coming out of nowhere, leapfrog technology, and product copying. I also find that products get into the marketplace without having been validated by sufficient tying and fishing experience and field-testing. And though I would say our ethics compare favorably with just about any other field I can think of, one should not be so naive as to assume that all of the claims for a particular product are gospel, and that one's tying and fishing success will automatically be enhanced. When I think about the amount of stuff I had to examine, experiment with, tie with, cast with, and fish with, in order to write this book, I can say that there is no way that I could have fished enough, in a sufficient variety of situations, to field-test everything adequately. If I had tried to take that route, the book would have been ten years in the writing, and much of it would have been dated if not obsolete by the time it came out. Also, my publisher, Nick Lyons, would have had me jailed for breach of contract!

And just how do you test a material in the angling environment? How much fishing, by whom, under what sort of conditions, and for what type of fish? For example, one evening I took some dry flies to a stream not far from my home in Manchester, New Hampshire. My objective was more a matter of seeing how they cast, floated, and behaved, rather than how well they caught fish. It was a pleasant, mid-spring evening. Caddis started coming around 6:30 and later there were some spinners from an earlier mayfly hatch. So in addition to having a stream to work in, I had a bunch of rising trout.

But what about these trout? They were hatchery rainbows of nine to eleven inches, stocked only a couple of days earlier. They took everything I threw at them. Was this a valid test? Hardly. But neither would it be fair if I were on a different sort of river, where there were, let's say, wild brown trout, and they refused all or most of the flies. It might have been the manner in which I was presenting them. It might have been that I had a poor match for the naturals. It might have been simply a case of mean-spirited, jaded trout, who watch six fly shops pass over their heads every Saturday.

Now, if I had a week to fish that river, and could demonstrate to my satisfaction that flies tied with certain materials were taken in overwhelming preference to similar flies tied with other materials, then I'd be in a position to make a definitive statement. True, that would still be classified as anecdotal knowledge, but once you have enough consistent experiential data, it begins to have meaning and validity.

As for tying itself, I have relied on the sum total of thirty-five years at the vise, plus all that I've learned from teaching the craft to a great many people, and studying under the tutelage of some outstanding practitioners. Also, I spent many hours at the vise, running materials through various tests and exercises. That, essentially, is how the information for this book was developed.

At this point, I want to express particular gratitude to George Kesel, who works at Hunter's Fly Shop in New Boston, New Hampshire. George is a truly excellent fly tyer, and a widely diversified one. He ties a lot of patterns that I don't. He also sees everything that passes through the shop, including the flies of some very talented customers. And on top of all that, he fishes a lot.

George was good enough to go through the entire manuscript, and his observations and suggestions were most valuable. It was a lot of extra work for an already busy guy, and I want to state for the record that his work is highly appreciated.

One of my problems in writing this book has been the unavoidable involvement with brand names, and the frequent necessity of making direct comparisons. I wish I could leave this entirely to the marketers and advertisers. The problem is that things constantly change; new stuff comes on, old stuff disappears or is altered and (hopefully) improved. I could describe an undesirable attribute in some product, and by the time the book is published, the defect could be corrected, and I'm stuck with an outdated critique. How, other than by mentioning product names, can I identify and compare products, and relate them to photographs? There has to be some tangible frame of reference. But please don't try to use this book as a catalog, because I'm not trying to write it that way. Change is constant and accelerating, and certainly materials will come and go even before this work is printed. I'm aware that I lightly chided the suppliers a few paragraphs ago about redundancy. But let me also say this: you'll probably get as tired of reading the caveat, "At this writing" as I did of using it. But that's life in the fast-changing materials lane!

Where possible, I focus on functional analogies that assess materials against a norm, or standard, such standards having been established by my experiences with the various materials available in a particular category. Obviously, in this imperfect world, there will be trade-offs. One material will be better than another in certain respects, but not as good in others. A perfect example is tinsel; the Mylar type versus traditional. I'll address such matters.

You see, it's not very important that you know, for example, how many companies make fly-tying hooks, and the identification numbers of all the models. *The bottom line is that you are able to judge the quality points of those hooks, and select, in an informed manner, the one that's best for the particular fly you're tying.*

I hope to pass along many valuable tips on handling the various materials, both traditional and contemporary. There seems to be no end to the potential for improving one's tying skills, methods, and techniques. I know I'm still striving to improve mine. Some of these tips appear in my previous books, but I'm not conceited enough to assume that everyone has read them, nor do I want to try to leverage readers to buy them. Besides, it's tedious to be bouncing back and forth among a whole bunch of books. The more complete and instructional a book can be, the better. Plus, there's all that new stuff—and also, I keep getting better!

So please remember that this book is essentially driven by practicality, not faddishness or new-for-newness' sake. In fly tying, as with many things, form follows function. You might consider this analogy: *if it eats grass, gives milk, and says moo, it's a cow*! In other words, if a particular material looks and behaves like another material, feel free to substitute. It may work better than the original. For example, there are synthetic wrapping materials that are easier to work with and produce better visual effects than silk floss.

In striving to achieve the visual and physical effects I desire, I do so with great attention to feasibility. Usually, there are more ways to tie a fly than to skin a cat, and when I can get what I want with an easy-to-use material, as opposed to one that's nasty to work with, that dictates my choice.

At this point, I'd like to acknowledge some of the folks who helped with this project. There were many, and their contributions were substantial. Thanks to Dr. Ted Roubal for allowing me to take advantage of his expertise in dyeing and bleaching, and also to Ted Hebert for telling me about the use of hair dyes, and for valuable input about hackles. I also thank Tom Whiting and Charley Collins for sharing their feathercraft.

Thanks to the various hook manufacturers mentioned in that chapter for their input, and likewise to all of the merchants within our business who contributed or loaned items and materials for inspection and photography. And where photography is concerned, thanks to Arthur Rounds and Tom Knight for superb film processing, and to Tim Savard for the great shots used in the hackle pages, and for advice and counsel.

Thanks to Dr. Jim Payne, the veterinarian who provided insights into the rabies situation with regard to handling animal carcasses, and also to Leon

Verville, wildlife taxidermist, for sharing his expertise on treating and caring for pelts.

Most of all, thanks to the gang at Hunter's Angling Supplies: proprietor Nick Wilder; wife Leila; George Kesel, whom I mentioned earlier; and everyone else who works there. They were not only most cooperative in providing assistance in many forms, but also kindly tolerated my frequent interruptions of their already busy routines. It's done with now, gang; I promise!

I hope this book will be of value over a long period of time in helping the tyer/consumer deal with the incredible array of materials that are now, and will be, available in the ever-expanding realm of fly tying. Happy hackling.

—DICK TALLEUR
February 1995

Fly-Tying Vises Today

Where fly-tying vises are concerned, the past ten years have seen much development because enough people have become interested in fly tying to create an expanding market.

Let's begin by clearing up some semantics. There are two main types of vises—stationary and rotating (also known as "rotary"). However, within the stationary category we have vises with the ability to revolve. It's important to be aware that this isn't the same as rotating. A functionally rotating vise is one that facilitates *full and free 360-degree rotation with the hook on the same axis as the centerline of the jaws and shaft of the vise, and is so designed to allow the tyer access to the hook from the rear.*

While of benefit to the experienced tyer in certain applications, true rotating vises have a few drawbacks. But let's leave them until later and look at the more traditional type of vise: the stationary model.

Mounting Mechanisms

The choice of C-clamp or pedestal mount is up to you. Realizing that this information is Sand-Box 1, I nevertheless suggest the following considerations:

- C-clamp allows adjustment to vise height to match up with the chair used by the tyer, and his or her physical characteristics
- C-clamp is lighter in weight, a consideration for the traveling angler
- Pedestal obviates worry about thickness, shape, and "overhang" of desk or table; it will sit on any flat surface
- Pedestal does not interfere with lap drawers
- With a pedestal, the vise is over the tying table, and dropped items usually land there; with a C-clamp, the vise is mounted in front of the tying table, and dropped items usually wind up on the floor, or in a waste receptacle

- A C-clamp allows tying in a parked car, because it can be attached to the steering wheel (I've sat out many thunderstorms thusly)
- The C-clamp may be of benefit to the novice tyer, who doesn't always apply thread tension directly downward

While pedestal-mounted vises aren't height-adjustable *per se*, it is possible to correct the relative positioning of the tyer to the vise as follows: if the vise is too low, put something under the base, such as a book; if the vise is too high, put a thin cushion on the chair seat, thus elevating yourself. I might mention that an office chair with a height adjustment feature is ideal for fly tying.

Many vises offer conversion kits that enable switching between the two types of mount. This is simple enough, but somewhat costly, as it is necessary to change mounting rods, the C-clamp rod being considerably longer than the pedestal rod.

There's another type of vise mount that was actually developed outside of the vise-making industry. It was designed by Joan and Arthur Stoliar of New York City, who also designed the Folstaff and several other ingenious and useful angling products. It replaces a pedestal base, and employs a lever-activated suction device that causes it to adhere to any smooth surface, such as glass, tile, a highly polished wood tabletop, or simply a piece of plastic. This vise mount is part of a traveling kit called the Fly-Tyer's Carryall, and carries that name, but it is also sold separately. It is lightweight, compact, and highly transportable—ideal for the traveling tyer.

The HMH *standard vise. Also available with optional brass base.*

Features

First, a listing of basic features that any vise should have:

- Adjustment for hook wire diameter (size of hook)
- In C-clamp models, sufficient width to accommodate most tables
- Collet angle adjustment

Second, a listing of more advanced features:

- Revolving capability
- Interchange between C-clamp and pedestal
- Interchangeable jaws

Note that I put collet angle adjustment in the first group. I might get some arguments over that, but in my experience, the ability to change collet angle is really important, as it enhances access from the rear to various sizes of hooks. Smaller flies are becoming more popular all the time, and tying them is not at all difficult if you can get at the hook with your fingers.

Vises come in various sizes. Smaller ones, such as the fine-quality HMH Spartan Voyager, are very handy for traveling. However, they may be a bit tricky to use in certain respects, as the reduced length of the collet tube causes the hook to be mounted closer to the vertical rod than on larger vises. This can interfere with certain operations, particularly when the collet is adjusted to a sharp angle, in order to allow easy access to smaller hooks. However, I consider this a manageable problem.

Jaw Closure Mechanisms

Vise manufacturers employ several designs for closing the jaws. The most common is the cam-lever/draw-bar type, in which the downward operation of a lever, interacting with a simple wiper cam, causes the jaws to be drawn rearward into a tube, or collet, thus closing them. In some lower-priced vises, a screw wheel is substituted for the lever, which helps keep costs down. Rotating this wheel creates the same effect as pushing down the lever. It's a little slower, but it works just about as well.

Another mechanism also utilizes the screw principle. It consists of a round knob or wheel that, when turned, causes the jaws to close. However, it is much different from the one referred to earlier, in that there is no cam, collet, or draw bar. Instead, there is a simple lever, which behaves something like a seesaw; when one end goes one way, the other end goes in the opposite direction. In this case, it is an asymmetrical seesaw, which employs the basic principle of leverage. The end that effects the jaw closure is much longer than the jaw itself, which enables the application of sufficient force to hold a hook effectively.

This mechanism requires the use of a second, smaller screw knob, the purpose of which is to allow the tyer to change the dimension, or distance between the two sides of the jaw at the point of axis. This is an important part of the design, as it facilitates adjusting for various wire diameters. The operator must become familiar with this adjustment feature, if the vise is to accommodate a wide variety of hook sizes.

This operation may seem a bit tedious, but in practice, it's pretty simple, once you become accustomed to it. This technique is employed on several low-priced vises, and also on some sophisticated ones—specifically the Renzetti line of rotating vises, which I'll examine later. This design is a spinoff from the traditional wood clamp; it holds hooks securely.

The Renzetti two-jaw system, which is incorporated in their Master model, uses a screw mechanism to push the jaws into a collet, thus closing them. The Dyna-King employs a similar collet closure, but does so by way of a cam lever, rather than a screw.

Yet another design for jaw closure involves the use of a powerful, internally mounted spring, which causes a levering action similar to that just described. At this writing, only one vise that I know of uses this design: the Regal, which is produced by the Regal Engineering Company. It is unique, and deserves special comment, which will follow a bit later in this chapter.

Jaw Options

Some vises offer interchangeable jaws. One model in particular, the HMH (Hunter's Multi-Head) offers the convenience of screw-in-screw-out jaws. At one time, it was hard to keep these jaws properly aligned during tying, but this

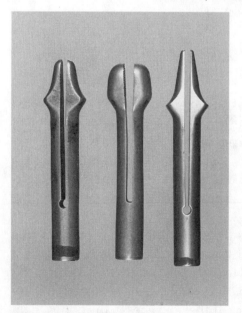

Several jaw sets for the HMH.

difficulty has been reduced to negligible proportions by the addition of a small neoprene washer that fits around the jaw bar, just beyond the threaded area. This can easily be retrofitted to existing jaws.

A further word about this product. Just as I was finishing this book, word reached me that Angling Products Incorporated, the company that manufactured the vise for the past ten years, has sold the operation to a group from Maine. I contacted them and was most pleased to learn that they plan to continue to produce the HMH vises, except that the HMH II, which is essentially the same as the main product but without screw-in-screw-out jaw change capability, will be discontinued. They will continue the Spartan, but will probably change the name to the Voyager.

The name of the new firm is the Kennebec River Fly and Tackle Company. As the name implies, they have plans for other fly-fishing products. We wish them all the best.

Changing jaws on the Spartan Voyager and HMH II vises isn't at all difficult. Basically, it involves loosening the hook-size adjustment, removing the screw that fastens the lever to the draw bar, and perhaps loosening an additional hex screw that keeps the draw bar aligned within the collet tube.

Jaw design is, of course, of great importance. There's more to this than simply accommodating hook size, which in this context essentially means wire diameter. There's also the matter of shape, which affects both hook-holding and hook-access attributes. There is an interaction here with the important angle-adjustment feature found on better-quality vises.

A more subtle but quite important aspect of jaw design is the manner in which the jaws close on a hook. All but the heaviest wire hooks are vulnerable to breakage in the barb area. This is critical on high-carbon, fine-wire dry-fly hooks, especially on those models where the barb is unnecessarily large, which involves a deeper slicing of the metal. If the jaws close tightly on that spot, the hook can be broken or, worse, weakened. That is one reason that where possible, I mount dry-fly hooks by only the bend, thus avoiding the barb area.

In a well-designed jaw, the slot extending from the front of the jaws where the hook is mounted back into the area compressed by the collet is slightly tapered. The effect is to grasp the hook by the rear of the metal, with clearance in the barb area. This only partially avoids hook breakage, and I still advocate discretion in mounting, especially in the case of dry-fly hooks.

All vises are adjustable for a range of hook thicknesses, some more so than others. However, the mere ability to close the jaw on a hook doesn't mean that one can work on it effectively; there's the matter of access. This is related to two features: jaw design, or shape, and collet adjustment angle. The latter is particularly important when small hooks are being used and the tyer must work close in.

Adjustments

As I've already mentioned, many stationary-type vises have a revolving feature, whereby the collet/jaw assembly can be turned 360 degrees, thus allowing the tyer to inspect, and perhaps even work on, the back side of the fly. This is particularly useful when tying Atlantic salmon flies, streamers, and other types of flies where front–back symmetry is critical. It should be kept in mind that the more severe the setting of the angle adjustment, the more difficult it is to use the revolving feature, because the jaw/collet and the hook shank are on different axes. As mentioned above, it is beneficial to be able to set the collet at a severe angle for working on small hooks, since this allows better access from the rear.

When using larger hooks, as is usually the case with salmon, saltwater, and streamer flies, the angle can be set on a flatter plane, making the revolving feature more viable. This still does not equate to or approximate full rotating operation, but it does allow access to the far side of the fly, if for nothing more than a visual check and some moderate tweaking.

I might mention that another way to check for, and make adjustments in, front–back symmetry is to swing the entire vise around on its mounting shaft, so that it is positioned for left-handed tying. This works much better with a pedestal base. I've learned to do some simple operations with the vise in this position, which means I wrap the thread left-handed and toward myself. This is helpful in getting things like wing veilings, cheeks, shoulders, horns, and the like into position.

Some of the adjustments referred to require one or more tools—usually a small screwdriver and hex wrench. The more sophisticated models may require several hex wrenches of different sizes; these are, in most cases, included by the manufacturer, along with instructions. Keeping track of these items is a pain, especially when traveling. I've always felt that the manufacturer should design and produce a specialized, unified tool set, perhaps along the lines of a multi-bladed jackknife, but so far I haven't been able to convince anyone to produce one.

Getting back to jaw shape, there are those that may be considered more-or-less universal, in that they will, with proper adjustment, accommodate a wide range of hook diameters, and allow adequate access to fairly small hooks. The photo depicts several of these. It is feasible to mount heavy hooks in jaws of this type, if one is careful to position the hook farther back in the slot, where the metal is thicker and stronger. My Spartan travels with me a lot, and I can securely mount hooks with wire diameters of up to sixty thousandths of an inch. This is a pretty heavy hook, indeed; for example, the Partridge Model M heavy salmon hook in size 4/0 measures .055.

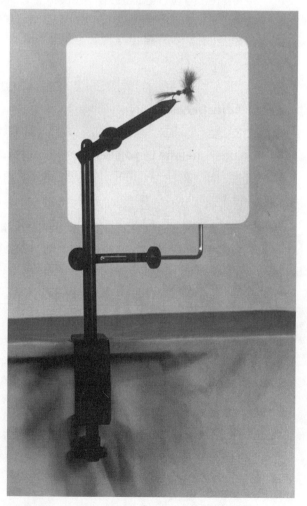

The Griffin; a good-quality inexpensive vise. Note attachment of the Abby backdrop device, referred to in Chapter 2.

Of course, strict attention must be given to jaw adjustment, and you mustn't force anything. I hope that the HMH people don't get upset with me for disclosing that I do this. I don't think I've damaged any jaws, since I've yet to have a set break. But do be careful.

At two opposite ends of the HMH spectrum are very heavy and very delicate jaws that accommodate huge and tiny hooks, respectively. The delicate ones are a joy when tying on size 20 or smaller. Please resist the temptation to leave them in place when tying with larger sizes. Some manufacturers offer jaws and collets that are matte-finished, rather than chromed. I prefer this, since they're restful on my eyes. They also help eliminate glare from photographic lighting if you plan to do any macrophotography involving a fly-tying vise.

There are vises to fit every budget—in the non-rotary category, at least. The less costly ones are adequate for typical work. Naturally, one can't expect the precision, ease of adjustment, durability, number of features, product life and overall performance with, say, a $30 vise as compared to a $200 model, but for a young beginner or occasional tyer, they will do the job. Perhaps the main thing is to know what sort of hooks you'll be tying with, so you can verify that the vise you're considering will readily accommodate them.

I've used the HMH line as a yardstick here, because I'm most familiar with those products, and they incorporate the features and designs I wish to illustrate. I also consider them to be of excellent quality. True, they are also right up there in price. But the quality, features, and warranty justify this. It's up to each tyer to make these evaluations, and to decide what best fits his or her needs and budget.

A Unique Design: The Regal

As I mentioned earlier, the Regal vise employs an internal spring mechanism for closing the jaws, which it does automatically. In other words, you apply

The business end of a Regal, shown upside down to display the mechanism.

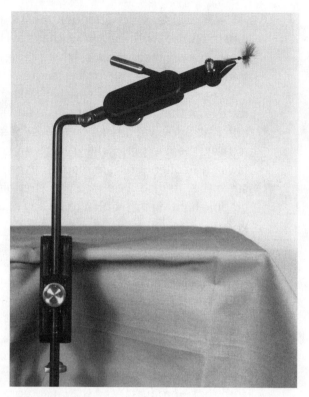

The Regal, full view.

pressure when opening the jaws, rather than when closing them. Then, you relax your grip on the lever, and the spring does the rest.

The standard jaws have a curved groove inside, for the purpose of holding hooks with absolute security. There is a degree of compromise here, in that the shape fits certain hook bends better than others. However, this can be rectified by adjusting the angle of the vise proper, so that the hook shank lies on a flatter plane.

For holding larger hooks, I must give this feature an excellent rating; once the hook is entrenched in that groove, it is effectively immobilized. This is particularly important when spinning hair, which involves a lot of thread tension. Understand that this feature isn't operable below a certain diameter of wire. You can't use it on medium-to-small hooks, and certainly not on a dry-fly hook. But in that case, you don't need it; you simply mount those hooks up front, ahead of the groove.

The Regal comes in both pedestal and C-clamp models. A lightweight model with mini jaws for working on small hooks is also available. These jaws have less spring tension than the standard jaws, which mitigates against breakage of small, delicate hooks. If you only tie from size 12 on down, these jaws are the only ones you'll need. I don't recommend that small, fine-wire hooks be mounted in the standard jaws.

The Regal has both angle adjustment and rotating capability, but it is not a true rotary vise. It comes with a materials holder that consists of a conically shaped spring that sits atop the jaws, where the axis bolt comes through.

Many tyers, myself included, find this most intrusive, and discard it immediately. It is possible, with a little effort, to mount a standard circular-spring materials holder behind the jaws of a Regal, even though at first glance one might assume it won't fit.

Many production tyers use the Regal, because hooks can be mounted quickly, and with minimal or no adjustment. There are just a few precautions:

- Don't try to mount a hook too far forward in the jaws; it may shoot across the room like a piece of shrapnel
- Release the lever gently when mounting smaller hooks
- Don't try to put smaller or lighter wire hooks in the groove
- Use the mini jaws for lighter work

The True Rotary Vise

Automation of certain fly-tying operations has long been the dream of vise designers and manufacturers; over the years, many have tried to perfect a device that would accomplish this. Let's take a look at a modern rotary vise, and see how they've done.

At this writing, the most popular rotary vise is made by Andy Renzetti. There are several models currently available: the Traveler, at around $125, the Presentation, at around $300, and the Master, at around $550. The latter includes a number of advanced features, such as cam-operated jaws, sealed ball bearings for added smoothness, an additional jaw angle adjustment mechanism, and a two-way actuator, for easy adaptation to left- or right-handed operation.

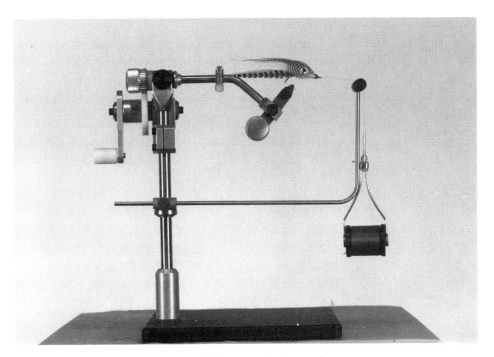

One of several models of the Renzetti. Note bobbin rest, referred to in Chapter 2.

As implied, the Traveler and Presentation models must be ordered for either left- or right-handed operation. C-clamp or pedestal mounting is available. The jaws utilize the two-screw-type adjustment feature, which enables these vises to hold hooks from very heavy to the finest wire, and in a complete range of sizes. Both models have a tension adjustment, which controls the amount of resistance the main shaft has to rotation. Both operate in either the rotating or stationary mode.

An optional accessory that's available for the two higher-priced models is a crank that attaches to the rotary actuator. This makes true rotary operation easier and faster, since the gears spin the hook at a 2:1 ratio. When using the crank with a pedestal mount, take care to set the rotary tension adjustment fairly light; otherwise, the amount of force required to turn the handle will cause the vise to move around.

Here are the main advantages this type of vise offers:

- Full rotation for increased speed on tedious operations, such as wrapping stranded material onto a large hook
- Use of supplemental bobbins, which enables the tyer to apply such delicate materials as floss without touching it with the fingers
- Capability of inspecting and working on a fly from any vector, while maintaining it in level position, on a true axis
- Effective control of adhesives, through the rotating feature, which permits working with hot glues, epoxys, and such
- Ease of applying head lacquers

Now for the minuses:

- Hook mounting and adjustment is a bit slower than with stationary cam lever vises, except on the Master
- Because rotary operation necessitates keeping everything on a single center line, the superstructure of the vise somewhat inhibits access to the hook from the rear. This can be reduced on the Master model via the angle adjustment feature, but only in the stationary mode.
- Operating in the rotary mode requires that the thread bobbin be suspended in front of the jaws in the bobbin rest. This requires securing the thread by either a couple of half-hitches or a three-turn whip-finish knot.

I must state—and this is my personal view—that I am bothered by the latter two items. I like to be able to get at the hook from the rear without having to alter my hand position, or thinking about dodging anything. I also find having to fool with the bobbin rest cumbersome, and I particularly don't like having to secure the thread by tying a knot of some sort. In many instances, after making a double-wrapped body with floss, tinsel, or other material, I want to back off the thread—that is, unwrap the wraps I tied on with, so as to reduce bulk and keep everything smooth. With the rotary, not only can't I do this, but I have an additional knot to deal with.

Even so, the advantages of true rotary operation are very nice, if you do appropriate kinds of tying operations. (Running floss up and down a long-shanked streamer hook with the crank mechanism is the closest thing to a sexual experience a guy of my age might have.) Bob Popovics, the reigning genius of saltwater fly tying, wouldn't give up his Renzetti unless someone pried his cold, dead fingers from around it. Bob does a lot of great things with plastics and adhesives, and the ability to rotate the hook is a great asset in controlling and shaping these substances.

I would advise the beginning tyer to proceed with discretion as regards the full rotary vise. Beginners have enough to do without having to contend with a more complex tool for holding the hook. Later, the tyer may wish to try a rotary vise, and see how it works. For certain things, it's the best, and I'm pleased to own one.

The Renzetti line of products are, from the standpoints of quality and workmanship, excellent. There is another rotary vise on the market that I haven't used, but I have heard good reports about it from fellow tyers. This is the Nor-Vise. I understand it offers an option whereby it can be hooked up to a variable-speed electric motor, which cranks the vise automatically! If you're a rotary guy, you should check this out.

Care and Maintenance

This will be short, because fly-tying vises don't need much care. The main thing is to follow previous instructions regarding adjustment. The one thing that can hurt or ruin a vise is forcing the jaws to close on too big a hook for the setting. This stresses several components, mainly the jaws. Not only will you impair the instrument's ability to perform its function, you may also invalidate the warranty.

With conventional vises, adjust whenever you get full closure with the cam lever just past vertical—in other words, somewhere between the 5:00 and 6:00 position. Check the instructions that come with the vise for further details.

With vises that use the two-screw mechanism, the procedure is to set adjustment with the front screw, then effect closure with the rear one. Don't try to cheat. The Regal needs no adjustment. Vises that employ other closure mechanisms come with instructions. Heed them.

Also very important: with vises that have interchangeable jaws, use them for the specific tasks for which they were designed. This is particularly critical with the so-called special-purpose, or midge jaws. They have little tolerance for oversized hooks, and are easily damaged.

Tools, Gadgets, and Gizmos

There are enough fly-tying gadgets on the market today to load, and possibly sink, a battleship. By the time this book is in print, some will have fallen by the wayside, and others will have come onto the scene. I'll address these devices by going into specifics on the ones I use, have tried and found to be useful, and for which I see strong market acceptance.

Bobbins

In choosing and using a bobbin there are three essential concerns.

First, use the tool properly. Beginning tyers should develop skills in handling the bobbin and should avoid falling into bad habits, such as touching the thread with the fingers as it feeds out of the tube. This makes wrapping more difficult in addition to possibly abrading the thread.

Second, proper adjustment is essential. The bobbin should feed out thread with moderate resistance but should not be so loose that it feeds thread by virtue of its own weight. New bobbins invariably need to be loosened up. Beginners may want to watch an experienced hand do this first, so as to get the hang of it. You gently bend out the limbs, one at a time, until the desired setting is achieved. If the limbs rub against the edges of the spool, the angle of the bend should be changed a little. Now you know how to adjust a bobbin!

Third, the tool should be free of defects. This means that the mouth of the tube must be smooth, so it won't cut the thread. I encounter a lot of this in my beginner's classes. If you notice that your thread frays a lot and breaks easily, try a few little experiments:

- Put another spool of thread in the suspect bobbin, do some wrapping, and see if the problem continues. If not, you probably have a bad spool of thread.

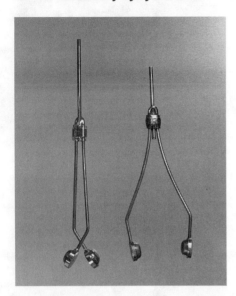

Long-tube and standard-tube bobbins. Note that the long-tube model has not yet been adjusted to accept a spool of thread.

- If the second spool frays or breaks easily, try both in another bobbin, preferably one that you've been tying with problem-free. If this solves the problem, you know it's the bobbin.

- If you continue to have problems, take your threads and bobbins to an experienced tyer or local fly shop and have them go through the same procedure. Also, have the tension adjustments checked, as well as your technique—you might be a bit heavy-handed.

The basic bobbin employs a metal thread tube. Other models use ceramic tubes, and still others feature little ceramic donuts at the mouth of their tubes. The metal ones are the most prone to having a burr or sharp edge within the tube. However, now and then this flaw occurs in ceramic ones. If this is the case, just return the tool.

Bobbins are also available with extra-long tubes. I've never found the need for one, but I don't tie every kind of fly. Maybe there's an advantage to this in bass-bug or very large streamer tying.

Tube diameter in bobbins varies. The narrower the tube, the more precise the behavior of the bobbin. Those with wider tubes will accommodate materials other than thread, such as floss, lead wire, and even fine yarns. There are times when this is beneficial. Just remember that when you apply a spooled material with a bobbin, each wrap is accompanied by a twist, unless you are using a full-rotating vise.

You'll also want a bobbin threader. These are all about the same. I prefer the model with the wire loop on one side and the reamer for cleaning out bobbin tubes on the other.

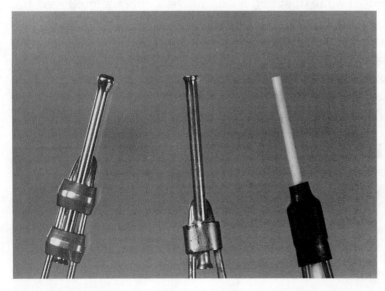

Several choices of tube type: ceramic insert, flared tube, and full ceramic tube.

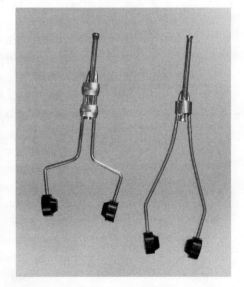

Alternative models. On the right is a floss bobbin.

Hackle Pliers

Maybe I'm getting old and cranky, but I just can't understand some of the hackle pliers that are now on the market. Here we have a tool that's even simpler than the bobbin. Artifacts found in archeological digs are considerably more sophisticated! We can fly around in the cosmos, and store *War and Peace* in a tiny silicone wafer, but we can't make consistently good hackle pliers.

Remember what I said in the preface: form follows function. Let's consider the two basic tasks hackle pliers must perform:

- Grip a feather securely enough so that it doesn't slip, but not so hard as to crush or break the quill.

- By virtue of its weight, maintain enough tension on a wrapped hackle so that it doesn't loosen and so that the tyer can let go of the pliers and do something else.

That's it! And still I find that there are pliers that do not perform these two prehistorically simple chores.

Thank God the time-tested English hackle plier is still with us. Find out who sells them, and buy one. Get the full-size, not the mini version—the latter is too small and too light. Tiny hackles can be wrapped perfectly with regular-size hackle pliers. It's the jaws that matter.

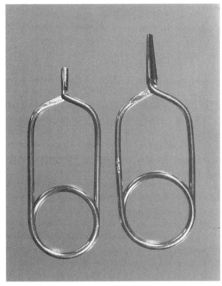

Two English-style hackle pliers, with different jaw lengths. One has been retrofitted with heat-shrink tubing.

Once you've got your pliers, pay a visit to your friendly hardware store and buy some narrow-gauge heat-shrink tubing. Disengage the jaws of the pliers, and slide the tubing over one jaw. Cut it to length, and apply a little heat, so as to shrink the tubing tightly around the metal. Reengage the jaws. Now you have a dependable tool that will not only perform the two basic functions, but many others as well. For example:

- Making and spinning a dubbing loop
- Twisting peacock herl with thread for reinforcement
- Holding the butt end of a feather while folding it, or extracting barbs for tailing or hackling
- Grabbing the end of a broken thread, to maintain tension while rebooting

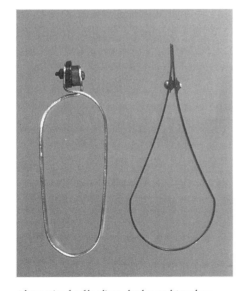

Alternative hackle pliers; duplex and teardrop.

It would be inappropriate if I failed to mention that tyers differ with respect to their personal techniques, and thus may prefer a different type of hackle plier. The teardrop-style tool is popular, and I have nothing against it. However, as I've told you, I'm an English-type tyer.

Scissors

Wow, are there scissors out there today! We have great variety, both in terms of function and price. If you're the typical trout- and salmon-fly tyer, your Number One scissors will be fine-tipped, very sharp, and of excellent quality. Then you'll get another pair for rough work, to protect and preserve the Sunday-go-to-meetin' pair.

Don't buy cheap scissors—they are a bad investment and a functional disaster. Once, I bought such an instrument. In the shop, they looked just dandy—nice-sized finger loops with long blades tapered to a very sharp point. For a little while, they worked fine. But soon they became dull. Handyman that I am, I tried to sharpen them with a fine stone. It literally ate the blades! The metal was of such poor quality that after a dozen strokes, the edges were gone.

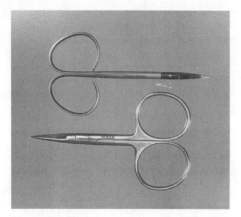

Typical fly-tying scissors. Note the expandable finger loops on one pair.

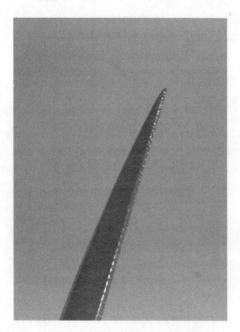

Close-up of scissor blade showing tiny serrations.

Where finger loops are concerned, they should fit your hand so that you are comfortable. Some people like large loops and a loose fit. Others, myself included, prefer a tighter fit for better control.

When tying, I keep the scissors in my right hand virtually all the time. However, I don't want them to slide all the way down to the base of my fingers—I want them seated just below the first knuckle of my fourth finger, and about at the bottom of the nail of my thumb. My hands are neither large nor small; I'd say they're about average for a normal American male. Therefore, I don't require very large finger loops.

People with large hands may need more room. There are a number of scissors on the market that have oversized finger loops, and also several brands that have adjustable finger loops. As a matter of fact, you can make almost any pair of scissors adjustable by cutting the finger loops where they join the main limbs.

Fly-tying scissors come with either straight or curved tips. The choice is yours. I have come to prefer the curved type for most work, especially when I'm tying salmon flies, where some discreet trimming and shaping of materials is often required.

Scissors are available that have fine serrations along one blade. This causes the blades to grip materials and cut them quickly, rather than having them slide along ahead of the closing blades. This feature is also effective when trimming hair, as on a Muddler head, Bomber, or bass bug.

And that raises another issue. There are several makes of scissors on the market that have blades with tungsten carbide edges, or inserts. These are a pricey spin-off from the surgical field. They are very sharp and, of course, tungsten carbide is extremely hard stuff. However, I find the blades to be somewhat slippery. Materials tend to slide along, rather than stay in place and get cut with precision. Also, sharpening tungsten blades is no task for an amateur, so when they eventually become dull, you will have to send them back to the manufacturer for a tune-up.

If you do opt for scissors with tungsten blades, be careful of them, since they are brittle. Whatever you do, don't drop them on a hard surface, and don't use the tips to pick or pry at anything.

As mentioned above, it is ideal to have at least one pair of heavy-duty scissors at hand for cutting hair, metallic materials, synthetics, and anything that will take a toll on your precious delicate scissors. More scissors are ruined by being splayed than by being dulled, and trying to cut materials that are too bulky will do just that. Switching scissors is somewhat of an inconvenience, especially if you tie with scissors in hand, as I do. But try to discipline yourself and your scissors will thank you. Failing that, if you're going to cut a piece of heavy oval tinsel or something with your Class A scissors, at least do so well down into the blades, staying away from the tips.

We have now examined what I consider to be the must-have tools: vise, bobbin, scissors, and hackle pliers. Now let's look at a grouping of more specialized devices. While not absolutely essential, all have their place, even if they are one-trick ponies, and some, such as bobbin threaders, hair eveners, and whip-finishers, make vital operations much easier and contribute greatly to tying efficiency and ease.

Whip-Finish Tools

These devices are for making the finish knot on the head of a fly, something I did by hand for the first 25 years of my tying career. They fall into two categories: the Matarelli, and the ones that aren't a Matarelli. I don't say this facetiously. There are two very different principles involved.

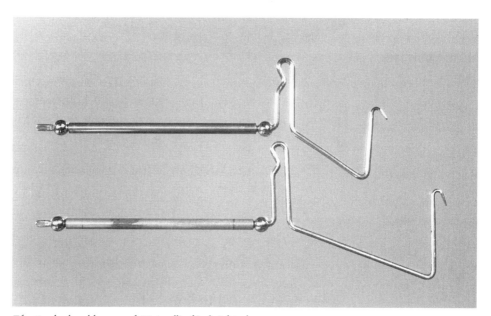

The standard and long-reach Matarelli whip-finish tools.

The most well-known of the not-Matarellis is the Thompson whip-finisher. It takes some getting used to, and frankly I never paid my dues and reached any appreciable level of skill with it. However, those who have developed expertise love the tool, and can make a whip-finish lightning fast with it. Instructions are included with the tool. It should be noted that the Thompson can apply a whip-finish only at the head of the fly, whereas a Matarelli, particularly the long-reach model, can place one almost anywhere.

The design of the Matarelli device is considerably different. The part of the tool that actually forms the knot rotates within a brass tube. To start the whip-finish, one holds the tool so that it doesn't rotate inside the tube until the thread is mounted and in position. Then the tool is released, and one simply wraps. The "dismount" is accomplished by tipping the tool slightly, so that the thread slips off of the part that held it in position during wrapping. It is held taut by the small hook at the tip of the instrument.

At this writing, the Matarelli is available in two sizes: regular, and long-reach. I use the long-reach for everything. However, I should point out that the small one also does a good job, and is more compact, which the traveling tyer always appreciates.

Bobbin Threader/Reamer

This little tool is for drawing the tying thread through the tube of the bobbin. You can fashion a makeshift one out of a piece of fine wire or monofilament. There is a model, however, that has a threader on one end and a reamer on the other, with a short piece of bead chain in the middle, connecting the two. The reamer is required periodically for cleaning out wax buildup in bobbin tubes. This feature makes the device well worth buying.

If you use ceramic bobbins, be careful when reaming out the tubes. It is possible to crack or nick them if you're a bit heavy-handed.

Hair Eveners

Often referred to as stackers, this tool renders the tips of a bunch of hair even, which helps to make nice, neat wings. I highly recommend the preliminary step of stacking dry-fly hair wings. The sightly result is sufficient reward in itself, but the most important benefits are:

- Full utilization of all of the hair in a given bunch forms great-looking wings with less material, and less bulk at the vortex
- Bringing all the hairs into proper position accurately tells you just how much hair you're working with

The most important factor in a hair evener is the inside diameter of the tube. There are a lot of cute little stackers out there, and they may be okay for working with small bunches of fine, straight hair. But for more sizeable amounts, and for hair that's crinkly, you'll want a wide tube. Be careful—some

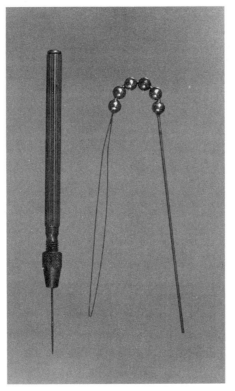

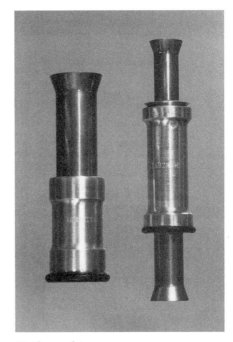

Two useful tools: a bobbin threader/reamer, and a common pin vise, used as a dubbing needle.

Stackers, or hair eveners.

stacker tubes look a lot wider than they are, because they are made of heavy material. Remember that it's the *inside diameter* that counts. Renzetti stackers are very good in this regard.

Hair Packers

The function of a hair packer is to compress and pack spun-on bunches during the construction of a trimmed-hair fly. The most common type consists of a metal bar with holes drilled in the ends that allow it to be slipped over the eye of a hook. Before these came on the market, we used to use the tube of a ball-point pen and it worked pretty well.

A couple of years ago, a terrific fly tyer named Chris Helms gave me a new packer that he designed to try out. It's an ingeniously simple device, consisting of a doubled-over piece of flat brass stock, with the ends bent to form a pair of "jaws." Each jaw has a triangular notch, which accommodates the hook shank. To use this packer, you compress the two sides, so that the jaws come together around the hook shank, or nearly so. It is then possible to pack the hair.

This is an easy packer to use, but a word of caution: be very careful not to chafe the thread when jamming the jaws against the hair, since this will cause thread breakage, and ultimate disaster.

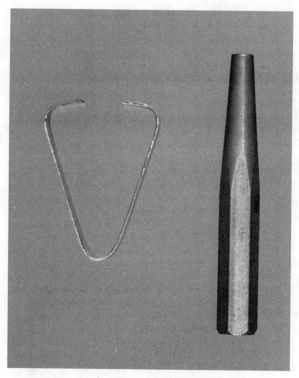

Hair packers.

Materials Clips

These handy little devices mount over the barrel of the vise, and are used for holding various items, such as tinsel, out of the way until it's time to wrap them in place. The most common model today is nothing more than a small spring. The materials are wedged into the slots between the coils. The problem here is that some materials are of such fine diameter that they won't stay in the slot.

There is a model—the HMH materials clip, designed by Bill Hunter—that neatly solves this problem. It consists of two springs of different diameter. The smaller one is mounted inside the larger, but this only extends halfway; thus, half the circumference of the device has wider slots, while the other half, by virtue of the double spring, has narrower ones. This materials clip will hold even the finest tinsels.

Backdrops

I find it desirable to have a neutral background against which to tie. Of course, you can create this in any number of ways and it can be whatever color you choose. For example, if you are tying Light Cahills, there's nothing like a piece of black velvet to make the pale-colored materials stand out.

There is a device on the market that mounts onto tying vises that have ⅜-inch-diameter shafts. It's called the Profile Plate, and is produced by the Abby Precision Manufacturing Company of Cloverdale, California. It is adjustable for both height and distance, and is not overly intrusive. The standard plate is a soft white. Additional plates are available in black, pale blue, and pale green. You can also make your own plates out of mat board, and clip them into place.

This is a very useful tool. It not only provides the desired type of background, but also reflects a small amount of soft light, which helps bring out definition and detail by backlighting the fly. It's also portable, a feature I find particularly appealing.

Hackle Gauges

Over the years, many gadgets for measuring hackle, dry-fly in particular, have come along, and many are still with us. While I own several, I never use them, because one of my few talents is that I'm an astute judge of proportions. This is nice, but it hardly compensates for the biggies that Nature shorted me on, such as athletic talent, good looks, and a metabolism that responds only to a diet short of utter starvation.

However, while the basic function of a hackle gauge is measuring the radius of dry-fly hackles for various hook sizes, some of them offer other features as well. For example, the Du Bois Fly Fisherman's and Fly Tyer's Gauge also measures hackle length for wet flies, wing lengths and tail lengths for wet and dry flies, and hook gap sizes and shank lengths over a fairly wide range. This is nice, if you agree with Mr. Du Bois' proportions. I feel he's about a size over on the dry-fly gauge.

Most of today's hackle gauges have a pin of some sort around which you wrap the hackle to simulate its position on the hook. This is very convenient. The Griffin tool offers the added convenience of being mountable on the vise shaft, and also features a hook gauge. However, the gauge only goes down to a size 16, and is based on the Mustad Model 94840. As we will see in Chapter 5, that scale doesn't apply universally.

The Hacklemaster, designed by the great tyer/angler/guide of the Beaverhead, Al Troth, is intended for the volume tyer who wants to sort hackles ahead of time. It mounts in the vise jaws. Al provides instructions on how to proceed. For someone interested in speed of production and obtaining absolute maximum yield from each cape, this is a valuable little tool.

Yet another design is offered by a company with the intriguing name of Worry Wood. In addition to a pin-centered dry-fly gauge, it has scales for measuring various other components, including streamer wings. The base is a heavy metal plate that sits firmly on the tying table.

I've described these products by name because each is a little different from the other, and they provide an appreciation of what's out there, even if one or more of them won't always be available.

A hackle gauge is very important for beginners. It is rare that a new fly tyer has such visual acuity and sense of proportion that they can judge proper hackle sizes right off the bat. Later, as experience sharpens visual skills, the tool can be set aside. Photo illustrations of various hackle gauges follow on the next page.

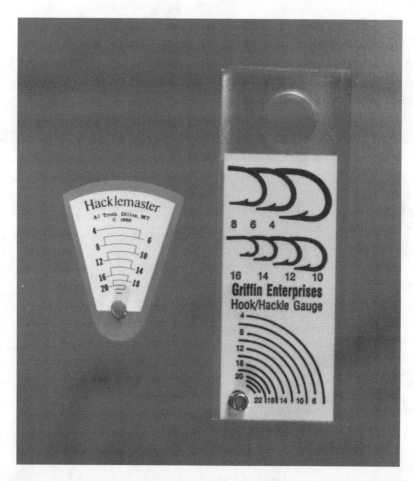

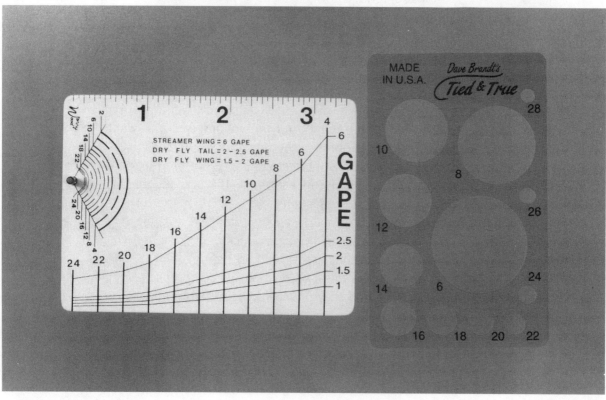

Various hackle gauges. Take your pick.

Wing Burners

For shaping realistic dry-fly wings, these gadgets are great. There are several types available. Your choice will depend on just how sculptured you want your wings to be. I don't think it makes any difference to the fish that the wings on a dry fly have exactly the shape of those on a natural insect, as long as a believable silhouette is presented.

My wing burner of preference is a homemade set I fashioned out of thin brass stock one can buy in hobby shops. The wing formers are symmetrical in shape, so that by centering the quills, I can burn both wings at once. The design is such that the quills hang out the bottom, and this makes it easy to position them.

Other than these comments, there's not much more to be said about wing burners. Pick the ones that appeal to you or make yourself a set. There's not much that can go awry.

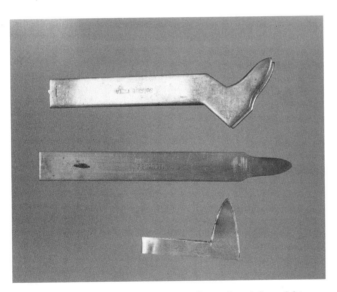

Typical (and non-typical) wing burners. The small upright model is one I made myself.

More wing-burners, for nymph wing cases and highly stylized mayfly wing imitations.

Tweezers

These are handy items to have on a tying table. They are quite useful for picking up small objects, such as tiny hooks. They also can be used in certain tying operations. A flat-nosed tweezer is good for flattening the quills of feathers such as streamer wings, golden pheasant crests on salmon flies, and for other similar operations, before tying them in.

Be careful of bargains. I have some inexpensive tweezers that looked great in the store, but the metal was so soft that the tips bent under minimal

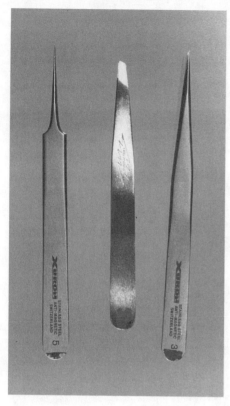

Tweezers.

stress. Considering that these are lifetime tools, it pays to go for quality. The Tweezerman brand is very good.

Bobbin Rests

Some tyers have a problem working around the bobbin when it is hanging down from the hook in proximity to the work area. In such cases, a bobbin rest will make life easier. This tool attaches to the base or mounting shaft of the vise, and can be shoved out of the way when not in use.

I've never found that I needed a bobbin rest, but if it helps you, go for it. In the case of fully revolving or rotating vise operation, it's a necessity.

Parachute, or Gallows Tools

These gadgets provide a sort of third hand, which secures the wing post while freeing both of the tyer's hands for wrapping parachute-style hackle. While it is possible to tie parachutes without this device, it does make life easier, especially for the inexperienced or occasional tyer.

In *The Versatile Fly Tyer*, I demonstrated how to make a simple parachute tool out of spring steel wire. Someone picked up on the idea, and now there's a commercial version on the market called the Skyhook.

Dubbing Blenders

These are strictly a spin-off from the food processing industry. There are any number of compact machines that are designed for pulverizing coffee beans, chopping nuts, and so forth. They are dissimilar from the traditional blender in that the receptacle and blades are at the top, rather than down at the bottom of the machine. That kind doesn't work for mixing dubbing—don't even try it.

Making dubbing blends with this sort of device is easy, fast, fun, and very useful. The process is described fully in Chapter 7.

Finger-Smoothing Items

Burrs, hangnails, and callouses are the bane of tyers the world over. People who do manual work, especially outdoors, often experience serious problems with this. Hand creams provide only partial relief. Significant burrs that interfere with tying need to be smoothed out more effectively.

A pumice stone will do the job quite nicely. In more persistent cases, the smoother side of an emery board will do the trick. These are rougher than pumice stone, so use them with discretion.

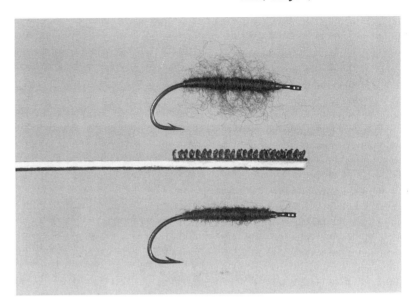

The Velcro dubbing teaser, and its effect, before (bottom) and after (top).

Dubbing Teasers

In many cases, a fly is rendered more effective by fuzzing up the dubbed body. The old books suggested tediously picking out the dubbing with a needle or bodkin. Then someone wrote about using the burred instruments dentists use for doing root canals. This would be dangerous; such tools will cut thread like a hot knife cuts through butter.

Again in this situation, I resort to a homemade gadget. Using Zap-A-Gap I glue a piece of "male" Velcro to the smoother side of an emery board. After the adhesive is dry, I cut the board lengthwise into strips, in order to reduce its width.

This simple tool is one of the handiest ones on my tying table. It is particularly good for fuzzing up dubbed sections of salmon fly bodies. I can tease out the imitation seal fur on a Green Highlander even after having wrapped the body hackle into place. I know no better means of doing this.

Combs

Fine-toothed combs are great little gizmos for the tyer. As I've explained elsewhere in this book, they are used to remove underfur and short hairs from bunches of deer hair, calf tail, and materials of that sort. They are often sold as moustache combs, eyelash combs, or just plain fine-toothed combs. The degree of fineness varies, and it's important to consider what sort of material you'll be combing since combs that are too fine won't work on coarser hairs. A photo illustration of two fine-toothed combs follow on the next page.

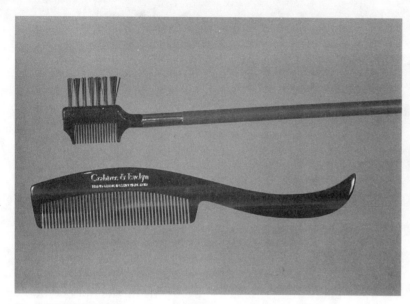

Small, *fine-toothed combs.*

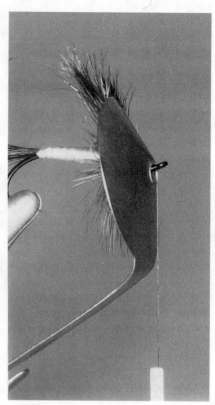

A *hackle guard, in position.*

Hackle Guards

These little gadgets are something of a crutch—but if one is limping, a crutch comes in very handy! Their function is to isolate the very front of the hook shank, holding material out of the way, while a whip-finish is applied. Usually they are sold in sets that accommodate hooks of different sizes.

I seldom see hackle guards used by competent tyers. However, they can be of great benefit to the beginner, who's having trouble enough learning the whip-finish, without having materials in the way to boot. I still resort to them on occasion when tying Muddler heads, because deer hair has a tendency to get mixed up in the finishing process.

Bodkins, or Dubbing Needles

These are very traditional tools and at one time, they were used for various tasks, such as the picking-out of dubbed bodies. Hence the name "bodkin." Today, they are more or less relegated to the application of head cement. In fact, I don't even use them for that. I've gone to tiny brushes, or if I need more delicacy, a sharp toothpick which is, in effect, a throwaway dubbing needle.

If you want a dubbing needle on your tying desk, I would recommend purchasing a pin vise at a hardware store. In this tool, you can mount any type of needle or pin that you desire, and replace it with another when it becomes crusty.

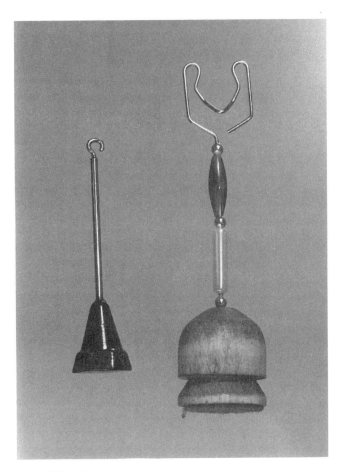

Two dubbing twisters.

Dubbing Twisters

I find that these gizmos are similar to those vegetable slicers you see advertised on TV. They look fantastic in the demo, but when you get them home, it's a different story.

I can only say that these items conflict with my adherence to the KISS principle: Keep It Simple, Stupid! I sense a bit of technological overkill here. I have never found a device that spins a dubbing loop as well as a good English hackle plier or grips as well as an electronics clip. But in deference to the clever folks who design and produce these tools, I'll say no more than this: if you do opt for a dubbing twister, I recommend the simple "shepherd's crook" style, which is consistent with the KISS principle.

Lamps and Lighting

It is important to have good light for fly tying, especially if you're getting along in years, and the old orbs aren't what they used to be. Over the years, I've tried a number of lighting devices, some of which have worked out better than others. The three main types are:

- **Incandescent light**
  Advantages—inexpensive, many choices, similar to natural light
  Disadvantages—gives off a lot of heat, can take up a lot of space

- **Fluorescent light**
Advantages—cool, restful on eyes, long-lasting
Disadvantages—bulky, somewhat costly, distorts colors

- **Halogen light**
Advantages—similar to natural light, very bright, very compact, very concentrated in spotlight configuration
Disadvantages—can be glary, quite pricey

Despite the high cost, I've gone to halogen overhead lighting in my tying room. I've installed a compact rail-type ceiling fixture that will accommodate up to four sealed-beam spots or floods. I prefer the spots for tying, the floods for lighting up the rest of the room, where my supplies are stored. So I have two of each in the fixture. Not only do I have wonderful light, I no longer have a lamp in the way on my desk!

As mentioned above, fluorescent light is very restful on the eyes. And while not as concentrated as halogen, it can be an efficient means of lighting up a tying area. You can install ceiling fixtures, but if that wouldn't suit the space you have, a good table lamp will suffice. They tend to be bulky though, so you'll have to contend with that problem.

Common incandescent light is okay, but it takes a fair amount to adequately illuminate a tying area. Either that or the source of light must be quite close, which isn't so pleasant, because of heat and bulk.

If you travel and take along your tying stuff, you'll want to include a lamp. God only knows what you're liable to find at your destination! There are quite a few portable lamps on the market, some of which are sold in fly shops. My favorite is a very compact microhalogen model put out by Zelco of Mount Vernon, NY. It uses a small 20-watt halogen bulb, which provides an amazing amount of light. A pedestal base and clamp are both included. Best of all, this excellent device breaks down into small components that can almost be carried in one's pocket.

Some tyers want magnification as well as illumination from their lamp. There are several models that offer this. One that's been popular over the years features a circular fluorescent bulb which surrounds a large magnifying glass. I shudder when I see someone hauling one of these things into the classroom where I'm teaching fly-tying, because they take up so much space. But if that's what the person needs, I'm not going to argue.

Recently, a lighting/magnification device appeared on the market that is much more compact and in all respects better suited to tying than the huge, cumbersome, circular fluorescent models. It's called the Giraffe, and the brand name is Goodwin. It is available with only a lamp, or with a magnifier also. An interesting feature is that one can use a number of different bulbs, including a Chromalex bulb that is color-corrected to the Kelvin rating of daylight.

If you think that a vision problem may be compromising your tying, I'd recommend several steps be taken, before you go for magnification. Get your eyes checked, and explain to the doctor what you're doing. A cheap pair of diopters from the local drugstore may suffice, as they have in my case. Keep in mind that once you've come to depend on a magnification setup, you're virtually married to it, and that becomes most burdensome when traveling.

Dispensers

The two main types of dispensers commonly encountered at this time are dubbing dispensers and spooled-materials dispensers. I've included a photo of both. If used in conjunction with the right sort of materials, they both work.

With dubbing dispensers, the material feeds out through small holes drilled into the tops of the compartments. Some dubbing is of such texture that it will keep feeding continuously as you tease it out of the hole. Other dubbings are too short-fibered for this, and for them, this type of dispenser doesn't work.

The other dispenser consists of a box with six spools in it. They can be filled with whatever material you choose: chenille, yarn, tinsel, braid and mesh, even various types of wire. The materials feed out through slots, which are V-cut at the bottom, to enable securing the tag ends. It seems to work very nicely. I'd be a little concerned about using it for floss though, since that material may be abraded by the slots.

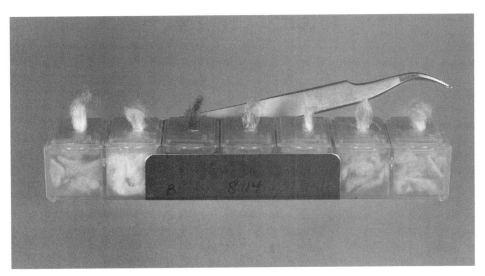

A *dubbing dispenser.*

A *spooled-material dispenser.*

Organizers

There are all sorts of items for sale that will help you keep your tying materials organized. In my case, nothing seems to help much, but that's me, not the products!

A *desktop organizer.*

The item in the photograph is nothing more than a closed-cell foam block, with cutouts for various sizes and shapes of instruments, tools, bottles, and so forth. For that purpose, it's quite adequate. For all the rest of your junk, you'll need some sort of system.

There is a large assortment of special-purpose boxes, kits, and even desks available, in a very wide price range. If you get into custom cabinetry, you can spend thousands. So it's up to you. Each tyer has his or her own set of needs, not to mention widely diverse physical accommodations. It makes quite a difference if you are tying in the corner of an already crowded room in a city apartment, or in a finished loft in a large house that's probably bigger than a lot of apartments in their entirety. If space is at a premium, you might look into some of the clever modular tables that are available.

Adhesives

This chapter might easily be entitled, *Better Living Through Chemistry*. Adhesive substances of various types have played an important role in fly tying for centuries. Waxes in particular have been widely employed and were vital back in the days of silk thread and vise-free tying. The British tyers of the 1800's made up some very effective formulas which inhibited decomposition of the organic thread and helped hold things in place. Such notable American figures as Harry Darbee and James Leisenring made up their own waxes, and were quite particular about them.

Waxes

Waxes are a good starting point. Today, there are certainly plenty of choices, ranging from the stickiest to the most gentle. It's up to the tyer to choose one that works best for a particular application. And believe me—the stickiest isn't necessarily the best!

Choice of wax relates to the hands of the tyer, as well as the task at hand. Some people have soft, smooth fingers with a high level of natural moisture. Such people need little, if any, wax for most applications. Other people, particularly those who have worked outdoors for long periods, have very dry skin and rough fingers. For them, waxes help soften and smooth out the skin and also aid in getting materials to adhere to the thread.

I dislike having wax on my fingers, and when I do use it, I usually apply it to the thread. I don't use the terribly sticky stuff—I find no reason to. I use wax only for dubbing the most slippery materials such as seal hair, fur containing a lot of guard hairs, and some of the modern synthetics. Sometimes it helps the dubbing hang on the thread for a moment, while a spinning loop is formed. I suggest that wax be applied only to the portion of thread where the dubbing takes place.

Applying wax to the thread has several advantages. For one, it allows the use of unwaxed thread. Waxed thread has a certain resistance to head cement or lacquer, and inhibits thorough penetration and effective bonding. This can prevent the head coating from sticking to the thread, which eventually results in discoloration and chipping. The viscosity of the cement also plays a role here but we'll address that in depth a bit later.

As mentioned above, there are many types and consistencies of wax available. I know one that's so sticky you can remove the cap, touch your finger to it, and thus pick up the whole thing, container and all. However, it spreads smoothly and evenly when applied to the thread, and is a pleasant product with which to work.

A few criteria for choosing wax:

- It is important that wax spreads onto thread in a smooth, even, thin layer, with no buildups or hunks. Otherwise when the tyer begins to work the dubbing between the fingers, the places where there are excess amounts will become messy.
- Wax should only be sticky enough to get the job done. Wax that's too sticky may not spread smoothly, and will probably mess up your fingers. It may also bind onto the thread during application.
- Wax shouldn't be too hard, like paraffin, or it simply won't do the job
- Wax shouldn't overly discolor lighter-colored threads
- Wax should hold up well over time, and not become too hard or too gooey or break down into its separate components
- Wax should be conveniently packaged. I prefer the extrusion-type tube, similar to Chapstick.

Head Coatings

Here again there's a wide choice both in terms of type and color. Most tyers prefer the clear type. However, streamer-fly, saltwater-fly, salmon-fly and steelhead-fly tyers often require various colors to obtain the desired effect.

The main function of head cement is to bond with and protect the thread that forms the head of the fly. This requires a certain amount of penetration. Therefore, the most critical consideration isn't so much the brand of product, but its viscosity. The cement has to be runny enough to soak into the thread layers. However, it shouldn't be so thinned out that it runs all over the place and has poor bonding and coating properties.

Most head lacquers and cements have fairly volatile thinners, and once the bottle is opened, it doesn't take long for the substance to start thickening up. It is therefore essential to have a supply of the proper thinner on hand. The trick is to find out which thinner this is. According to Federal labeling laws, it's supposed to be written on the container, but often this information is rather cryptic.

The most commonly used thinners are toluol (toluene), Methyl Ethyl Ketone (MEK), acetone, and plain lacquer thinner. All of these can be purchased in hardware stores. Most fly shops carry the thinner for the cements they sell, but purchasing it in small quantities is extremely expensive.

A convenient device for adding thinner to a bottle of cement is a common eye dropper. Add the thinner in small amounts, shake the cement well, and test it before adding more. Do not allow the level of cement in the bottle to become too low, or the substance to become too viscous before thinning, and don't over-dilute.

Many tyers, myself included, use nail polish for certain applications. Modern nail polish is a complex chemical compound. The resins, acetates, butyls, and other ingredients give it body and texture. This results in a hard finish and lustrous appearance. However, the penetrating properties of nail polish may not be too good, especially if it isn't thinned properly.

Due to the complex makeup of nail polish, its thinners are likewise compounds. Reading the back of a Sally Hansen bottle, I see acetone, toluene, alcohol, and some other substances. This implies that a simple thinner alone is not entirely effective in thinning out this product, and may result in breaking down the formula by changing its chemical balance. Therefore, I advise using the nail polish thinner recommended for the specific product.

Nail polish comes in a wide array of colors and shades. However, one of the problems in buying all but the clear type is that most stores use fluorescent lighting, which causes color distortion. This also causes problems in selecting other items where color is a concern, particularly dun capes and saddles. I will address this in Chapter 10. In the case of nail polish though, you may find that the shade you thought you were buying isn't the one you wanted. For example, I tie a number of flies that call for red heads, notably the Silver Doctor. If I rely on fluorescent lighting when selecting a shade, the head will probably turn out to be more pinkish than I want. I now know several brands that I like, and if I can find those specific brands and colors in the store, things work well.

But this shouldn't discourage you—nail polish can produce great results—and you have the advantage of excellent packaging! I've yet to have a nail polish cap come loose or leak during travel, or a bottle break. The bottles are easy to open, and many are flat, a convenience for the mobile tyer. Also, they have a built-in applicator—the brush. When you buy the polish, this brush may be far too heavy for all but the largest heads, but it can easily be transformed into a delicate, wonderfully effective applicator in seconds by reducing its bulk with scissors or a razor blade. When I buy a new bottle of nail polish, the first thing I do is remove the cap, wipe the brush on a paper towel, and reduce it by 75%–85%. I also keep my empties and refill them with other types of lacquers and cements that don't have such nice packaging.

Obtaining a Beautiful Finish

Some tyers are completely pragmatic and don't care what the heads on their flies look like. Why not? Because the fish don't give a damn, except in the case of special effects, such as eyes. For practical purposes, a coat or two of properly thinned clear cement is all the fish require. But for tyers who are interested in appearance, here are a few thoughts.

The hairwinged salmon flies I crank out for fishing on Russia's Kola Peninsula are utilitarian and without pretense. However, I do like a nicely finished head on them, especially the red ones. To obtain this, I use one coat of clear for base and bonding, two coats of colored lacquer, and finally another coat of clear, for a protective finish.

Here are two *very* important concerns: both substances must be at proper viscosity, and must be applied in *thin coats*, allowing them to *dry completely*! Head coatings—nail polishes and lacquers in particular—that don't contain sufficient thinner don't dry or harden properly. Often the outside dries, forming a sort of skin. The tyer, thinking the head is cured, either applies another coat or takes the fly fishing. But what's actually happened is that underneath the head is still gooey, and the least little squeeze when handling the fly will pop the skin.

Earlier in my career, through carelessness and ignorance, I messed up some beautiful "wall flies" this way. It's an awful temptation when finishing off a head to just gob on a thick droplet of lacquer, which looks gorgeous while wet. But later, if you pick the fly up by the head, there are your fingerprints, impressed into what you thought was a bowling-ball finish!

I must also point out that a good black finish isn't all that easy to come by. You should be particularly skeptical of black nail polishes, as some of them aren't really a *black* black. Also model paints found in hobby shops may look great in the bottle, but they can be tricky to work with.

My favorite black is an oldy but goody—a British product called Cellire. The solvent is ordinary lacquer thinner, which is cheap and easy to find. Cellire also comes in clear, yellow, and red. I like the first two, but the red is weird—a sort of V-8 juice shade. Cellire is good stuff in and of itself, but for a really brilliant, durable finish, I follow the clear-colored–colored-clear procedure just described.

Glues and Reinforcing Compounds

Modern tyers use various things to strengthen materials, change their texture, strengthen assemblies, and effect finishes. Let's look at the more prevalent ones.

Epoxy

This is a trade name that has become generic, like Xerox. Epoxies are two-part catalytic adhesives, meaning that hardening is caused by a chemical interaction that takes place when the resin and hardener are combined. No evaporative-type solvent or thinner is present.

Epoxy is well noted for its strength. The two-part polymer finish used on the wrappings of most of today's better fishing rods is a type of epoxy. Besides its durability, epoxy has a couple of additional attributes. Since it has no thinner, it doesn't shrink and cause curling when drying and one coat normally does the job. Its main drawback is an extended drying time, but with the faster type, that's no big deal, especially considering that only one coat is required for a smooth, sightly, durable head. The particulars on working with epoxy are covered in detail in Chapter 15.

George Kesel uses epoxy to finish all of his salmon, saltwater, streamer, and wet-fly heads. George does a fair amount of commercial tying, and this one-step finish saves him time. He has also found that it eliminates chances of error—that is, getting lacquer where you don't want it, especially on salmon flies that are headed for the framing shop. Nice idea.

Many saltwater tyers use epoxy to protect, and even form, components on flies that will be exposed to the lethal teeth of creatures such as bluefish and barracuda. This has evolved into a major school of fly tying in and of itself. Witness the popularity of the whimsically named MOE (Mother Of Epoxy) flies. Innovative tyers such as A.J. Hand and Jack Montague have developed this type of tying into an art form.

Several recent books describe the techniques for making these flies, most notably Lefty Kreh's *Saltwater Fly Patterns* and Frank Wentink's explicit and detailed *Saltwater Fly Tying*. These books also cover the construction of hot-glue flies, which employs a similar methodology.

One thing to remember—epoxy goes on rather thick, and attention must be given to maintaining even distribution and avoiding "blobs" caused by gravity. Rod makers do this by placing newly finished rods on a machine that slowly rotates them until the two-part coating has set up. With flies, you may not have to resort to anything that high tech, but you will at least need to remove excess that runs to the bottom within the first 30 seconds or so after application. You may have to do this two or three times in quick succession.

When coating bodies, and with many procedures that employ epoxy, a fully rotating fly-tying vise is a valuable asset. It allows the tyer to revolve the fly on a true axis, facilitating the shaping of the fly and the even distribution of the epoxy.

It is important to mix the resin and hardener thoroughly, and in the *exact proportions specified on the package*. For a mixing surface, use something you can dispose of. If I have a dozen streamers ready to receive head coatings, I take a toothpick and mix an appropriate amount of epoxy on a small piece of card-board such as a file card and apply it as quickly as possible, removing the blobs of excess as they form, and setting the flies aside to harden. Work within the range of normal room temperatures—extremes can alter the hardening process.

Super Glues

These volatile but highly useful adhesives have many valuable applications in fly tying. There are a number of them on the market. Basically all these adhesives are quite similar, but there is one, at this writing, that I prefer for fly tying. The brand name is Zap-A-Gap, and it's manufactured by Pacer Technologies, of Rancho Cucamonga, California.

When Bill Hunter owned his shop in New Boston, New Hampshire, he did a lot of experimenting with super glues in connection with protecting line/backing splices. He settled on Zap-A-Gap for several reasons, the two most critical being its viscosity and its behavior in water. It is considerably less runny and more "forgiving" than the standard super glues, hence its name. It also does not weaken when wet as others may, even after drying completely.

Throughout this book, you'll find many suggested uses for this stuff, such as reinforcing and reconfiguring hairwing salmon flies, reconstituting and reinforcing jungle cock, and forming preassemblies. Here are a few additional suggestions:

- Use as a substitute for head cement. Care must be taken to use very minute quantities, to prevent the glue from leaching into places where it's not wanted. It does not produce a pretty finish, but it does form a very tough bond, and you can always dress up the head afterwards with something else.

- Reinforce the wing/hackle assembly on parachute flies. A tiny drop at the base of a post wing after the fly is completed effectively protects an otherwise fragile area. You can also correct for any hackle that may have ridden up the wing post using a simple tool formed from a paper clip.

- Reinforce Wulff-style hairwings. Simply touch a tiny drop to the "V" where the two wings come together and let it soak into the thread wraps used to form the wings. This helps prevent the wings from starting to lean forward later.

- Coat and secure underbodies, such as lead wire

- Compensate for web in dry-fly hackle. This technique is described in Chapter 10.

- Use as an adhesive on the thread wraps that cover the connecting wire or monofilament that joins the two parts of tandem flies.

However, there are a few things to keep in mind. Zap-A-Gap, and most current versions of the so-called super glues are cyanoacrilates, which means that they contain cyanide. As such, they can be dangerous, so be careful about avoiding contact with eyes, mouth, and skin. I've also found that this family of adhesives interacts unpredictably with certain other materials. For example, if you use a Magic Marker to change the color of the head on a fly and then apply a cyanoacrilate, it will immediately turn the head a bizarre color. So you can't use a cyanoacrilate in that case. However, I haven't noticed that dyed materials, even my own home dye jobs, are affected in this manner.

Zap-A-Gap dries more slowly than most other glues of this type. You can buy an accelerator, but that's just one more messy, weird chemical to deal with. The interaction between the glue and the accelerator also releases cyanide gas as a by-product. I don't know that the quantity is lethal, but it is something to consider. If you want it to dry faster, Zap-A-Gap responds to being rubbed with a toothpick and this effectively accelerates the process.

Packaging of course can change, but at the moment, Zap-A-Gap comes in a small plastic bottle with an elongated snout. The cap is actually an extrusion of the tube, and initially is protected by a plastic shell. To open the container, one removes the plastic shell, and then twists the cap free from the snout. The hole thus exposed may be partially blocked by some plastic fibers and these should be removed with a sharp instrument.

And here I'll pass along a neat little tip. The factory-made opening is often too narrow, and when I open a new bottle, I take a razor blade and cut off a little bit of the snout to widen it. This allows to glue to run back down into the bottle without clogging the opening. *Very* helpful!

Zap-A-Gap will stay liquid for a long time if it's kept upright with the cap in place. Once a certain amount has been used up—let's say half—the air that replaces it begins to interact with the remaining glue in the bottle, and it begins to thicken. This can be counteracted by keeping the bottle in the refrigerator when it is not in use.

If you should get some super glue on your fingers, a little acetone on a paper towel will remove it. Acetone will also remove epoxy-type glues from fingers if it is used before the epoxy sets up.

Spray Adhesives

In the art world, sprayed-on coatings are used to protect drawings done in softer mediums, such as charcoal and pastel. These sprays also have application in fly tying. At this writing, the popular favorite is Tuffilm. That could, and probably will, change at some point. But the idea is to find something that bonds and lends strength to the feathers to which it's applied.

One of the most common applications is treating feathers that are going to be used to make nymph wing cases, such as goose or turkey wing quills. This is easy enough—you simply hold the feather by the quill butt with a pair of pliers, spray it lightly on both sides, and set it on a piece of waxed paper. When it's dry, repeat. Work in a very well-ventilated area with lots of air flow, but allow drying to occur at room temperature.

Here's another example of what can be done with spray coatings. Let's say you're tying the Juicy Fruit, a beautiful and effective saltwater pattern. It calls for teal or mallard cheeks with painted eyes. I spray-coat the cheeking feathers as described above, which makes them very receptive to a painted eye. Then I spray coat them lightly once more. Incidentally, stick-on eyes can also be used on the Juicy Fruit, with an assist from Zap-A-Gap, as described in Chapter 15.

Spray coatings contain a fast-drying thinner, and lose considerable volume in drying. Because of this, they tend to make things curl a little, so be very conservative in application. Use only as much as you need. Multiple light coats are better than a single soaking one.

Strong Glues for Reinforcing and Reconfiguring

Further along in the book we will cover more uses of these: Pliobond and silicone cement in connection with treating jungle cock, and epoxy types for protecting heads and other fly features.

Pliobond is an interesting and versatile adhesive. I've used it for many years and in quite a number of ways. Its unique properties allow you not only to strengthen and protect feathers, but in some cases, to actually change them.

Here's an example. Take a typical soft hen feather or something similar, such as a grouse or partridge body feather, and strip off the fluff near the base. Holding it by the butt-end quill, dab on a small amount of Pliobond and stroke towards the tip, preening the feather outward and working the glue into the fibers. Apply sufficient pressure to cause the feather to slim out dramatically. In a matter of ten or so seconds, the glue will become tacky to the point that you can't stroke any more. Now you have a long, narrow, reinforced, malleable feather. Do a bunch of them and set them on waxed paper to dry.

Feathers prepared this way make great shells and wing cases for nymphs. They are tough, have nice natural colors, and can be folded and configured into realistic-looking body parts. They match up well with other feathers that may be used for legs, tails, and other features.

While it is easier to treat wing quills and feathers of that type with a spray adhesive, Pliobond produces a much more durable result. Simply smear it on with your fingers, preening towards the edge of the feather and working the glue into the fibers. Again, set it aside on waxed paper to dry thoroughly. Later, strips of the desired width may be separated with a needle point and used for nymph backs and wing cases.

Yes, this is a slightly messy process. I strongly suggest the use of throwaway vinyl gloves, rather than bare fingers. When finished, simply discard them—they're that inexpensive. You should also note that the thinner that's worked best with Pliobond for me is Methyl Ethyl Ketone (MEK).

Goop/Shoe Goo

Another very tough adhesive is Goop, also known as Shoe Goo. Both of these, as you might expect, are registered trade names. This stuff is *really* strong. Back when I was a long distance runner I used it on my shoes, and it stood up under unbelievable punishment. My joints didn't!

The version of this material I'm familiar with is slow-drying, requiring twelve to twenty-four hours to set. It seems to lose a considerable amount of its bulk in drying, and therefore tends to make feathers and the like curl if used as a coating. However, when used over firmer materials, it forms an extremely durable covering that will resist even the murderous teeth of a bluefish. It is very effective for gluing eyes onto deer-hair flies. It can also be used to form molded flies but in my opinion the epoxies and hot glues are more suitable for this type of work.

Thinned with toluol, Goop/Shoe Goo makes a very useful general purpose fly-tying adhesive. It penetrates thread very well, and is a high-bonding head cement. It is also good for coating and reinforcing feathers and like materials. The added thinner reduces the drying time to a fraction of that of the uncut glue.

Silicone Rubber-Type Glues

In addition to common bathtub sealer, two popular adhesives of this type, at this writing, are Jolli-Glaze and Sof-Coat. They are available in craft stores, some hardware stores, and fly shops that cater to saltwater tyers. They are really tough, yet also soft and flexible, and lend themselves to taking various forms, thus being of great value in modern fly tying. They come in many colors as well as clear. The latter allows the use of additives, such as sparkly glitz and dyes.

There are several major applications for this type of adhesive. It can be used as a "stand-alone" for making molded/shaped components, or as a protective coating. For example, it can be applied to wool and hair heads and bodies, giving them a slicker appearance and different texture. It also protects vulnerable components such as glued-on eyes, and makes flies less air-resistant. I am particularly impressed with the texture thus created, which is much like the body of a real creature.

Photoflo

As one might deduce from the name, this is actually a product from the photographic industry. It is used in darkroom work to remove all developer chemicals from film, and to "slick" it out before drying.

Bob Popovics, a great innovator of saltwater tying, uses Photoflo when working with silicone glue. It enables him to smooth out body coatings and forms without having the silicone glue stick to his fingers. This is essential, because silicone glue is like the proverbial tar baby. Bob reports that the Photoflo dries very quickly, so that additional coats of silicone can be added soon after its application.

Vinyl Gloves

The preceding reminds me that adhesives, even while very useful in contemporary fly-tying, are not always the most pleasant substances to work with. Most of them are very gooey indeed and they tend to mess up one's fingers something awful. This can be prevented by wearing thin vinyl gloves. Such gloves are available everywhere these days. They are inexpensive and are thin enough to allow delicate manipulations. Vinyl is better than true rubber because very few adhesives will stick to it. Just ask anyone who has tried to resole a vinyl wading shoe!

Lead Wire

The best boss I had in my many years with AT&T was an intriguing and often enigmatic character named John Taylor. He was brilliant but had a proclivity for telling the truth to people who didn't want to hear it. John loved proverbial sayings—his own brand, preferably. One of his favorites was: "Don't wish too hard for something, you might get it." I always had a problem with that one, but finally I think I'm getting the message.

American fly tying has traditionally made wide use of added weight. This is logical. We have a lot of great big rivers and deep lakes in which much of the time the only way to catch fish is to get the fly *down*. We tend to be a pragmatic lot and we're not hung up on arbitrary traditions or protocols. Thus the Weighted Fly.

The principal method for weighting flies is lead wire. We wrap it on or lay it in strips to form underbodies. It gives our flies both weight and, in some cases, shape. My Perla Stonefly nymph relies on lead wire for its flatness.

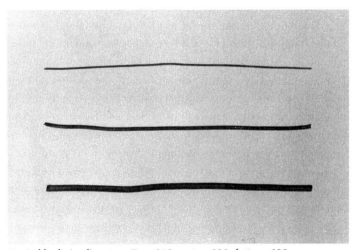

Typical lead wire diameters. Top, .010; center, .020; bottom, .035.

Within the past generation, we've had to face up to the fact that lead isn't good for us or for other creatures. This has profoundly affected the kind of paint we use, the kind of shotgun shells we buy, and lately, even the kind of split shot we crimp onto our leaders.

So getting back to John Taylor, we who are environmentalists wished for something—specifically, a public mentality that would demand a clean environment. Finally, we're getting our wish. After years of study and much debate, nontoxic shot became mandatory for waterfowl hunting. And it probably won't be too long before lead wire gets legislated out of fly fishing and tying as well.

I have searched my soul, what there is of it, and I can't see where lead wire, in the quantities we use it, has any appreciable effect on the environment. Speaking for myself, I doubt that I would introduce as much lead into the environment in twenty years of fly-fishing as I used to in a few weekends on a duck and goose marsh. We are not dumping the stuff into the food supply as do hunters who shoot over shallow marshes full of wild rice and other natural foods. However, we've been raising visible and audible hell for many years with all sorts of polluters, telling them what horrible guys they are. Now we are in a position of having to be consistent with our preachings, even though what we are doing has a minimal effect or perhaps none at all.

The first shoe has already dropped. Lead in any form is banned in the national parks. No lead split shot and no flies weighted with lead. Think about that. How do we get our beloved Woolly Buggers to sink now? Super glue stones to our leaders?

Already the industry is scrambling around, looking for a replacement. In the case of split shot, this was simple. We now have nontoxic shot and it seems to work just fine. At this writing, Dinsmore is the predominant brand. However, nontoxic wire is a whole different ball game. I've tried some prototype alloy products and they are absolutely lousy. No one could tie an acceptable weighted fly with any of the stuff I've seen so far.

We need some new technology. How long this will require, I have no idea. One would hope that it comes sooner rather than later. Meanwhile, it would be nice if we could go on tying the way we've been doing all along. In my opinion, the damage to the environment would be imperceptible.

Yeah, I hear the voices calling: "Hey, you're the guys who want to shut down the lumber companies for the sake of some weird little owl. Now it's your turn, and you beg for exemption. How about a little integrity, huh?"

Okay, I accept that often one's position is a matter of whose ox is being gored. But looking at the situation objectively, if what we are doing has far less of a negative effect on the environment than washing the dishes, why not give us some time so we can come up with an answer? After all, the automobile industry has been permitted to phase-in environmental improvements in cars over what is now three decades, and counting. We're really pretty small peanuts.

Thus spoke Zarathustra, or in this case, an old fly tyer, trying to cope with change. Let's just hope rationality prevails in this case.

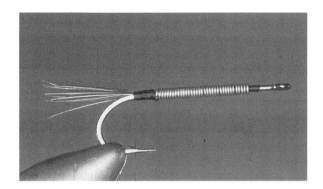
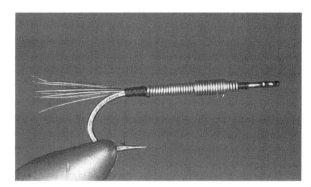

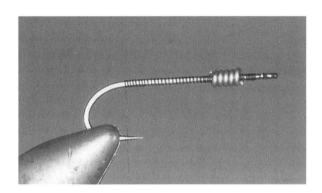
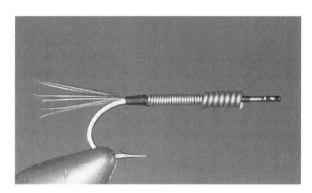

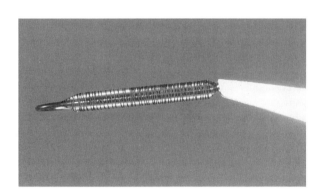

Typical applications of lead wire. Note that where appropriate, the thread has been built up, to equalize diameters, and eliminate bumps.

Hooks

If there is one thing I wish for on almost a daily basis it is some form of standardization in hook sizing and descriptive terminology. Someone should lock all of the hook manufacturers in a room and restrain them from eating, drinking, or going to the toilet until this mission is accomplished. If this had been done many years ago we would have a true system today. But at this moment in time, with so much expensive technology in place, no one is going to change simply for the sake of standardization. So it looks as though we're stuck with the Tower-of-Babel situation that exists at present.

What should have happened, and didn't, is something like this. Take a very common size and design of hook—let's say a size 12 dry-fly hook with a model perfect bend. Of the various shapes used in hook bends, model perfect is the only one that has a finite description—it's a semicircle. Agreement is reached that the gap (gape, for you traditionalists) is a certain dimension—⅜ of an inch, or for metric countries, the closest metric equivalent, which is five millimeters. Then it is established that a standard-length shank will be twice the gap.

This would establish a benchmark. From there, meaningful variations could be extrapolated. For example, a 1X long shank would be, in essence, a size 12 gap with a size 10 shank. And so forth.

Even more bothersome, and in my opinion more critical, is the lack of standardization in wire diameters. A similar set of terms is employed: 1X fine, 3X fine, and so forth. This should tell us what to expect in the way of wire diameter or more important, weight. But it fails to do that because the "X" rating system has no consistency. Using a rather costly and highly accurate machinist's micrometer, I found that one manufacturer's 4X fine wire was heavier than another's 1X fine, in the same hook size. This is an atrocity.

There is no point in my going on about this much further, because nothing by way of help will come of it. But I'll leave you with this: know your hooks!

Examine them, ask questions, even get yourself a micrometer of your own. It's the only way you're ever going to be sure of the specifications of the hooks you buy.

Also, you should know that there is more than one scale by which hooks are sized. For example, if you are buying hooks expressly designed for Atlantic salmon flies, or bass flies, you'll encounter a scaling system that's quite different from the one used for trout hooks. The Wilson salmon dry-fly hook made by Partridge is much larger in gap than a trout hook of the same numeric size. For instance, a size 14 Wilson has a slightly wider gap than a size 10 regular dry-fly hook! Just so you know.

A Little History

At this writing, we have many more choices in hooks than in 1959, when I first sat down at a vise. However, a few significant suppliers are now long gone and some of the hooks they produced were quite excellent. The following story provides a bit of history.

Ray Bergman, the well-known author/fly tyer from Nyack, New York, imported a line of hooks from Redditch, England, which he marketed under his own name. It was a fairly complete line, and included salmon hooks as well as models for all sorts of trout flies. He used a descriptive system based on the color of the label. I'm not sure what the rationale was because in some cases there were variations of hook types that bore the same label color. However, the Gold Label and Red Label hooks were mostly dry-fly, although designs did differ.

The Gold Label hooks had a slightly different shape, being just a bit sproatish at the bend. They were a little longer in the shank, which essentially compensated for this. The eyes were always nicely formed, but were not tapered. The Red Label hooks featured a model-perfect bend, had a slightly shorter point, slightly smaller barb, and a tapered eye. Very beautiful indeed.

It was interesting for me to note, going through my History Hook box, that some Bergmans were labeled "Sinfalta," rather than labeled by color—although they still carried the various label colors. I have another box of Sinfaltas with a gold label that have a turned-up tapered eye and a model-perfect bend. Interesting.

I noticed that the Sinfalta's box simply stated, "Made in England," rather than "Made in Redditch, England," as the Gold Labels' box did. I wonder if Bergman might have switched manufacturers at some point—there were several to choose from. I believe they were all located in Redditch, as the hook-making business was an outgrowth of the needle-making trade that flourished there for centuries. Partridge, Sealy, and Alcock were the major producers. They made hooks under their own names, as well as for others, including Hardy, Bergman, Herter's, and briefly Orvis. Partridge is the sole survivor in Redditch today.

Meanwhile, just across the water, Norwegians were developing hook-making machinery so efficient that it would eventually enable them to dominate the industry. O. Mustad and Sons of Oslo make hooks for practically any type of fishing you can think of. In terms of volume, they are the leading supplier of fly hooks in the world. However, in recent years they have not only lost market share but prestige to British, and lately, Japanese manufacturers.

Before switching to other makes, I experienced a lot of malformed fly hooks from Mustad. They often displayed poor workmanship in critical areas such as the eye, barb, and point. I also had some Mustad dry-fly hooks that were the result of bad metallurgy. Some were soft, others brittle.

At one time, they were better. I have some old Mustad hooks that have very good workmanship. I don't know what happened. It may have had something to do with World War II. I understand that during the war the Mustads completely dismantled their factory and hid the machinery to keep it out of German hands.

However, to Mustad's credit they seem to be trying to upgrade their line of fly hooks, the dry-fly models in particular. They now offer a premium line called Accu-Point, which uses the modern chemical sharpening process. They cost more than the standard line but considering the cost of the other items that go into a fly, the price of the hook isn't all that much.

About twenty years ago along came the Japanese, and in a very short time they were grabbing major market share. Tiemco was first, offering a fairly complete line of high-quality hooks. Soon to follow were Dai Riki of leader material fame, and Kamasan, which is now Daiichi. There is definite evidence of improved technology here. The workmanship is consistently high quality, with few culls, and the metallurgy is excellent. The hooks are also very sharp thanks to chemical sharpening, a technique the Japanese developed. I believe that all fly hook manufacturers are now doing chemical sharpening, on at least some of their fly-tying hooks, in one form or another.

It is curious that the USA, with all of its technical capabilities, and with more sport anglers than any other country, doesn't have a major fly-hook manufacturer. The only name that comes to mind is Wright-McGill. They are perhaps better known for their baitfishing and saltwater hooks. But they do have a limited line of fly-tying hooks, particularly for wet-fly and saltwater-fly tying, that appear to be of good quality. I don't understand Wright-McGill's reluctance to get into the mainstream of the fly-hook market, since I believe they have the technology to become a formidable competitor.

But let's examine today's hooks from a functional standpoint, considering shape, weight, metallurgy, point, barb, eye, and other important features and qualities.

Dry-Fly Hooks

From a design standpoint here's what I like to see in a dry-fly hook, and why:

- A model perfect bend, so the entire shank length can be utilized, while the tail still sticks straight out the rear, and is not driven downward at an angle by the slope of the bend

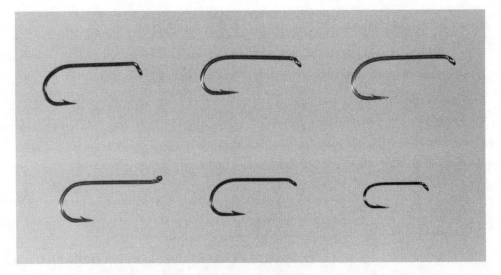

A selection of dry-fly hooks. Top row, left to right: Mustad AC94833, size 10; Daiichi 1180, size 10; Tiemco TMC 100, size 10. Bottom row: Belvoirdale Dry Fly, size 10; Partridge E1A, size 12; Orvis Big-Eye, size 16.

- Fine-diameter wire, appropriate for the size of the hook and its intended use. Ultra-fine wire hooks are great for fishing in places where the trout don't get very large.
- A highly tempered, bend-resistant wire, consistent with hook size and wire diameter
- A short point, again consistent with wire diameter, but not so short as to be too stubby to penetrate with slight pressure, or impractical to re-sharpen
- The sharpest possible point, for obvious reasons
- A very small barb, sometimes called a feather barb, to minimize damage to the mouths of fish and to reduce hook-weakening at that spot, thus better facilitating debarbing
- A perfectly finished, properly closed eye, turned down approximately 30 degrees, that will accommodate both Turle-type and Clinch-type knots

A word about eyes. I purposely said nothing about the size of the eye, but there is a consideration here. Orvis has a line of hooks that have proportionately larger eyes in smaller sizes. I think this is a fine idea, provided it isn't carried too far. My concern is that a great many anglers, including myself, like to use one version or another of the Turle knot for tying on dry flies, small ones in particular. A correctly tied Turle knot always forms around the "neck" of the fly, so that the leader comes straight out of the eye. If the knot should slip forward and form in front of the eye, it is seriously weakened. Even worse is when the knot slips right through the eye. This will happen when the eye and the diameter of the leader material are incompatible. So if one is fishing a 7X tippet with a size 20 fly, but the eye is a size 12, there is the potential for trouble.

To my knowledge, the enlargement of the eyes on the Orvis hooks isn't that extreme, and there have been no reported problems.

Those of you who are hookophiles may have noticed that I didn't say anything about forged bends or tapered shanks and eyes. Forging the bend simply means flattening the wire on the sides and creating an ovate, rather than a round cross-section. This is supposed to enhance strength. Forging is something of a hand-me-down from the days of iron work, and on larger hooks it may actually afford some benefit. However, on trout hooks the difference isn't even measurable—this from someone in the business, who tests such things.

Tapered shanks and eyes are nice, but not much more than that. At one time, tapering probably was beneficial in that it enabled the hook maker to conserve on metal, using more in the bend where strength was critical, while removing some from up front. It does result in a very neat eye, with less outside diameter for equivalent inside diameter. However, with modern metallurgy, finer wire can be used throughout, so that tapering, which complicates hook making considerably, is no longer so important. But I'm speaking of dry-fly hooks—with heavier-wire models it's still an asset, and I'd like to see more of it.

As a lover of fly tying, I'm very particular about hook attributes that affect the tying itself, as well as the fishing. Perhaps the most critical is the workmanship around the eye. Few things are more frustrating than a poorly closed, ragged-edged eye, especially when coupled with too severe a turn-down that starts ahead of where the eye is actually formed. This causes the thread to slide down into the eye when the tyer is attempting to finish off the head, abrading the thread and making a horrible mess. I counsel you to avoid such hooks; there are alternatives.

Hooks for Mini-flies

For those who tie and fish very small flies, there is another critical design consideration—effective hooking. This is mainly a matter of having sufficient gap for the hook to become engaged when a fish takes. It isn't a problem until you get down below a size 18. Then the gap is beginning to become small enough that the materials used in tying the fly may actually block it.

Attention to tying techniques, choice of materials, and fly design can relieve this problem to a large extent. For example, I use thread for bodies on many of my small dry flies, and I'm very careful with hackle. We get this wonderful stuff from Hebert and Hoffman that is so stiff it can actually interfere with hooking. I ran into this problem on the Griffith Gnat, a great favorite of mine that calls for a palmered hackle over a peacock body. I now start the hackle a little further forward, thus clearing the point of the hook.

But even with the most enlightened approach a hook with insufficient gap still won't hook up effectively. The answer is in design—specifically, the changing of the gap-to-shank length ratio. Here, the hook maker must depart from the 1:2 gap-to-shank ratio referred to earlier in this chapter, and reduce the gap *less* than the shank, proportionately, with each reduction in hook size.

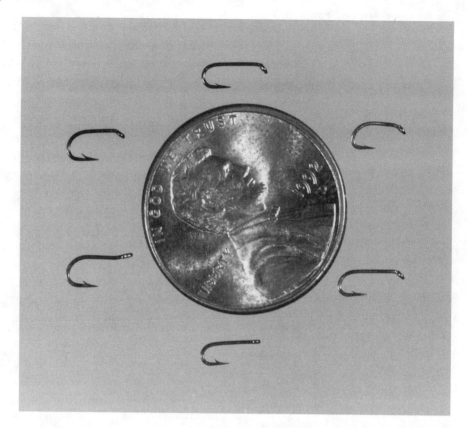

Mini-fly hooks. Top row, starting at 10:00: Partridge K1A; Daiichi 1100; Daiichi J220. Bottom row, starting at 8:00: Belvoirdale Midge; Mustad 94859; Tiemco TMC 100. All are size 24.

All major manufacturers offer small and tiny hooks. Unless something has changed that I'm not aware of, Mustad's ubiquitous model 94840 is simply reduced in linear ratio all the way down to size 28. In my opinion this doesn't leave enough gap for dependable engagement. They also offer a turned-up-eye (TUE), model 94842, which at least gets the hook eye out of the gap area, but that's not the entire answer. Neither is their model 94859, which appears to be the 94840 with a straight, rather than turned-down eye (TDE). In my experience the gap is still inadequate, and the straight eye negates the use of the Turle knot.

Daiichi offers several small hooks that depart from this linear design to improve hooking effectiveness. The model 1480 is interesting—it combines a shorter than normal shank with a limerick-style bend that sets the hook point further back, thus enhancing gap. The smallest size is 24, but the short shank facilitates tying equivalents to 26's and 28's.

Daiichi also has a model 1640 that I find interesting. It has a straight eye which disallows the Turle knot, and the smallest size is a 20. However, it has a 2X short shank, so you can tie an equivalent size 24 on the size 20. If Daiichi were to make this hook with a 30-degree turned-down eye and add sizes 22 and 24, they would have a formidable mini-fly hook. Tiemco offers a similar model.

Partridge offers a very effective departure from linear gap-to-shank ratio with their Marinaro midge hook, coded K1A. These are offered in sizes 24, 26, and 28 only. The Partridge L3A, which is quite adequate in gap and is available down to size 22, covers the remainder of the mini-hook range quite nicely.

Wet-Fly and Nymph Hooks

Variation in hooks for subsurface flies is much wider than with dry-fly hooks, since the range of images we tyers are trying to imitate or create is far greater. In addition to the many nymphs and larval forms of aquatic insects, there are hellgrammites, crayfish, aquatic worms, leeches, shrimps, and scuds, even snails. We also seek to imitate forage fish, but let's save that for the streamer-fly hook discussion.

Generally, hooks of this type employ heavier wire than do dry-fly hooks. How much heavier? That depends on several factors, the most important of which are how much weight you want the fly to have, and how strong the hook needs to be. Too thin a wire would be prone to bending under pressure, depending on its tempering. This becomes more important with longer-shank hooks, which are used for large nymphs and streamers. Too fine a wire here will allow a strong fish to twist and bend the hook, which normally results in a lost fish and a ruined fly.

The criteria mentioned above with reference to dry-fly hooks also applies here, in terms of points, barbs, and work around the eye. However, the shape or length of the point should bear a direct relationship to the diameter of the wire. With fine dry-fly wire a shorter point can be used without sacrificing pen-

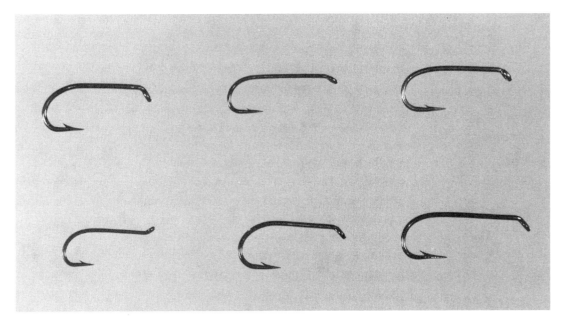

Nymph and wet-fly hooks. Top row, left to right: Mustad 3906, size 8; Daiichi 1560, size 10; Tiemco TMC 3769, size 8. Bottom row: Belvoirdale Wet Fly, size 12; Partridge G3A, size 8; Mustad 3906B, size 8.

etration. With heavier wire though, more of a gradual taper is required. This also facilitates repeated resharpening, which is rather important. Wet flies usually last longer than dry flies. They are more ruggedly constructed and usually are fished on heavier tippets. They are also more likely to be dulled by contact with underwater objects, which is exacerbated to some degree by the slightly softer metal used by some makers.

The shape or bend is not as critical as it is with drys, since we aren't so concerned with the position of the tail. Most wet-fly hooks use a sproat or modified limerick bend. Not that there's anything terribly wrong with a model perfect bend—those hooks will catch fish too. To a large extent, it's a matter of eye appeal. Most tyers, myself included, feel that wet flies and nymphs appear more graceful when tied on hooks with a compound bend.

Various shank lengths are employed in tying subsurface flies, due to the considerable variation in the size and shape of the organisms we seek to imitate. For example, short-bodied nymphs, such as the clingers of the Epeorus family, fit nicely on a "standard" (that word again!) length hook. On the other hand, the elongated nymphs of the numerous stoneflies lay out nicely on 2X, 3X, and even 4X shank hooks.

Availability of these hooks is no problem, since every major hook maker offers quite a wide range. However, here's where you'll run up against the lack of standardization mentioned earlier. One maker's 3X-long is another's 2X-long. Just be sure to look the hooks over carefully and decide which one best fits the shape of the f! you want to tie.

Good-quality work around the eye is just as important for wet-fly hooks as for dry, although one doesn't get that impression when examining some of the hooks on the market. For some reason certain hook makers think that the eye on a wet-fly hook should be turned down at a severe angle. I can't under-

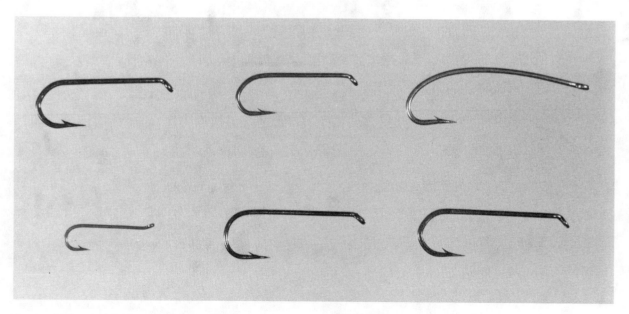

Longer-shank nymph hooks. Top row, left to right: Mustad 9671, size 8; Daiichi 1710, size 10; Tiemco TMC 200R, size 6. Bottom row: Belvoirdale Nymph, size 16; Partridge D4A, size 10; Mustad 9672, size 8.

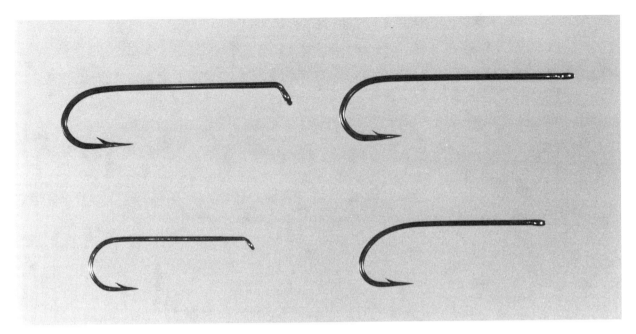

Long-shanked hooks. Top row, left to right: Mustad 79580, size 4; Daiichi 1750, size 4. Bottom row: Partridge H1A, size 6; Partridge D3ST, size 4.

stand this, because the same considerations with regard to knots apply, as do those relating to the tying work around the front of the fly. In fact, I like to use straight-eyed hooks on my large nymphs and like flies, because the knot I'll use in fishing will probably be an Improved Clinch or some kind of loop knot, rather than a Turle.

With heavier wire hooks, a tapered eye is a nice touch. It reduces the overall size of the eye without sacrificing inside diameter, and enables the hook maker to form a more neatly closed eye with fewer ragged edges.

Streamer-Fly Hooks

As we all know, streamer flies are essentially imitations of forage fish. Many of them fall into the attractor category, but that term is for our convenience. Can you imagine a smart old brown trout thinking, "Gee, that's a gorgeous attractor fly. I'm going to eat it!" Hah!

A word about how predatory fish take—or at least try to take—a small fish, and thus, an imitation of one. Ideally, they try to turn on it and, if it's small enough, scarf it up with a powerful engulfment of water. If the forage fish is too large to be popped down like a canape, the fish will try to grab it and work it into a head-first position. Pike, pickerel, and other warm-water predator fish are very good at this. This action enables the predator to slide the meal down its gullet without interference from sharp, spiny fins.

The point—no pun intended—is that an extremely long-shanked hook isn't necessarily effective for engagement. However, neither is it an impediment. From a tyer's standpoint, a longer-shanked hook accommodates and positions the various components of a streamer. It also allows the use of

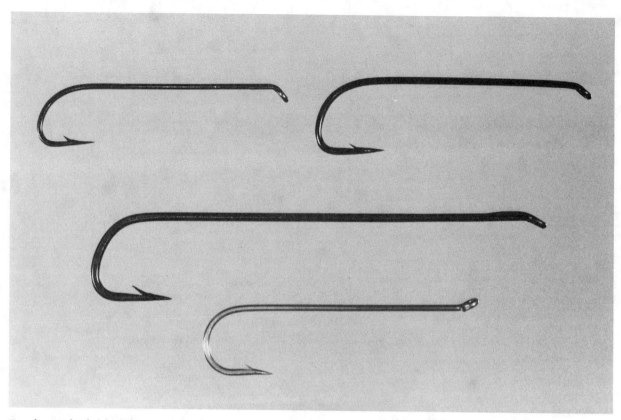

Even longer-shanked hooks. Top row, left to right: Mustad 9575, size 4; Daiichi J171, size 2. Middle: Partridge CS15. Bottom: Belvoirdale Streamer, size 2.

longer hairs and feathers for the "wings" without them extending too far behind the hook, which contributes to tangling during casting. The end result is also a beautiful fly.

I like streamer hooks from 6X to 8X in shank length, with either a straight or moderately turned-down eye. I much prefer a looped eye, because the double wire affords a more comfortable base for mounting both feathers and hair. Of course the return wire has to be smoothly tapered, with no drop-off at the end. There are hooks with stubbed-off return wires, and they are a nightmare to tie on. In comparing notes on this subject, George Kesel and I found that we had both resorted to the same tactic—a Dremel tool with carborundum or diamond discs. Tedious, but effective. This instrument is very useful for other things as well, such as sharpening larger hooks, tying scissors, knives, and other instruments.

As for wire diameter, it should be stout enough to resist being bent or skewed during a hard battle with a powerful fish, but it shouldn't be so thick as to inhibit hooking. Wire diameter also influences how quickly and deeply the fly sinks, but there are other methods for adjusting that, so it's a secondary consideration.

As I mentioned earlier, the point needs to be sufficiently tapered to facilitate effective penetration and allow resharpening without creating bluntness. The barb doesn't need to be very pronounced, but there should be one.

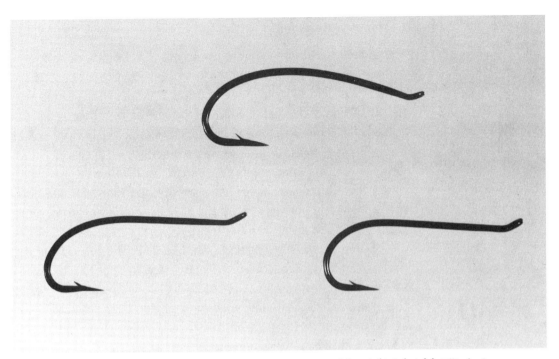

Typical stout-wire salmon-fly hooks. Top: Daiichi 2161, size 1. Bottom row, left to right: Belvoirdale F/R, size 1; Partridge M, size 1.

Barbless is fine for small flies, but not for larger, heavier ones. Ask any salmon fisherman. However, the barb does not need to be disproportionately large either, as some manufacturers seem to believe. In fact, this creates an impediment to penetration, and causes other problems as well.

There should also be sufficient throat—the wire from the rear of the barb to the bend—to allow adequate penetration, so that the barb becomes well engaged in the tough, cartilaginous tissue of the fish's mouth. This is one of the reasons that a compound bend, such as the sproat or limerick, is the preferred design for this type of hook.

Salmon-Fly Hooks

Here, we will examine the hooks used for tying Atlantic salmon flies. This is an intriguing topic. Consider that with very few exceptions, these hooks are all black in color. This is referred to in traditional circles as a black japanned finish. Why use this black finish? I can only deduce that it creates rust resistance. In the glory days of British salmon fishing a century or so ago, those incredibly beautiful and complex flies represented, in many cases, a half-day's work, so for the hook to rust and ruin one would have been unthinkable. Also I would imagine that in certain cases these flies were used in tidal waters at the mouths of rivers, where salinity accelerated rusting.

Design and Rationale

The archetypal single (double hooks are also common) salmon-fly hook features a looped eye and a sproat, or modified sproat bend. The shank length varies considerably from model to model. In trout hook terms, from about 2XL to 4XL. Some of this is the whim of the maker, but there is also a rationale involved. For example, long-shanked models are commonly called low-water hooks. Their original purpose was to facilitate the tying of a small fly on a larger iron, for summer fishing when water levels were low. With today's superior metallurgy, we simply use a small hook. However, the popularity of the low-water style carries on, as the longer shank accommodates the multi-component bodies of certain flies.

Some hooks have straight shanks, others have curved ones. I'm sure there is, or was, a reason for this. The various books we have that describe salmon-fly patterns and tying methods show a range of designs. Some of these are rather unusual, and apparently, the hook makers have tried to accommodate the fly tyers in this regard. I also think that some of these innovations in shape were done for purely aesthetic reasons.

Rather than attempt to describe the various hooks and their respective shapes and idiosyncrasies, I'll refer you to the photographs. These illustrations cover the great majority of what's available at this moment. What the future might bring, one can only guess.

With reference to the photos, I'd like to point out a few things. Note that there are some remarkable innovations in hook point design, particularly in the Bartleets by Partridge (see page 65). This is apparently intended to im-

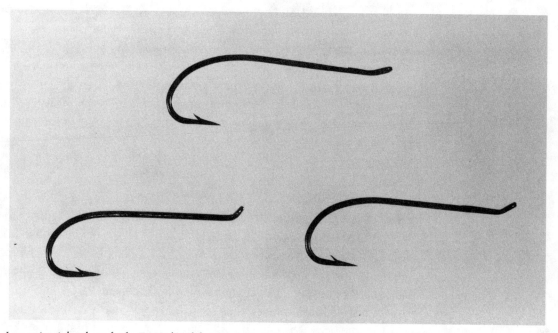

Low-water style salmon hooks. Top: Belvoirdale L/W, size 1. Bottom row, left to right: Daiichi 2421, size 2; Partridge N, size 2.

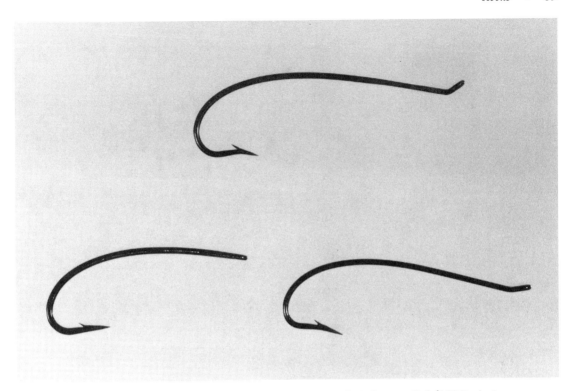

Different style salmon hooks. Top: Daiichi Alec Jackson Spey 2051, size 1 1/2. Bottom row: Daiichi 2151, size 1; Partridge Bartleet, size 1.

prove engagement performance. While I feel the Partridge Bartleet is a bit extreme, I must state that I had a good experience with this hook in Russia.

It was 1993, and some obtuse characters in the Russian bureaucracy in Murmansk had decided that they didn't like foreign anglers, after all. In addition to harassment from the fish inspectors, this attitude was manifested in pervasive regulations. At the last minute, by which time everyone had tied or purchased all of their flies, word came down that only de-barbed single hooks would be allowed. We rolled our eyes, heaved a sigh, and complied.

I was managing a camp from which we fished two rivers, the Pana and the Varzuga. These rivers have few really huge salmon but an enormous number of small- to medium-size fish. I must say that the last time that much steel was in the air on the Kola Peninsula was during the German bombardment in World War II. *Salar* would leap, shake his head, and the hook would fly across the river. Our takes-to-landed ratio was abysmal.

I had some Bartleets with me, and decided to give them a try. I tied up a few Winter's Hopes, the hot pattern at the time, in large sizes. The oddly shaped points seemed to resist dislodging much better, and my ratio improved. I did learn that one has to take care when de-barbing a Bartleet, as it's easy to break off the point at the barb.

Conversely, I've heard from several experienced salmon fishermen that Bartleet-style hooks are most ineffective in hooking fish with kypes. That doesn't surprise me. But then again, the presence of a pronounced kype presents a problem no matter what type of hook is employed.

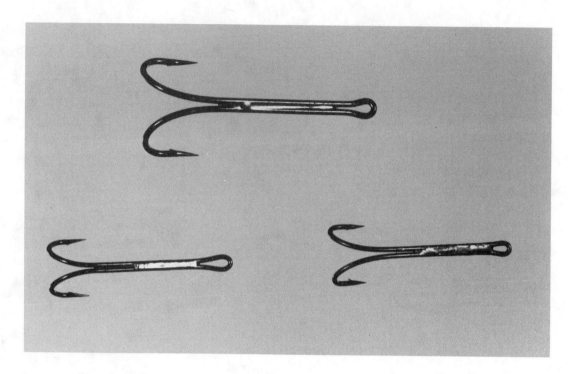

Salmon doubles. Top: Belvoirdale DLW, size 1/0. Bottom, left to right: Daiichi 7131, size 4; Partridge Q, size 4.

To this point, we've been talking about single hooks. What about doubles? The argument has been going on for eons about whether they actually hook better than singles. Obviously, the positioning of the two points is a plus; one never knows exactly what angle a salmon will come from. However, what about penetration? The anti-double set contend that the added pressure required to drive home two points causes poor engagement. They also believe that a salmon can fight against a double hook by shaking its head and working the points against each other to loosen them.

My opinion is that size and wire diameter have a greater bearing on engagement than single or double points. I've caught a fair number of salmon on both styles, and my experience indicates that I lose more fish on large, very heavy-wire hooks, whether single or double and particularly when de-barbing is required. In Iceland, Canada, and Labrador, I've fished a lot of small to very small doubles, and the salmon seem to have a much more difficult time dislodging them. I think this is due to effective penetration, and the fact that there's nothing for the fish to leverage against. It's easier to throw a baseball than a ping-pong ball.

The double hook offers one more advantage. That is the manner in which it accommodates the riffling hitch. For those who may not know, this technique involves throwing one or more half-hitches around the "neck" of the fly, causing it to ride the water at an angle. Which side the hitches are tied onto depends on which side of the river you're fishing from. The fly tends to ride high in the surface film, leaving a little wake, like a tiny swimming animal. This drives salmon wild on certain rivers, especially in Iceland and Labrador.

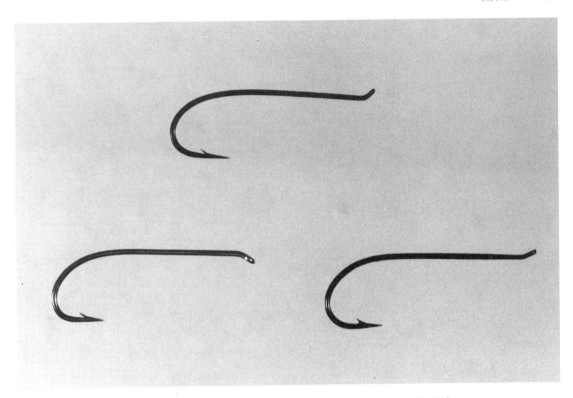

Salmon dry-fly hooks. Top: Tiemco TMC 7989. Bottom, left to right: Partridge CS42; Partridge Wilson.

Some credit Lee Wulff with originating the riffling hitch, or Portland Creek hitch, as it's sometimes called. Others say that Lee learned it from the natives in his Newfoundland days. Word has it that they had a lot of old British flies that had been tied on blind-eyed hooks, using gut eyes. When the gut eventually gave way, the fishermen simply half-hitched the flies to their leaders. After all, a good fly was far too valuable to throw away! It was then discovered that they worked better than before. A nice tale—I'd like to believe it.

Doubles are offered in several styles and also in several weights. There isn't nearly the diversity that exists with singles, but there needn't be. Basically there are standard models and low-water models, the latter being longer in the shank and made of lighter wire. Given a complete range of sizes, that's really all we need.

Quality Concerns

In addition to the considerations that apply to all hooks—metallurgy, sharpness, eyes, barbs, and points—doubles have one more. That is the quality of workmanship in the brazing process, which is how the two shanks are joined. Of all the operations in hook making, this one gives the most heartburn to the manufacturers.

So far, no one has automated the procedure with total success. Eventually, I'm sure they will. Meanwhile, it's a tedious, costly, technique-intensive process—and a somewhat imperfect one. We see a lot of double hooks with pretty rough brazing, which shows up as lumpy, uneven, or sometimes overly

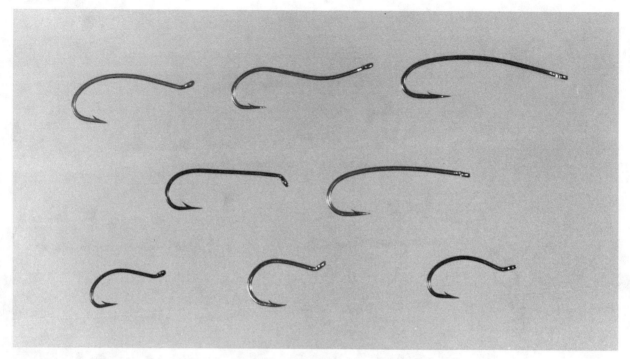

Specially-shaped hooks for special purposes. Top row, left to right: Partridge GRS7MMB, size 12; Daiichi 1770, size 8; Daiichi 1270, size 6. Middle row: Mustad 94831 long-shank dry; Tiemco TMC 2312 1X fine Hopper, size 8. Bottom row: Belvoirdale Caddis, size 14; Daiichi 4259 egg, size 6; Partridge K2B Yorkshire Sedge, size 12.

thick shanks. Making good-looking bodies on such hooks is a real challenge. However, it's not all that critical, since nobody makes doubles for framing. These flies are fishing weapons. The most important point is that the brazing forms a good bond, and that there isn't a lot of lumpy metal up front where the finish work on the fly takes place.

This applies to single hooks also. A well-designed hook will have enough length in the shank and in the return wire to allow the tyer to complete the head without crowding the eye. In fact, flies tied expressly with riffling in mind should be tied off a bit short of the eye to accommodate the hitches.

Special-Purpose Hooks

With all the innovation going on in fly tying today, it's not surprising that a large number of odd-looking hooks have appeared in the marketplace. Beyond the usual concerns relative to sharpness, strength, and quality of workmanship, the fly tyer needs to know what these hooks are used for, and what types of flies they're best for.

An innovation that's come onto the scene fairly recently is the increased use of color variations in hooks. Daiichi is particularly creative in this respect. At this writing, the beautiful Alec Jackson salmon hook is available in black, bronze, red, gold, silver, and blue. This not only makes for pretty effects in "wall" flies, but provides a color-compatible base over which light and bright materials can be wrapped, without concern about discoloration when the fly gets wet. Perhaps some colors that are harmonious with subaquatic insect life are in the offing—that could be interesting.

Saltwater Hooks

In addition to the universal criteria set forth for all fly hooks—sharpness, metal quality, workmanship—there are a few additional considerations of importance for saltwater hooks.

Not long after the great increase in popularity of saltwater fly-fishing in the 1970s came a series of hook critiques. One of the most strident arguments had to do with the use of stainless steel. The theory was that these hooks were *persistent* over a long period of time, meaning that a fish that broke off was stuck (no play on words intended) with the fly. Unless it could somehow rid itself of this fly, the fish would develop an infection and eventually die.

The September 1992 issue of *Saltwater Flyfishing Magazine* carried a report on a study done by the Maryland Department of Natural Resources, Tidewater Administration. Tests were performed on the following hooks: bronze, nickel-plated, stainless steel, and cadmium-plated. The results indicated that, while none of the hooks biodegraded quickly, bronze and nickel did so the soonest. Stainless steel, while virtually impervious to corrosion, was the *easiest* for the fish to get rid of. None of these hooks resulted in a mortality among the fish tested.

Cadmium was a different story. It was found to introduce a toxic substance to the fish, and a twenty percent mortality rate was observed.

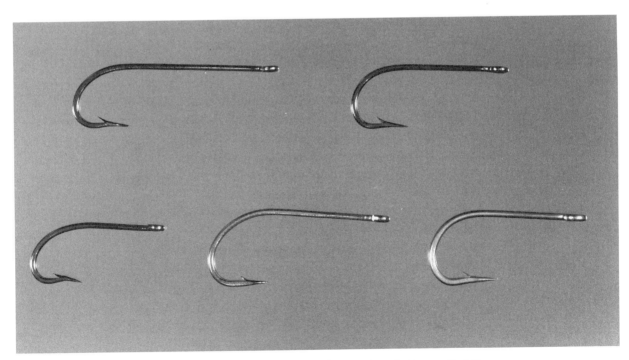

Saltwater fly hooks. Top row, left to right: Mustad 34011, size 1; Mustad 34007, size 1. Bottom row: Partridge CS52, *size 2; Daiichi 2546, size 1/0; TMC 800S, size 1/0.*

No one wants to see fish endangered by the inherent technology of the hooks used to lure and engage them. However, accurately evaluating the effects of various metallurgies is very difficult, since one must consider not only how long the hook remains in the fish's mouth, but what goes on during the entire time it's there. A bronzed hook *does* react quickly to the corrosive effects of salt water, but even if it dissipates in a relatively short period of time, it has chemically affected the fish.

Perhaps we have to bite the bullet here. Like it or not, we are engaging in a blood sport. Not on the same level as bullfighting maybe, but still, fishing is a type of violent physical interaction. Much as we might not like to admit it, even the most skillfully handled fish, hooked and played optimally in all respects, can be mortally injured. We strive to minimize this. Statistics overwhelmingly support the efficacy of fly fishing in this respect. Still, sadly, we lose a few. Should we give it all up? The fish on this planet might better be served by eliminating thirty-mile-long drift nets, and impassable impoundments. We're the smallest of potatoes.

The problem can be mitigated by de-barbing. You'll need a stout pair of flat-jawed pliers. Or, you can do what I've done and buy a Dremel tool, with abrasive discs. These will zap the barb on a heavy hook pronto, and are also great for reshaping and sharpening the point.

So let's use the most practical hooks available, and do the best we can to safeguard the fish via skillful handling and compassion. Stainless steel hooks are the strongest and sharpest, and respond to resharpening and reshaping better than whatever else is at hand at this writing. They may be persistent, but the same studies that found cadmium to have toxic properties indicated that stainless steel hooks were a very minor factor in saltwater fish mortality.

There's not a lot of variety in saltwater fly hook design, and unless some revelation occurs subsequently, a few models will suffice. Typically, short-shanked hooks are the order of the day, because fish of the sea are not like spring-creek trout; they don't pick at their food, they engulf it, and move along before something engulfs them. The most popular hooks equate to a 1X or 2X short trout hook. Really long-shanked hooks, analogous to freshwater streamer hooks, would be a liability, because of torque. Ocean fish are enormously powerful, and they would promptly make pretzels out of them. About the longest hook commonly used at present is the Mustad 34011, which equates to a 2X or 3X long trout hook.

It boils down to sharpness and quality of metal. Until recently, true devotees of saltwater fly fishing spent more time working on sharpening their hooks than they did tying materials onto them, reshaping, and honing. Very tedious, but hardly a waste of time if the result were to be a successful engagement with a titanic tarpon or a paranoid permit.

Now, with chemical sharpening, such arduous work isn't necessary. The enhanced hooks offered by Daiichi, Tiemco, Partridge, and Wright-McGill can hardly be improved upon, even by the most talented of hook mavens. Therefore, I have placed my Dremel tool and diamond discs in moth balls, and I'm devoting my time to tying the flies themselves.

Bass-Fly Hooks

As much as I respect this marvelous and highly popular gamefish, time restricts my opportunities to fish for it. So I have relied on George Kesel, my consultant at Hunter's Angling Supplies, for the essentials. George ties a lot of bass flies, and he ties them about as well as anyone. In his estimation, enlarged gap is of great importance, because of the bulkier bodies the flies usually have, and also because this facilitates spinning large amounts of deer hair.

Strength is certainly important, as bass tend to live in weedy, stump-infested spots, and love nothing better than to drag one's terminal tackle through such gauntlets. However, weight is also a consideration, because so many bass flies are floaters of one type or another. So we have strength vs. lightness, which mandates good metallurgy.

In recent years, the stinger design has become the most popular among bass-fly addicts. This model was introduced by Mustad, and is now available from at least a couple of other manufacturers. For those who like to use cork, closed-cell foam, and such materials, instead of trimmed hair, the humped-shank hook is still a favorite.

In conclusion, I might mention that heavier-wire hooks can cause damage to an improperly adjusted vise, or one with jaws that are inadequate for such work. Personally, I prefer a vise with interchangeable jaws, such as the HMH, so that I can go to the magnum set when tying saltwater or larger salmon flies. In any case, be sure to properly set your vise for the wire diameter of the hooks you're using. With respect to hook shapes and designs, the old adage about pictures being worth a thousand words certainly applies here. With that in mind, I'll let the photos and captions speak for themselves.

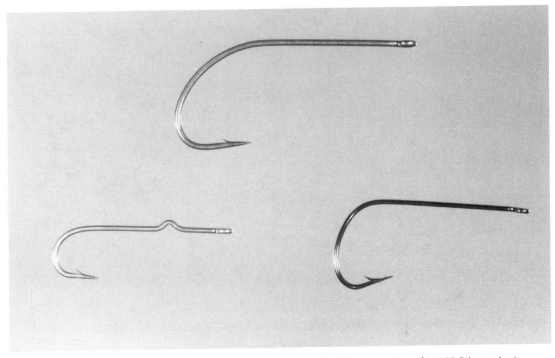

Bass fly hooks. Top: Tiemco TMC 8089, size 2. Bottom, left to right: TMC 511S, size 6; Mustad 37187 Stinger, size 6.

Threads

With only the rarest exceptions, the one ingredient that all flies have in common is thread. Offhand, the only flies I can think of that didn't require thread were those that Lee Wulff used to make, using polystyrene plastic and solvent to stick materials in place. These strange flies worked pretty well, but never became popular. Fly-fishing people are highly resistant to change.

Modern threads are terrific, and I can't conceive of anyone wanting to revert to the old silks of yesteryear. My most recent convert was Helen Shaw, when I was in the process of doing an article about her for *American Angler Magazine* a number of years ago. While amazingly innovative, Helen is in some respects very much a traditionalist, and a "fingers-only" tyer—that is, no bobbin. Her complaint was that modern synthetic threads didn't feel good to her hands. I gave her a few spools of 8/0 Uni-Thread, and asked that she give it an unprejudiced try. She did, and loved it.

I'd like to begin by setting forth my philosophy of thread. I'm not trying to hard-sell anyone, but you might give this some consideration. I prefer to use the thinnest thread that will serve for a particular job. I've satisfied myself that more wraps with finer thread are stronger than fewer wraps with thicker thread. Thin thread goes on more smoothly, and better facilitates the delicate shaping of things. It takes up less space, and makes neater whip-finishes.

At this writing, I'm doing almost all of my tying with 8/0 Uni-Thread. It reminds me somewhat of the silk I started out with 35 years ago, but is several orders of magnitude stronger, and presents no decomposition problems, as silk did.

For spinning hair, I often use 6/0 Uni-Thread, although it is quite feasible to spin very fine, soft hair with the 8/0, a nice advantage when tying smaller Rat-Faced MacDougals, Irresistibles, and the like. For very large flies I use heavier thread, such as 3/0, so as to cover space more quickly. I use these threads to build up heads on streamers where I intend to use a painted or stick-on eye, but usually I tie it on after the fly proper is completed with the 8/0.

This isn't a Uni-Thread commercial—all I'm saying is that at this moment in my fly-tying career, this particular thread has the attributes I think are important. It will be interesting to see how thread technology develops—who knows what may emerge in the immediate future?

Properties of Threads

Modern threads differ one from another in several respects. Four factors affect this: thickness, stretchiness, type of material, and waxed/not waxed.

The two most common materials at present are nylon, which the ever-popular Danville Flymaster uses, and polyester, of which Uni-Thread is composed. All of the nylon threads that I'm familiar with are prewaxed, because they almost have to be. Nylon is a slippery material, and has virtually no memory; it untwists readily when suspended by the weight of the bobbin. Thus, it behaves—or perhaps I should say misbehaves—much like floss in that it tends to separate into very fine individual strands. This can cause some vexing problems, particularly for the novice or occasional tyer who isn't sure why this is happening, and doesn't know how to cope with it. Once thread—or for that matter, floss—gets strandy, the little fibers begin to break. The result is a mess, especially if you're in the process of forming a whip-finish knot and must pull frayed thread underneath the wraps used to form the knot. Awful!

But there is another side to that coin. Some tyers who do a lot of cosmetic work for framings or display prefer Flymaster because it flattens a bit more than Uni-Thread and they feel that they can get smoother underlayers. While I acknowledge this, I also feel the difference isn't sufficient to offset the advantages of Uni-Thread's better strength-to-diameter ratio and handling qualities. It is rated 8/0, whereas Flymaster is rated 6/0, which is slightly heavier.

Uni-Thread can be purchased waxed or unwaxed, because waxing isn't necessary to mitigate untwisting with this material. Most people prefer waxed and usually that's what the shops carry. The only potential problem with this is that head cements may not penetrate and impregnate as well with the waxed thread. With Uni-Thread the amount of wax present is negligible, and if the cement is properly thinned there's no such problem.

I guess you've noticed that I'm using these two brand names as though they were the only ones in town. That's not quite the case, but presently they so dominate the field that there's not a lot of market share left for anyone else.

This could change as technology progresses. For example, I recently tried a thread marketed under the name of Georgio Benecchi. It's pretty good stuff. It claims a rating of 12/0. It's difficult to accurately rate these types of products because some of them spread more than others. My perception is that the overall thickness is little, if any, less than 8/0 Uni-Thread, but it handles differently, lying somewhat flatter. It is strong, and comes in several useful colors. My main complaint about it is that the spools they are presently using don't work well with bobbins.

I've tried a few other threads that are trying to break into the market at this time. The one thing they all have in common is strength. However, that's only one criteria. It's also important for thread to be easy to work with and accommodating to various fly-tying techniques. For instance, when I want to use soft wraps I don't want a thread that unwraps itself and jumps off the hook at the slightest relaxation of tension.

I also notice that the high-tech super threads, such as Kevlar and Dynacord, are terrible scissors-killers. I hate having to keep changing scissors just to save my good ones from destruction. So it is sometimes prudent to evaluate threads from a broader set of criteria than tensile strength alone.

Specialty Threads

There are a few special-purpose threads available that deserve mention. One such thread is made from Kevlar. This is a space-age material that in a different form is used in the nose cones of re-entry vehicles—it's that tough. Some deer-hair-spinning specialists use Kevlar because it's so strong it is, in effect, unbreakable—you'll bend or snap the hook first. This accommodates the heavy tension that is required to induce some types of hair to spin and flare.

Also—and this is the only thing I like about Kevlar—it's so slippery that when you want to pack your spun bunches to make a tighter body, the hair slides along almost as though it were on bare hook.

It should be noted that some deer-hair experts disagree that this is a desirable property. They contend that if the hair can slide when being compressed or packed, it will slide and loosen under fishing conditions. I won't argue that point, other than to state that my bombers don't fall apart, and they get worked pretty hard. I think that there are ways of compensating for this in the tying process.

On the negative side, Kevlar is pretty unruly stuff to handle. It has a tendency to loosen and back itself off with the least relaxation of tension, and spreads laterally like crazy. Also, it ruins scissors. If you decide to tie with Kevlar, use heavy scissors that you don't much care about.

Glo-bug enthusiasts also use Kevlar a lot or at least they did when that school of tying first evolved. My personal experience is that one can obtain equally good results with other more manageable threads, using whatever gauge is appropriate for the size Glo-bug being tied.

Another specialized thread is a Danville product called Flat Waxed Nylon. It's a thicker version of Flymaster, and well-waxed. Of the several threads offered by this supplier, I like this one the best. It's nice for larger flies, such as saltwater streamers, because it covers space effectively, has good stretch for enhanced gripping, and is strong enough to cinch down those wicked synthetic hairs we often use for such flies. Also, it covers lead wire very well, and smooths out nicely to accommodate painted eyes. It also facilitates the Glo-bug tying.

Flat Waxed Nylon is popular among spun-hair tyers. Keep in mind that it is necessary to spin the bobbin in order to "sharpen" the thread, as too much flatness inhibits neat flaring and packing.

I find that 6/0 Uni-Thread is sufficiently strong to facilitate the tying of both Glo-bugs and spun-hair flies. Its advantage is its smaller diameter, which translates to less buildup. In spinning deer hair I get better packing, and it's also easier to pass the thread through the bunch of hair when stepping forward. With Glo-bugs, I get less visible thread line where it passes over the center of the bunch of yarn. I consider all these advantages significant.

But before you all throw away your super-strong threads in favor of 6/0 Uni-Thread, please consider this. I'm a professional tyer. I've acquired high-level skills in thread management and related techniques. I can get away with things the average tyer can't. So, if using finer thread for spinning hair doesn't work well for you, forget it, and go for the tough stuff. I should also mention that the advantage of finer thread is most noticeable on smaller spun-hair flies, such as Irresistibles and Rat-Faced MacDougals, and the so-called wet bugs that are so popular with New Brunswick salmon fly fishers.

Monocord is another product from Danville. The name bothers me. I have always interpreted mono to mean one—monosyllabic, mononucleosis, monolith, monolog, and to the issue at hand, monofilament. But fellow tyers, this material is *definitely not* single-stranded. It is composed of a group of fine fibers, as all threads mostly are. Monocord may be a catchy name for the catalog, but it is not accurately descriptive of the product. I am also informed by shopkeepers that Monocord has a limited shelf life, and tends to weaken with age.

Monocord is tough stuff, a harder thread than any of the others mentioned, except Kevlar. It is available in three thicknesses: 3/0, A, and B, with 3/0 being the finest. It is suitable for those chores that require considerable tension—spinning hair, making Glo-bugs, synthetic hair, and other such jobs. It is offered in a wide variety of colors, but not all widths come in all colors. Check with your dealer for specifics.

Spiderweb

This is, I believe, the most specialized thread of all. It is ultra-fine, as the name implies. There is no rating on the label, but I've heard 18/0 casually mentioned. At this writing it comes only in white.

As one might guess, it is tricky stuff to tie with. I keep a couple of bobbins on hand on which I've reduced the tension by carefully bending out the limbs a little. A bobbin adjusted for normal (8/0-6/0) tension will cause Spiderweb to break right away.

Another of its attributes that can cause problems is its stiffness, which is surprising when one considers the diameter. It has a strong tendency to un-wrap and back off when "soft" wraps are used. This is bothersome, as variation in tension is an important technique.

But even with these caveats, Spiderweb is very nice for tying small to tiny flies. I use it for Tricos, little Baetis, small ants, Griffith Gnats, and other tiny flies. It also has another application. When tying "wall" flies—that is, flies that are intended strictly for mounting, where aesthetics is the main concern—I use Spiderweb for that delicate work at the rear of the fly—the tip/tag assembly, tailing, certain types of bodies, body veilings, and such. It really does help reduce buildup and bulk, yet allows the use of plenty of wraps.

Monofilament

At this point it is appropriate to talk about true monofilament thread. Both Uni-Thread and Danville now offer such products, and perhaps others soon will. At this writing, Danville has two diameters: fine and ultra-fine. The fine measures .006 inches. They come in two shades, which Danville describes as clear and smoky. Uni-Thread offers a product named Sea-Tru, which has a diameter of .007 inches and is clear.

These are special-purpose threads. As one might expect, this material handles very differently than any sort of true thread. It has a life all its own; relaxation of tension results in it leaping off the hook in writhing coils. It does not compress at all, and even the finer versions create bulk.

However, recently I received a sample from Uni-Thread of their latest monofilament product. It is a mere .004 inches in diameter, but is very strong. Its most remarkable attribute is its limpness; it handles almost like regular thread. I find it very useful for such tying applications that do not involve thread color, such as the rear of a tubing body assembly. Also, I have found it wonderful for spinning hair and for making Glo-Bugs. This product, and others like it that will almost certainly ensue, offer definite advantages to the tyer.

Monofilament threads also lend themselves to certain applications in saltwater fly-tying. In fact, the Uni-Thread people tell me that Bob Popovics, the talented and creative tyer from New Jersey, was responsible for Sea-Tru becoming a product. When the tyer wants everything on a fly to be glass-like and translucent, mono thread is the answer. Phil Camera frequently makes use of it in his interesting and instructive book, *Fly Tying With Synthetics*. I also know of tyers who rib quill bodies on dry flies with monofilament thread.

Dubbing

The word "dubbing" is commonly used both as a noun and a verb since it refers to both a material and a process. Dubbing materials, such as furs and chopped-up yarns, are among the oldest and most revered tying materials. Some of the most ancient ones, such as hare's ear, are still used with telling effect. However, there are also many modern ones that are excellent.

The old English term for these materials was "dubbin," and was used to describe the various materials used in making bodies on flies. You will still see this form of the word in the literature and on a few product labels.

From a fishing standpoint, there are a number of attributes one might look for in dubbing, and we'll examine those later on. From a fly-tying standpoint, there's one particular attribute that's of prime importance: texture.

Texture

The fly tyer's definition of texture addresses several important properties. They are a bit tricky to describe using classic English, so please allow me some latitude of expression.

- Fineness, softness, and the opposite, coarseness
- Slipperiness, or lack of it
- Length and strength of fiber
- Handleability—how it ties, how it interacts with thread

Notice that the list doesn't include reaction to light, water, and environmental factors. We'll get to that later. Here, we're concerned only with actual tying properties.

The texture of a dubbing material relates directly and dramatically to what one is trying to tie. A small, delicate dry fly demands very soft, finely textured dubbing with relatively short fibers, so that quantities can be strictly controlled. The amount of dubbing required to dress a size 24 dry fly is minimal, and materials that can't be applied in tiny wisps and packed or compressed neatly just won't work.

For example, some years ago a line of synthetic dubbing named the Andra Spectrum appeared on the market. It was a "breakthrough" material—clearly the best at that time. The proprietor of the product was a dentist from Connecticut named Fred Horvath. He knew his entomology, because the colors were very insect-oriented. To this day, his Pink Hendrickson shade is the best I've seen. In fact I prefer it to Art Flick's elusive urine-burned vixen fox fur. And if Art could see it, I think he'd agree.

Andra had only one negative characteristic: it was "strandy" (I warned you that I'd be extending the parameters of the English language a bit!). In other words, the individual fibers were rather long and very tough. The result was that like it or not, you were stuck with a bunch of a certain length. This varied from batch to batch. Reducing fiber length by cutting wasn't really the answer, since that only caused stubby rather than wispy ends. Thus, good as Andra was in some respects, it wasn't optimum for smaller flies.

At the risk of getting ahead of the story, I'll mention that several new synthetic products have recently appeared that don't have Andra's strandy quality. They dub like a dream. As for Andra, it went off the market a number of years ago. Now and then though, I see some in a shop. I heard that there are plans to bring it back, but if anything concrete has materialized, I'm not aware of it.

Having used the term "synthetic," I should develop this topic a bit further. Synthetic dubbing is essentially composed of man-made fibers, while natural dubbing comes from animal fur or plant fiber. Organic dubbing usually consists of fur or hair, although down and underfeather materials can also be used.

Natural dubbing runs the gamut from ultra-soft and fine (mole, beaver, domestic rabbit underfur, and kapok) to coarse, spiky, and tweedy (hare's ear, squirrel with guard hairs) to slippery and reflective/translucent (polar bear underfur, seal hair). Synthetics have been developed that imitate and in some instances go beyond natural materials. Various acrylics, such as Antron and Orlon, provide the shine and glitter of polar bear and seal. They are also easier to work with and come in practically every color imaginable.

Other synthetics offer the ultimate in soft, fine, eminently packable dubbing. Between these two groups is a wide assortment of textures, some of which are blends of natural and synthetic materials. I haven't yet seen a synthetic that closely imitates my beloved hare's ear, but the blends that combine hare's ear with a little sparkly stuff such as Antron are great.

Naturals

With that in mind, let's take a look at what's available in the smooth, easy-to-pack-tightly category. First, some naturals:

- Mole fur
- Rabbit underfur, without guard hairs
- Muskrat
- Beaver
- Otter
- Mink
- Fitch
- Foxes (various)
- Australian opossum
- Seal fur (as opposed to seal hair)
- Camel
- Wool
- Kapok

This is not a complete list, but those are the main materials. In all cases I refer to the *underfur* of the particular animal, with *all guard hairs removed*. Guard hairs are the longer, stiffer hairs that protect the underfur of many animals.

Some of these materials dub down finer than others. For example mole, rabbit, beaver, and mink have a fine texture and pack down very well. Camel, seal, and Australian opossum are a bit more coarse. Kapok, a plant fiber, packs very well. Wool varies widely, depending on the type.

Of the above, perhaps the most interesting and under-utilized is mole. It is of a rich blue-gray shade and is ideal for many classic patterns, such as the Adams. Its most striking attribute is the total absence of guard hairs. There are none! The fur is short, with a maximum length of about three-eighths of an inch on a prime pelt. However, because it is so soft and workable, that's long enough.

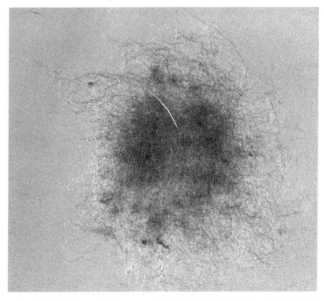

This soft dubbing would be very nice if it didn't contain those little "nits," or balls. These make lumps in the fly body.

One needs to know how to handle mole. Removing the fur from the skin is tricky. Don't try to pull it out or scrape it off with a blade of some sort because the soft skin will tend to come with the fur. Cutting it off with fine scissors isn't all that feasible either, because you can't really get close enough, and you don't want to lose fiber length.

I use small electric clippers, either the barber's variety or the ones sold in stores for trimming beards. Simply lay the pelt out flat and shear off the fur as close to the skin as possible. Then, fluff it up in a fur blender.

This technique can be used on most furs, and is particularly helpful in the case of soft, tanned hides. The downside is that if you want to remove guard hairs, the shearing action of the clippers may cause them to mix with the underfur before you have a chance to deal with them. So when you want to remove guard hairs, use scissors to cut off discretely sized bunches. Then follow one of the following two procedures, depending on what works best with the particular kind of material you're working with.

Separating Underfur and Guard Hairs

- Grab a bunch of hair/fur with your thumb and forefinger. With scissors, cut the bunch at the base, taking care not to let them mix. Then, grab the opposite end of the bunch at the base, where you just cut. This exposes the guard hairs, so that you can remove them with your fingers.

- With longer furs, such as fox and some types of rabbit, proceed as above, but continue to hold the bunch instead by the guard hair end. Then, use a fine-toothed comb to comb out the underfur.

In either case I like to fluff the underfur in a blender before using it, since this mixes up the fibers, and you don't end up having all the stubby ends from the cutting process in one place. It also texturizes the fur and nicely blends the subtle shadings that are often present in natural furs.

Storage

Furs prepared this way can be stored in a variety of containers. Small Ziploc bags are very convenient, and you can label them with a Sharpie or similar permanent felt marker. Empty film canisters are nice, particularly the semi-transparent ones. If you want to keep bunches of furs in one place, you can put them in the compartments of a plastic box.

It's also important to protect natural materials from infestations by insects. Traditional repellents such as mothballs or moth flakes work fine, but I've been told by medical people that longtime exposure to the gases produced by them can be hazardous to one's health. At this point I've gone to natural repellents such as sachets of herbal material that can be bought in many shops and catalogs. These seem to work fine on bugs, but may not repel mice, as mothballs and flakes do. I don't have mice in the townhouse condominium where I live. Those who have to cope with them might consider storing vulnerable materials in tough, tightly sealed plastic boxes.

Prepackaged Furs

More and more today, natural and synthetic dubbings are being sold in packaged form. Years ago I shied away from these because most of them were not properly selected, prepared, or they were not cost-effective. That's changed—most of today's stuff is selected by people who know and care about what they're doing.

The main thing is to make sure that the product you purchase suits the intended application. The surest way to do this is to open the package and closely examine the contents. In some cases (for instance Ziplocs) this is easy—in others, which involve staples or other types of closures it's a bit more problematic. But as any of my fly-tying students will attest, I'm *very* particular about my dubbing, and recommend that you become likewise. It's no fun trying to turn out a neat, compact dry-fly body with dubbing that's full of guard hairs or otherwise non-optimal material. And there are some packaged materials out there that can fool you. In particular, beware of rabbit that hasn't had its guard hairs fully removed. So have a care.

Synthetics

I will preface this section with the following statement: certain goods, consumables in particular, must include on their package labels information on the nature of their contents. Not so with dubbing. Although some suppliers tell us what's in the bag, e.g., rabbit/Antron, most packages of dubbing are essentially mystery bags.

I made a few inquiries to the people who produce this stuff and was rebuffed—they weren't about to divulge the makeup of their materials. I guess I can't blame them; copying and me-too tactics are rife in our business. Therefore, in discussing these products it's possible that I may err, and list something as a synthetic that's not entirely synthetic, but actually a blend. I apologize to any supplier who might be so misrepresented.

However, the main point is, does it matter? The answer is, damn little. What *does* matter—and this relates to my original premise—is how the material *ties*, and how it *behaves* under fishing conditions. I don't find it necessary to know the chemical components of a dubbing in order to determine its functionality. But I do have to do more than just look at it. I must feel it, and perhaps even spin a bit of it onto a piece of thread. In fact, I think it would serve any producer of dubbing to provide each dealer with a few sample packs, so that the inquisitive tyer can play a little. This would keep people from having to open bags and pick out tufts of dubbing to see what it's like. I consider this to be very important. These materials can be deceptive. Some that look as though they would be difficult to dub are actually easy, and vice-versa.

Evolution in the fly-tying materials business seems to be an annualized phenomenon. We've had The Year of the Glitz, The Year of the Hook, The Year of the Eyes, and other "special" years. Recently, we had The Year of the Dubbing. Quite a few suppliers came out with new and similar products at about the same time. It seemed almost telepathic. Some of them, blessedly, filled a

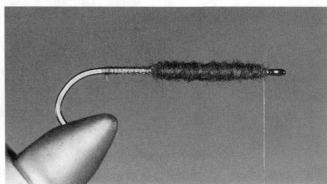

Soft dubbing spun onto the thread, then wrapped, using the single-thread method.

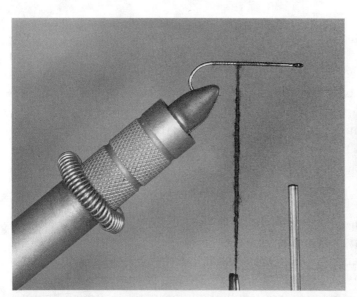

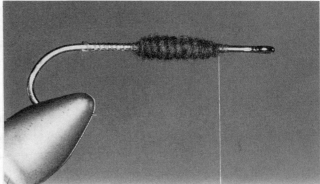

The same dubbing, twisted, then wrapped, using the spinning-loop method. Note compression and ribbed effect.

void—we were hurting for synthetic dubbings that packed tightly and smoothly for dry-fly work. All of a sudden, we had a variety from which to choose. Here are some of the better ones:

- Polytek
- Ligas
- Upstream
- Wapsi
- Spirit River
- UltraDub

Please note that several of these suppliers also offer coarse dubbings, so be sure you get the right stuff.

Polytek was actually available before the others, and had it been universally available and widely promoted it would have taken over the market, at least for a while. It's a product of Jack's Tackle, which is run by Jack Mickievitz, an interesting and innovative fellow. An excellent tyer himself, Jack knows his bugs, and his colors are quite useful. He eventually told me what Polytek was made of, and it's an amusing tale, but of course I'm not at liberty to share it!

Polytek apparently sent a wake-up call throughout the industry, and touched off a spate of new fine-textured synthetic dubbings, as you can see by the above list. Some pack down very tight, almost like cotton—Spirit River is a prime example. Others are somewhat coarser but still very nice to work with.

Ligas is particularly interesting. A number of years ago, Kenn Ligas introduced a synthetic dubbing material in about fifty different colors, and some of them were real killers. I particularly loved the Brown Drake mixture, which did a superb job of imitating the several important *Isonychia* nymphs common to the Northeast. I considered—and still consider—this particular product to be suitable for subsurface flies only because of its texture and lack of buoyancy.

Now Ligas offers a new material called Synchilla. At this writing Ernest Schwiebert of *Matching the Hatch* and *Nymphs* fame has partnered with Kenn to develop eighty-five colors. That's right, eighty-five! Several of them are designed to enable the tyer to imitate the egg masses of ovipositing insects which, believe it or not, can be very important. This indicates that the new Ligas is intended for both dry- and subsurface-fly application. Having worked with it extensively, I can report that this is mainly true, although it doesn't compress as smoothly as some of the other available materials. But its reflective and translucent properties along with its colors make this a landmark product.

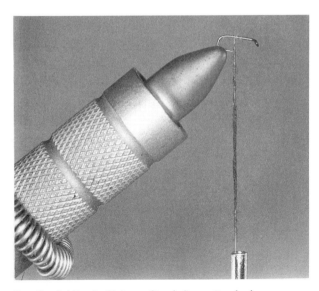
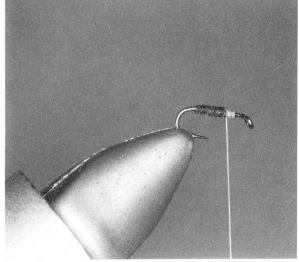

Very fine dubbing facilitates making bodies on tiny hooks.

I'm informed that the original Ligas is still available, Kenn having sold the product to another company to clear the way for his Synchilla operation. I'm glad to hear this, since I like some of the colors, especially the bright ones, which I use in salmon flies.

Over the years, a number of coarser and more brilliantly colored materials were introduced which were intended to replace natural materials that had become unavailable, notably seal and polar bear furs. These materials were widely called for in traditional dressings for Atlantic salmon flies. As it developed, the substitutes are actually better than the originals. They are much easier to work with, a fact that should bring a sigh of relief from any tyer who has tried to dub seal-hair fur. In terms of appearance and coloration they are at least the equal of the naturals. Besides that, all of this stuff was dyed anyway.

The first entry into this market was a product called Sealex, which was distributed by the famous salmon-fly dresser, Poul Jorgensen. It was a pure synthetic derived from a type of rug yarn, and it looked great on a full-dress fly. A few years ago, Poul sold the product to the Rocky Mountain Dubbing Company.

While I'm not sure it was intended as such, the original Ligas was and is an excellent seal substitute. The only problem is that it doesn't come in all of the colors called for in salmon-fly dressings. But the red is perfect for the butts on Silver Doctors and other flies, the green is super for the Green Highlander, and the fiery brown and black are ideal for segments of the Durham Ranger body.

If I might be forgiven a mild pun, a new product from England recently made a bit of a "splash" in the marketplace. It's called Synthetic Living Fiber (SLF) and is a Davey Wotton product distributed by Partridge of Redditch. For sheer brilliance of color it is unmatched at this time. As for being tyer-friendly, I recommend using the spinning loop method. You can also resort to wax, but I'm not crazy about that because it gets mixed in with the material and may detract from the brilliant coloration.

Perhaps this is an opportune time to talk a bit more about waxes. Certainly, they have a place in fly tying and serve a useful purpose. However, indiscreet application will always cause problems. Wax seems to stick to fingers more readily than to materials, and too sticky a wax results in the Tar Baby Syndrome. So I use it only when absolutely needed, and then very sparingly. I give a wide berth to ultra-sticky waxes. However, I realize that I came prewaxed from the womb. Some people, by virtue of nature, have very dry hands. For them, wax is a blessing, and in fact, a virtual necessity. Remember: just don't overdo it.

Rough Stuff

To date, nothing has equaled the universal popularity of the ubiquitous hare's ear dubbing. Originally it was obtained by scraping the fuzz off the ears of those large rabbits that are found in the British Isles. Later someone thought

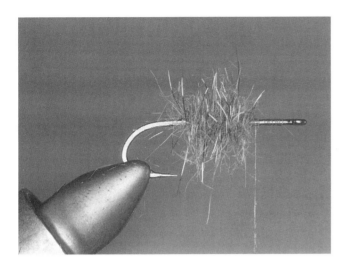

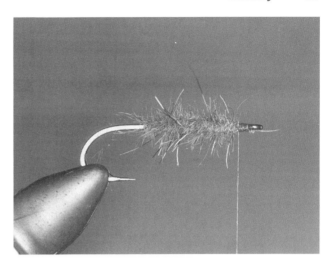

A hares' ear blend, wrapped with the single-thread technique.

The same dubbing, using the spinning-loop technique.

to mix in the tweedy hair and fur from the mask, or face. At this writing, you can still buy hare's masks, complete with ears, should you wish to go the traditional route. Whether they are the same historic breed of bunny, I can't say.

You can also make your own hare's ear mixtures, to suit yourself. Here's how I prepare the stuff:

- With scissors or electric shears, cut off the fur and hair from a rabbit pelt, selecting the shades you want. Include the rough stuff from the face and ears, as desired.

- From a squirrel pelt, shear off the material from right down the center of the back, guard hairs and all. Various species of squirrels will yield remarkably different effects. One of my favorites for this purpose is the large fox squirrel, which is plentiful in mid-America.

- Throw everything into a coffee-mill type of blender and zap it for a half minute or so. Shazam—dubbing.

- If you don't happen to have a blender of the type mentioned (don't use a regular kitchen blender), do this: throw everything into a bowl of lukewarm water, add a few drops of dish detergent, and stir it all thoroughly. Pour the material into a sieve, rinse out the detergent, and dry completely. This method also facilitates mixing in glitzy additives, such as Antron, and other synthetics. See Chapter 9 for more about this.

Most animals have guard hairs of some sort in some quantity, and leaving these in will result in a rougher sort of dubbing. Also, materials will vary in texture depending on what area of the pelt they came from. Belly fur is generally the softest.

Some furs and hairs used in fly tying, such as goat, seal, polar bear, woodchuck, and certain wools, are coarse and rough by their very nature. Most of these, except woodchuck, are employed in tying Atlantic salmon flies.

Today we have synthetic substitutes that not only keep us legal and respectable, but make tying easier. These will be covered subsequently.

Unless you simply enjoy do-it-yourself or have something very particular in mind, you needn't resort to a lot of dubbing mixing. The selection of packaged materials that adorn the walls of fly shops today is truly mind-boggling and generally you'll be able to buy what you want by the bag, at modest cost. Mail-order catalogs further extend these product lines.

Truly though, dubbing is interesting stuff, and much has been written about it over the years. In England, there was, and may still be, a traditional dressing known as the Tup's Indispensable. The original and authentic dubbing, or tup, as it was called, was the nap off the testicles of a ram, which had a unique pinkish cast. I would suggest a strong dose of sodium pentathol when collecting this material—for the ram, that is.

If you would like to further research the history of dubbing, I would recommend reading the works of the late-nineteenth and early-twentieth-century British authors, notably Skues and Halford. And from this side of the Atlantic, there are two short but highly intriguing and historic books that I recommend: *Tying and Fishing the Fuzzy Nymphs*, by E.H. "Polly" Rosborough, and *The Art of Tying the Wet Fly*, by James E. Leisenring. You'll be amazed at some of their techniques and by the lengths to which they went to obtain a certain effect. More recently, Sylvester Nemes has authored several books on the subject: *The Soft-Hackled Fly*, *Soft-Hackled Fly Imitations*, and *The Soft-Hackled Fly Addict*. They are highly descriptive and well done.

Road Kills, etc.

At one time, fly tyers did a lot of personal acquisition of fly-tying materials. Many of us hunted and trapped, and few could resist the lure of a fresh "pavement pizza," especially if it were a fox or a woodchuck. For years, I traveled with a skinning knife and a bunch of plastic bags in the trunk. Now, I limit myself to the occasional squirrel tail or pelt, and even that with all due caution. Caution regarding what? Please read and heed the following.

In the good old days, we fly tyers could blithely jump out of our cars and scoop up any creature unfortunate enough to have tried and failed to contend with vehicular traffic. I will always remember skinning out a woodchuck that the car ahead of me had clipped neatly along the side of the head, and having a New York State Trooper pull up and ask me if I was going to eat the thing!

Today, we have a new concern, or more accurately, a lethal and virulent revisitation from an old one: rabies. I'm very much obliged to Dr. Jim Payne, a veterinarian from Concord, New Hampshire, for providing me with detailed information and insights regarding the rabies situation.

In the Northeast, rabies is presently at epidemic levels. New York State recently recorded its first fatality since 1953—a young girl who apparently was bitten by a bat. Some animals are far more susceptible than others. Raccoons head the list, followed by foxes, skunks, and an occasional woodchuck. Actually, any animal can contract rabies, but except for those mentioned, they

Epoxy'ed head/eye assemblies.

The shrimp's shell is made from a feather coated with Shoe Goo, thinned with Toluol. This mixture is also used to protect the joints on the Del Brown Permit Fly. Both tied by Art Scheck.

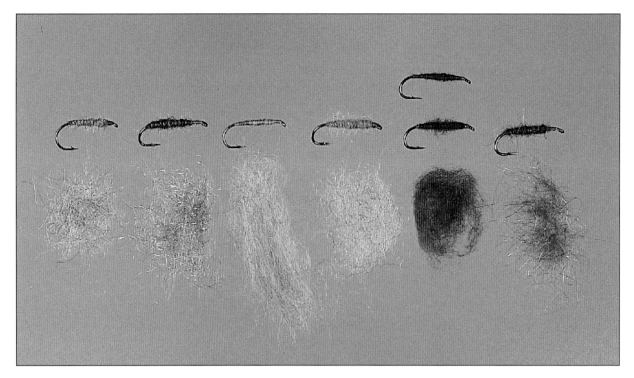

Dubbing group 1, left-to-right: (1) Oregon Upstream Innovations, Natural Nymph Dubb 30, Dark Scud; (2) Upstream, Inc., Caddis Emerger, Olive; (3) The Spectrum, Andra Co., Pink Hendrickson; (4) Ligas Scintilla, Ernest Schwiebert Series, Fiery Amber; (5) L&L Products, Ultra Dub, Rusty Brown; (6) Borden's Hare-Tron, Dark Olive.

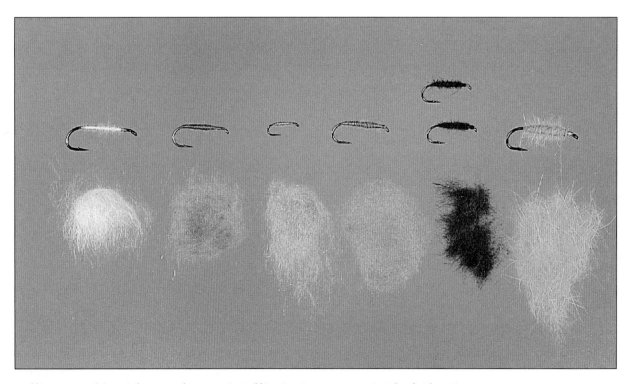

Dubbing group 2, left-to-right: (1) Rocky Mountain Dubbing Co., Cream Beaver; (2) Polytek, Ultra-Fine Midge Poly, Western Baetis; (3) Spirit River, Fine & Dry, Light Olive; (4) House Of Harrop (McKenzie), Callibaetis; (5) Sheared Mole; (6) Rocky Mountain Dubbing Co., Rabbit With Guard Hairs, Chartreuse.

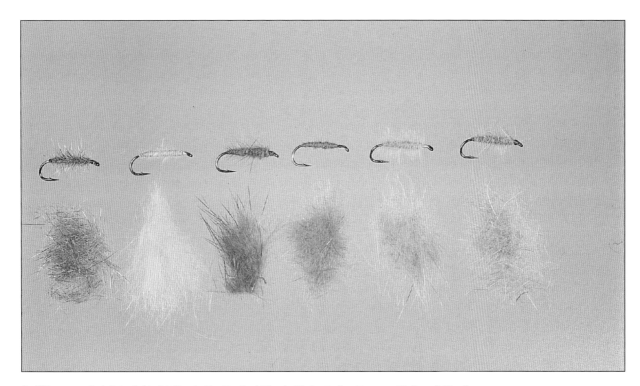

Dubbing group 3, left-to-right: (1) *Hare's Ear/Squirrel Blend*; (2) *Australian Possum*; (3) *Rough Muskrat*; (4) *Smooth Muskrat*; (5) *Fox Squirrel Belly*; (6) *Caucci-Nastasi Spectrumized Furs*.

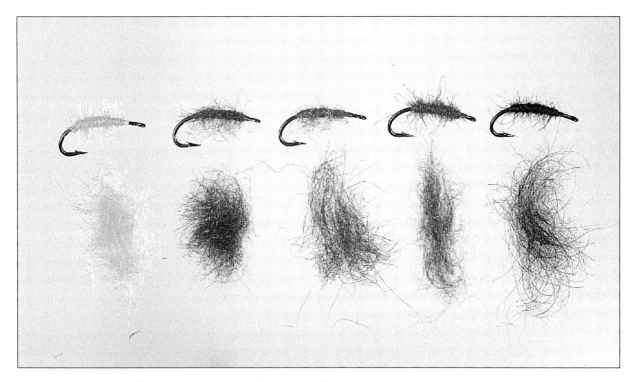

Dubbing group 4, left-to-right: (1) *Partridge SLF, Single-Thread Method*; (2) *Partridge SLF, Spinning Loop Method*; (3) *Natural Seal*; (4) *Original Ligas*; (5) *Angora Goat*.

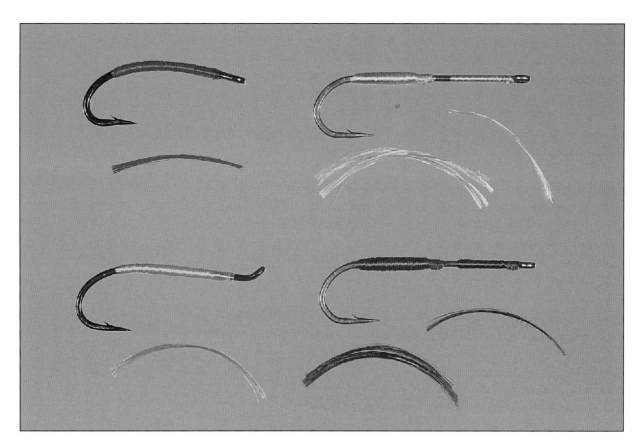

Floss assortment.

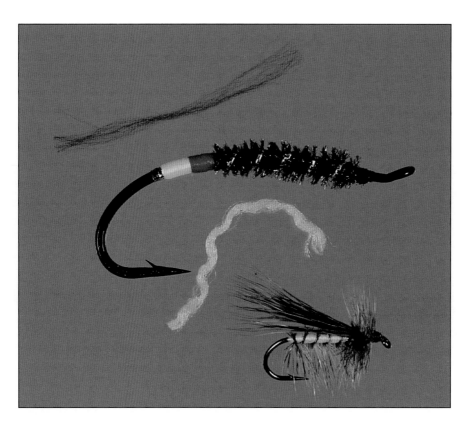

Stretch Nylon.

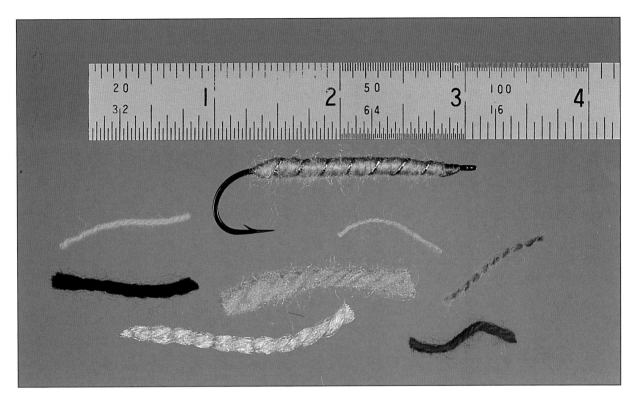

Assorted yarns, all from craft shops.

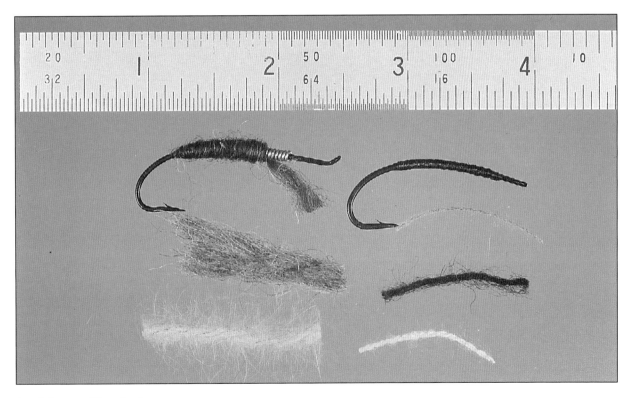

Assorted yarns, all from fly shops.

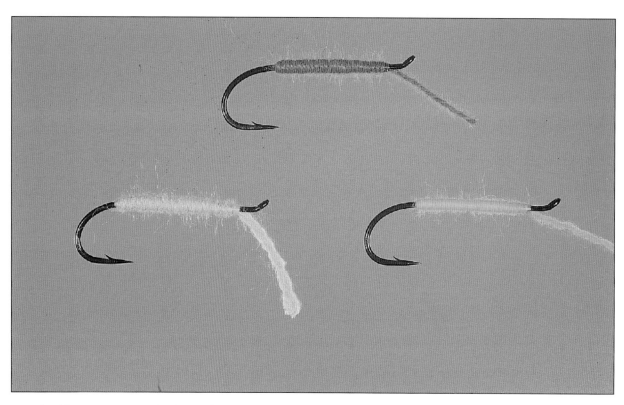

Examples of fluorescent yarns produced expressly for fly tying—similar, but from three different suppliers.

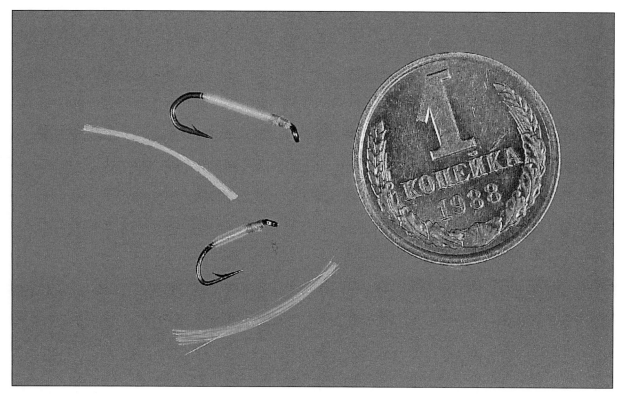

Mini-flosses for tiny flies.

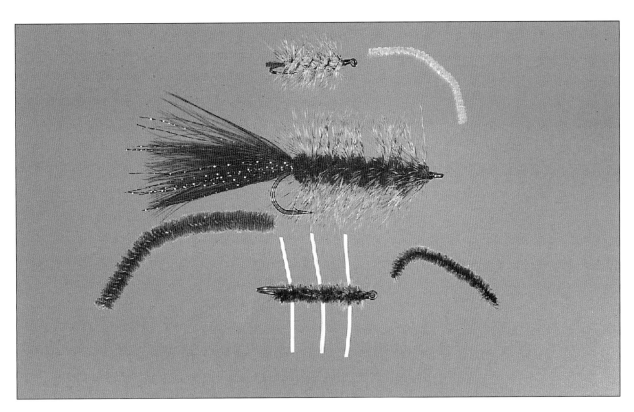

Chenille assortment.

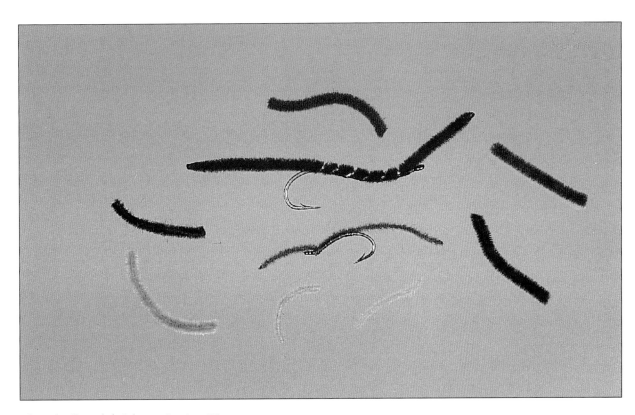

Ultra-Chenille, and the infamous San Juan Worm.

Antron and poly yarns, and several applications.

Poly yarn used as floss, and the Blue Rat, a Poul Jorgensen pattern, tied by the author.

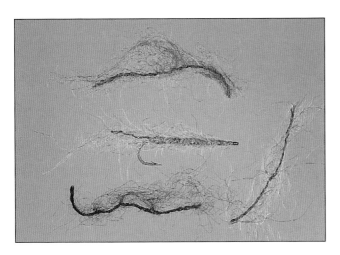

Leech yarn.

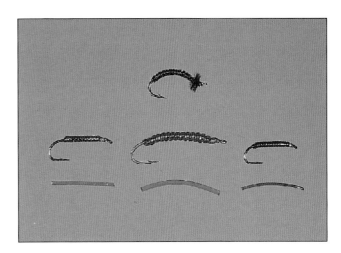

Several plastic body wraps.

Larva Lace, and Phil Camera's River Witch.

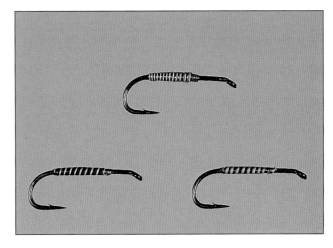

Left: moose mane; center: stripped hackle; right: stripped peacock from "eye" of tail feather.

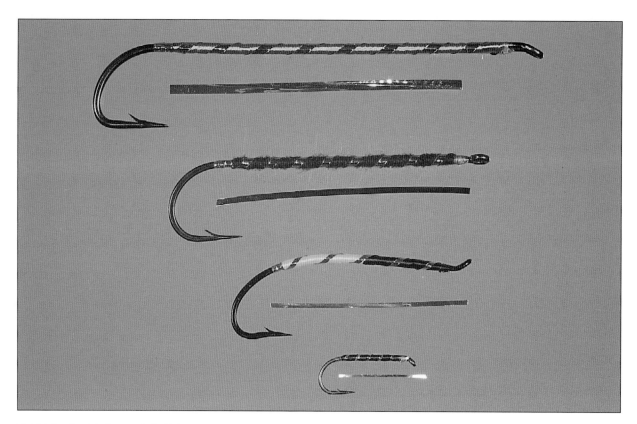

Flat Mylar tinsel, in four typical widths.

Typical applications of oval tinsel.

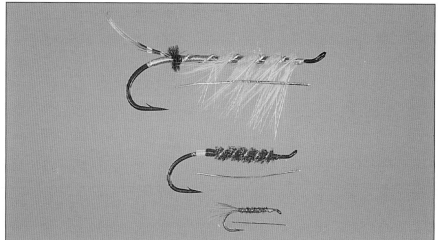

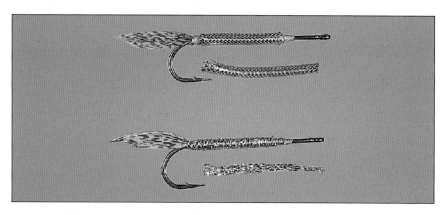

Top: gold Mylar tubing; bottom: gold braid, or mesh.

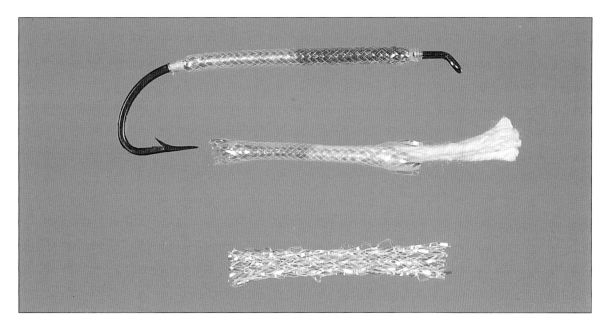

Pearlescent tubing, over contrasting underlayers.

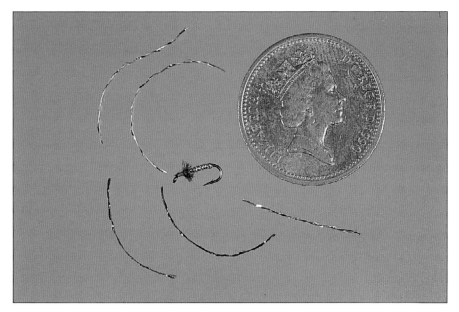

Miniature tinsels.

Corsair, a recently-introduced material.

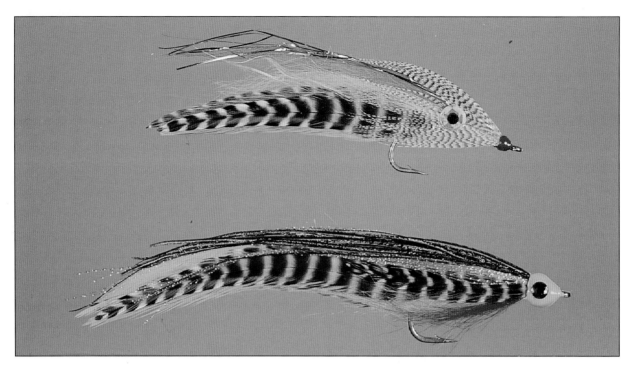

Flashabou (top), and Krystal Flash, used as highlights.

All-glitz flies, very popular for Alaskan salmon.

Light-Brite, used to highlight the white hair.

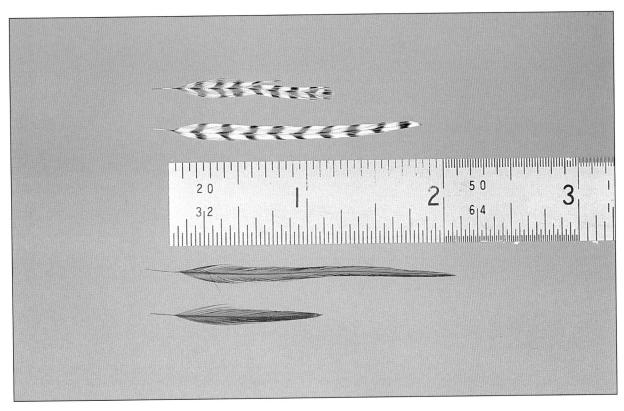

Modern genetic hackle, as compared to the imported hackle of 25 years ago.

Typical range of sizes in dry-fly quality on a good cape.

Feather from high-grade Hoffman saddle. The author has tied as many as a dozen flies, similar to the one shown, from one of these hackles.

Fifty wraps from a Hoffman grizzly saddle feather. Note how closely they are packed; this is due to the fine quill.

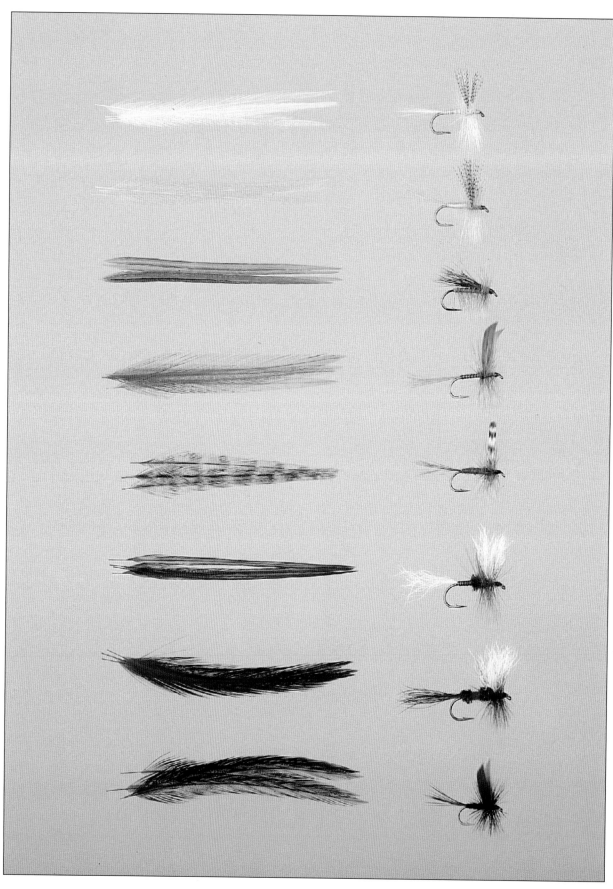

*Hackle Colors, Group 1, top to bottom: Cream (Hebert), Pale Cahill Quill; Straw (Hebert), Light Cahill;
Light Ginger (Hoffman), Tan Caddis; Ginger (Hebert), Ginger Quill; Cree (Hebert), Adams; Medium
Brown (Hebert), House & Lot; Coachman Brown (Hebert), Royal Wulff; Black (Hoffman), Black Gnat.*

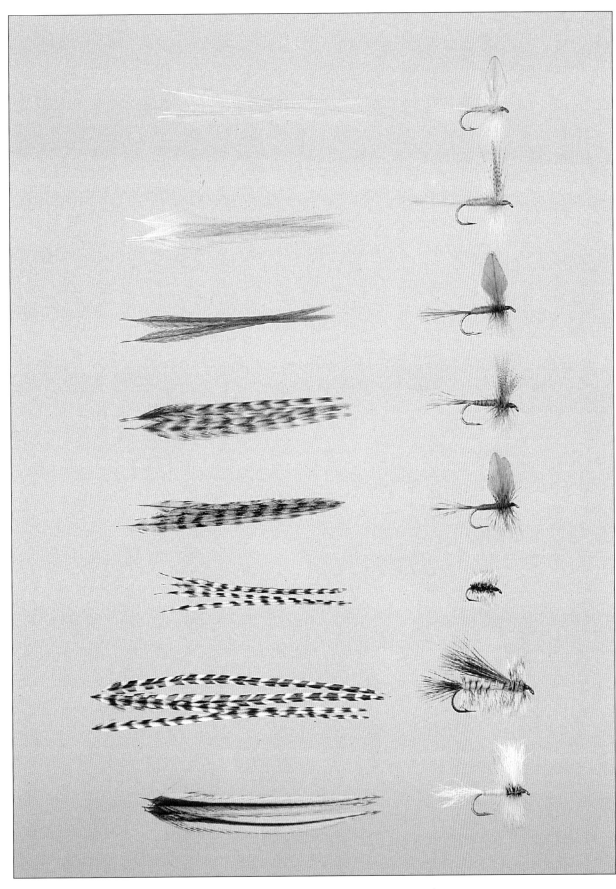

Hackle Colors, Group 2: Light Gray Dun (Hebert), Pale Morning Dun; Sandy Dun (Metz), Light Hendrickson; Medium Gray Dun (Hebert), Blue-Winged Olive; Barred Rusty Dun (Collins), Red Quill; Dun Grizzly, (Hoffman), Iron Blue Dun; Grizzly Cape, (Hoffman), Griffith Gnat; Grizzly Saddle (Hoffman), Stimulator; Badger (Hoffman), White Wulff.

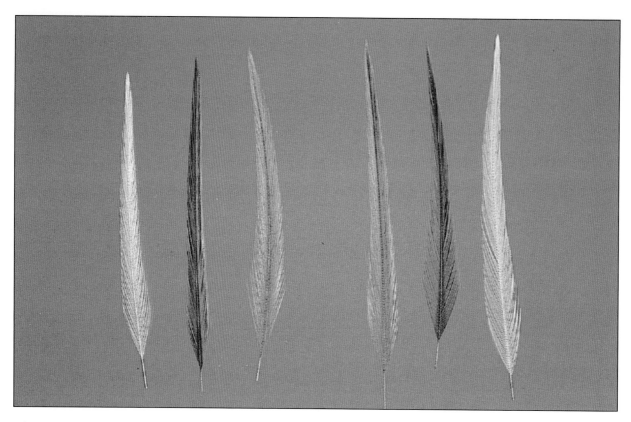

These are Hebert hackles. The three on the right are natural; the three on the left are dyed. Perhaps the fish can tell; I can't. No further comment.

Opposite ends of the spectrum in hackle quality. To distinguish between these feathers is easy. It's the close ones that make grading a challenge.

A short Hebert saddle feather, and a Wulff salmon dry fly, hackled with two of them. Note the stiffness and strength of the barbs.

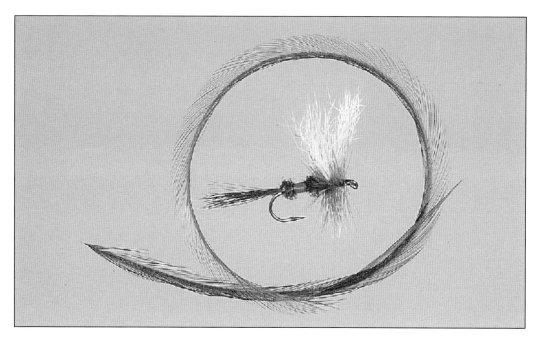

A long Hebert saddle feather, and a salmon dry fly, hackled with one of them.

Wet fly hackles of several types.

Hen hackles, dyed. Saddle hackles on top, corresponding cape hackles on bottom.

An array of wet-fly hackles. Top row, left to right: wood cock; four Hungarian partridge feathers: saddle, wing covert, cape, and rump, respectively. Bottom row: hen saddle; double-dotted guinea fowl; hen grizzly saddle; hen grizzly cape.

Cul de Canard (CDC).

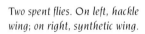

Two spent flies. On left, hackle wing; on right, synthetic wing.

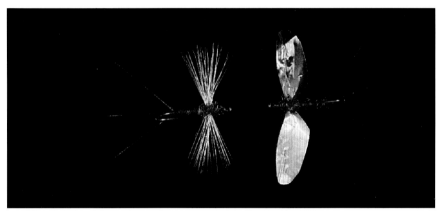

Caddis flies. On left, synthetic wing; on right, teal flank wing.

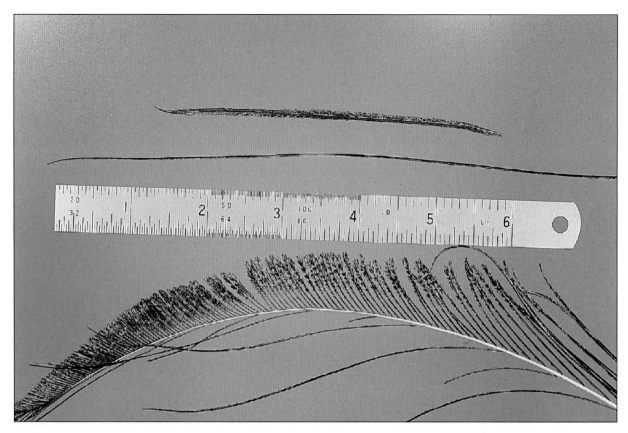

Peacock. Top; thick frond from tail feather. Middle; thin frond from bundled herl. Bottom; sword feather.

Top to bottom; aftershaft feather, ostrich feather, marabou, olive pheasant tail, natural pheasant tail.

Left to right: pheasant saddle, marabou, chicken rump hackle.

Left to right: pheasant rump, CDC, chicken marabou.

Artistry in spun hair; a frog, tied by George Kesel. This fly is an excellent example of how various materials, old and new, can be combined.

Top: A modernized version of an old classic, the Gray Ghost, redesigned and dressed by the author. Bottom;
Black Ghost Marabou, with eyes made from guinea fowl feathers.

A streamer fly, using pintail duck saddle feather.

Some hairs commonly used for winging streamers and salmon flies. Top; pine squirrel tail, fox squirrel tail. Bottom; gray squirrel tail, black bear body hair.

Bill Catherwood's Giant Killer, with sheep hair wings.

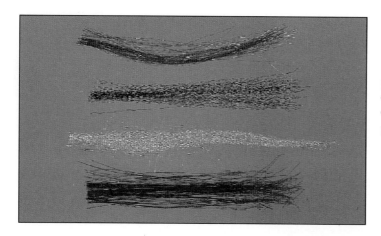

Four examples of synthetic streamer hairs. The top and bottom ones are unidentified. The two in the middle are; upper, Super Hair; lower, Polar Aire.

In the center is polar bear, flanked by two substitutes. On the left, Craft Fur. On the right, Super Hair.

Two saltwater flies, tied by George Chapman, that are prime examples of modern materials. Note use of markers to bar wings on top fly, and speckle body on lower fly.

More examples of the uses of synthetic hair.

Dumbbell eyes on the Lithuanian Bat, a great Alaska fly.

Color samples of Bugskin.

Bugskin flies, dressed by the author.

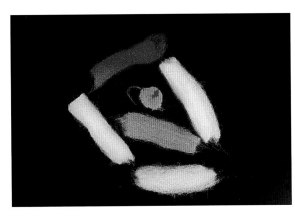

An array of Glo-Bug yarns, and a
Glo-Bug.

A Rabbit Matuka, with a wool head.

Samples of goose biots, and one of
the best-known flies that use them;
the Prince Nymph.

Closed-cell foam samples, and some flies that utilize this material.

Pieces of goose shoulder feather. These are from the first batches dyed by the author, using Dr. Ted Roubal's methods.

Left to right: a speckled hen saddle feather; the same, bleached by the Roubal method; the same, dyed yellow and orange. The dyes were formulated by Dr. Roubal.

Fur samples, dyed by Dr. Roubal, using dyes derived from natural materials.

Blue-Earred Pheasant feathers. The dark gray one second from the left is natural. The white one was bleached by the author. The rest were dyed by Dr. Roubal.

Hair samples, dyed by the author. Left to right: Norwegian Goat, dyed with Veniard Highlander Green; deer tail, dyed with Roubal orange; deer body hair, dyed with Roubal yellow; Norwegian Goat, dyed with Veniard Kingfisher.

Gray squirrel tail, dyed with Fly Dye Cardinal; natural color; off-white shade obtained by bleaching.

Simple, durable saltwater streamers, using craft-shop beads and Mylar eyes, under Epoxy. Originated and dressed by Chuck Furimsky.

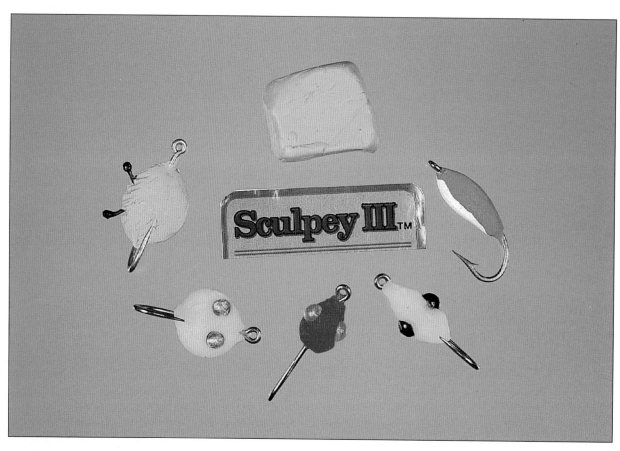

An array of clay bodies, made from Sculpey III.

This Furimsky Crab is made of Bugskin, over a clay body.

rarely do so. Bats are frequently infected, but do not act aggressively towards humans or other animals, as a raccoon or fox might. The incident in New York probably resulted from the child picking up a sick bat.

The rabies virus lives in saliva and in nerve or brain tissue. Almost invariably it is transmitted by biting. When the host dies, the virus lives for a while, depending on the temperature. In warm weather, it will die within a few hours. In winter, it may live for several days. When frozen, it can survive for up to a couple of weeks, and can again become active when the carcass is thawed. If you're a road kill collector, or if you trap or hunt, or if you intend to use animals killed this way, you might think about the above.

Based on this information, the following cautionary measures are recommended: first, before handling any animal, make sure it's dead. Use rubber gloves when handling a corpse. Clorox will kill the virus on contact, so if you can't resist scooping up a furry, flat goody, you should douse it well with Clorox before skinning it out. If you decide to keep it in the freezer for a while before skinning, leave it there for at least a month.

Raccoons have little of value to the tyer, and since they are the leading carrier of rabies, I would advise staying away from them. Foxes, woodchucks, and skunks have some usable materials, but should be handled with due caution. You probably won't be messing with a skunk carcass, since there's no effective way that I know of to eliminate their odor. Rabbits almost never contract rabies, nor do squirrels, but I would still be very careful in handling them.

Should you be unlucky enough to get bitten by any animal, you should go to a clinic immediately and get treatment, which consists of a series of shots. If possible, take the animal with you. If you shrug it off, and guess wrong—well, goodbye. Once rabies starts, it's not curable. With current levels running high, many communities throughout the Northeast have rabies clinics and hot lines. You should become familiar with these, whether you intend to avail yourself of any free tying materials or not. It's always possible that the dog or cat next door might get into a confrontation with a rabid animal, and become infected.

If you do get involved with skinning animals, even if you only take a small swatch now and then, you must learn to care for the pelts. First, get yourself a box of borax and some coarse kosher salt. Borax is both a desiccant and a natural preservative. Salt draws out moisture, and acts as a curing agent. Boraxo will work, but it is actually a cleansing product, and contains other additives. Plain 20-Mule-Team Borax is the right stuff.

It's of the greatest importance to cut or scrape all fat and grease from the skin. If there is any blood on the fur, rinse it off with cold water. Having done that, pat the material dry with paper toweling and then blow-dry the fur with a hair dryer. Now tack the skin to a board, and give it a good coating of borax, or a mixture of borax and salt. Allow it to dry away from moisture until it is completely cured. Inspect it from time to time, and add more borax/salt if required.

Skins cure very nicely if left out in the sun. However, you have to keep an eye on them. Borax is a pretty effective deterrent, but it doesn't guarantee that some scavenger won't grab the skin anyway. And be ready to bring the skin inside overnight or if the weather turns threatening.

Blends

Earlier I referred to dubbing blends that combine various materials, often mixing natural and synthetic. This has become very widespread, and quite a number of such products are now on the market. One of the early ones that's still quite popular is Spectrumized Fur Blends, by Caucci and Nastasi, the coauthors of H*atches*. Their position is that the combined effects of light, water, and gas and air bubbles associated with emerging insects produces a spectrumized effect. Thus their product consists of dyed furs in the basic colors, mixed in various proportions to produce certain effects under fishing conditions. Interesting stuff.

There are lots of blends to choose from, and they are very seductive-looking in their packages. I hope this isn't too confusing. New mixes keep hitting the market all the time, and there's little we writers can do to simplify this situation. Personally I have always liked more complex dubbings as opposed to flat colors, particularly for subsurface flies. I also like a bit of sparkle, particularly in emergers, caddis pupa, and like patterns. Gary LaFontaine, Gary Borger, Randall Kaufman, and numerous other authoritative writer/tyers advocate such materials. They are recommended reading for the aspiring flyfisher/tyer.

Thread Color

No examination of color in fly tying would be complete without addressing the effect of what's underneath the body material. Today we are fortunate to be able to buy thread of just about any conceivable shade. This enables us to compensate in large measure for the omnipresent hook, and also to blend in with, or complement, the color(s) we have chosen for the body.

If you are at all curious about the extent of the effect of the thread base, do this: dub a slender pale cream body onto black thread, and wrap it onto a typical hook. Do the same with white or pale yellow thread. Then, drop the two flies into a glass of water, hold them up to the light, and observe. It will make a believer out of you.

While I'm more concerned about the effect of thread color on subsurface flies, I'm also quite selective when tying drys as well. My main concern is that the thread doesn't cause the fly to darken too much when it gets wet. If I don't have an exact matching color, I just go a little lighter.

Salmon-fly tyers face a more critical situation with respect to base color vs. material color. For one thing, salmon hooks are traditionally black. This, combined with the delicacy of the fine, brightly colored dubbings and flosses that are so commonly employed in those types of flies, produces a conflict. In addition to being most circumspect about thread color, the more particular salmon-fly dressers are known to apply white or yellow paint to that portion of the hook that will be covered with pale materials. Some use an underlayer of tinsel in certain areas.

Today, several manufacturers are producing hooks that are other than black or bronzed. So far, we're seeing silver, gold, blue, red, and green. At present, this is pretty much limited to salmon-fly hooks, and the specialty models used for making egg patterns, such as the Glo-bug. It makes a lot of sense, and I think we'll be seeing a lot more of colored hooks in the near future.

Yarns, Chenilles, Flosses and Such

This chapter deals with materials for making wrapped bodies, including true flosses, floss-like materials, yarns, chenilles, and synthetic products. Tinsel and tinsel-like products are also used to make wrapped bodies; they are covered in chapter 9.

There is a danger that I might run afoul of tradition in short order. There is a belief among some Atlantic salmon-fly tyers that only the "original" materials should go into these flies, unless said materials are absolutely unavailable. One of these components is silk floss. I have a very high regard for these folks, and greatly admire both their work and their commitment to authenticity. However, being a practical sort, I don't personally adhere to that philosophy, nor do I recommend that others do so. One of the areas in which this manifests itself is that I prefer synthetic floss to silk.

Silk floss is still available. It certainly has its own unique charm, and imbues traditional flies with a distinct patina. It handles nicely, and wraps neatly, given a proper underlayer. The colors are slightly more subdued than those of synthetic flosses.

While it will not last forever, silk floss has a far longer useful life than silk thread. It should be stored in a dark, dry place, to prevent fading and decomposition caused by moisture.

Modern flosses are composed of synthetic materials, mainly rayon, Dacron, nylon, and polyesters. They tend to be somewhat brighter in color, and some are even available in fluorescent colors. They are a little more resistant to discoloration when wet than the silks; however, pale shades, such as yellow and orange, need the protection of a light underlayer, or else the dark hook shows through. White-out (correction fluid) works well for this.

There are a number of very good products on the market. One that's deserving of mention is Danville's Rayon Floss. It is packaged in two ways: smaller spools that contain four-stranded floss, and large spools that contain single-stranded floss. The four-stranded version is particularly convenient, since it readily adapts to whatever size fly or thickness of body is being tied; one simply uses as many or few strands as are required. You can always double over the single-stranded variety to achieve the same results.

I am satisfied with this type of floss, both in terms of the way it handles and the way it looks on a finished fly. Multiple strands, including all four as they come off the spool, present no insurmountable problems in wrapping. When they do seek to separate or spread, back off a turn or two and twist the strands a few times. This will bring them back together, so that they all traverse the hook as one.

Two problems that one must confront with any floss, silk or synthetic, are discoloration and fiber breakdown. Let's examine discoloration first.

This is caused by soiled fingers. If you want bright and beautiful bodies, you must keep your hands clean and free of bodily oils. I know several traditionalists who actually wear thin cloth gloves while working with floss. I don't go to those lengths, but I do keep a supply of those "wet-nap" things on my tying desk. They are very effective for cleaning fingers.

Having read the preceding, one might think: "Hey! I'll put my floss in a bobbin, and not touch it at all!" There are, in fact, bobbins expressly designed for floss, with wider tubes that are slightly flared at the tips. I've never enjoyed great success with them. For one thing, you have to get your thread bobbin out of the way. Also, you can't wrap as you would with thread because you put a twist in the floss with each turn. Both of these problems are overcome via the use of a full rotating vise; this is a case where that tool does offer an advantage. However, you may still find, as I have, that precise control is better effected with fingers than with a floss bobbin. Additionally, if the bobbin has even the slightest burr or sharp spot around the mouth of the tube—well, disaster isn't too strong a word!

Fiber breakdown refers to the hairlike, individual filaments that form the breaking strand of floss. This is a serious problem. The main cause is incorrect handling by the tyer, where the floss is allowed to spread too much, and fibers become independent of the group. Also, rough fingers will abrade floss very quickly. Tyers who do a lot of manual work, especially outdoor work, will have to use a pumice stone or fine emery board to smooth out those callouses. In extreme cases, the cloth gloves mentioned earlier may be the answer.

It should also be noted that silk floss, even the freshest and highest quality, will tend to fray more than synthetic floss. Not only are the fibers weaker, they are of different length, since this is a natural rather than a manufactured material.

Your choice of exactly which floss to use will be based, to a great extent, on the task at hand, meaning what you're trying to cover. Even the thicker, more forgiving flosses have a distinct tendency to take the shape of what's underneath. When you're working on smaller flies, and using thin strands, practically every little bump or wrinkle from the underbody shows through. This means that all of your cutting, trimming, and thread work has to be very clean if you want a smooth, well-shaped body. For this reason, and also because of its tendencies to misbehave, many tyers hate floss, and substitute other materials that are easier to manage.

As mentioned earlier, some of the newer flosses come in fluorescent colors. Some suppliers also refer to their products as having "hot" colors. These may or may not be truly fluorescent; fluorescent colors show up under ultraviolet light. I don't think that anyone has been able to prove that this has any discernible effect on the fish. However, I must say that a Royal Wulff with a brilliant red belly band that stays bright even when wet is a joy to behold. Anything that boosts the angler's confidence has to be of some value.

Miniflosses

I've coined this term to describe a number of new floss products that have come into the marketplace. They seem to be characterized by several common factors: they are synthetic; fluorescent or hot in coloration; and of thin denier. (In this context I use the term *denier* to mean thickness.) In fact, one of them, which is labeled Glo-Brite fluorescent floss, is so fine you can put it in a bobbin and use it as thread.

Gordon Griffith of England also offers a very fine-denier floss, but it is more like an actual floss, and should be used as such. Danville has a product they label Depth Ray Nylon. It comes in fluorescent colors, and is even finer than the Gordon Griffith. It is slippery, tends to spread readily, and is thus somewhat difficult to work with. But if you're up to it, the result is quite pretty.

The Uni-Thread Company has a line of Uni-Floss that is very brilliant in color, and in thickness falls somewhere between the Gordon Griffith and the typical flosses we're accustomed to. I'm not sure exactly what it's made of. It's a little more tricky to handle than silk or rayon, but the finished product is certainly most attractive.

All of these flosses are very good for work on small flies and minute tasks, such as making the belly bands on Royal Wulffs. Multiple strands can be used for larger applications. However, this works better with some products than others, since certain synthetic miniflosses don't lie smooth in multiple layers.

Stretch Nylon

At this writing, stretch nylon has been around for about ten years. Danville introduced it, and now, at least one other company, Uni-Products, produces a version of it.

I have to confess a strong preference for stretch nylon since it has several important advantages over floss. It is much stronger, resists fraying, wraps like a dream, packs beautifully, and holds its colors very well when wet. Most if not all of the colors are hot, or fluorescent. I particularly recommend it for use on salmon flies, which take a wicked beating. On Russia's Kola Peninsula, where the sheer numbers of Atlantic salmon cause flies to be run through the gauntlet, stretch nylon proved itself under fire.

Stretch nylon is also excellent for certain types of dry-fly work. It makes great belly bands on Royal-Whatevers, and is particularly good for making neat, slender bodies over which a hackle is to be wrapped palmer-style. It's also a good floater, because it does not readily soak up water.

Like floss, stretch nylon works much better when applied in two layers—that is, tied on at the front, wrapped to the rear, then forward again. However, it is possible, when a very slim body is desired, to cover with one layer, working back to front. It does this much better than true floss.

Polypropylene Yarn

It's appropriate to introduce this material here, since it represents a middle ground between the flosses and stretch nylons and the more common types of yarns we encounter. It was also something of a landmark product at the time of its introduction. We began to see polypropylene in the 1960's, first in stranded form, then as dubbing. This was the beginning of the so-called renaissance of fly fishing, and the shops were anxious for new things to sell. This particular material was an immediate hit, and remains popular today.

At first, we had to scour the knitting and sewing shops for poly yarn. I remember buying a large ball of it for under $2. It consisted of two main strands, one white, the other dark brown. To obtain colors, we had to dye the white stuff. But in short order, carded poly yarns popped up in the fly shops in a wide range of shades. We used them for certain types of wings, as well as wrapped bodies.

The essential property of polypropylene is that it doesn't absorb water. That's not to say that a bunch of it won't wick up water, through a form of capillary action. The point is that the individual fibers themselves are water-resistant. Thus, when a fly body gets water-soaked, one simply squeezes out the moisture, redresses the fly, and goes back to fishing. With the advent of another new product—the silicone desiccants that have now been around for a dozen or so years—this procedure works even better, and our dry flies have become drier in the bargain.

Another desirable attribute that we soon discovered with the advent of poly yarn is that it is smooth, and when applied in small quantities, it wraps very neatly. By thinning out the larger skeins, we are able to effectively tie very small flies. This revelation came at about the time when we were discovering that trout eat tiny insects in enormous quantities. For our size 24s and 26s, we needed only a few strands. It was a timely Godsend.

This is still the key to obtaining the best results from poly yarn. While somewhat similar to stretch nylon, it isn't as elastic, and the individual fibers are considerably coarser. It's slippery stuff, and does not compress very much under wrapping tension, so discretion in quantities is the byword.

Antron Yarn

By Antron what I'm referring to in this section is spooled Antron, as opposed to another form of this material, which is a sort of dubbing.

Spooled Antron is fairly similar to polypropylene in appearance and handling characteristics. However, it has the unique property of being trilobal, which causes it to refract light differently than other materials which at casual inspection seem to be about the same. I have seen it used for wrapped bodies and wings on spent flies. However, one of the more unique applications, and one that succeeds on some very picky fish, is the use of it as a dragging nymphal shuck imitation. This we find on the Sparkleduns that were introduced by the guys at Blue Ribbon Flies in West Yellowstone, Montana, back in the early 1980s.

Essentially this fly is a Comparadun with a short piece of Antron yarn tied on as a tail. With the sky light shining through, this looks very much like a shuck that some struggling mayfly is trying to cast. Trout are often very selective to these disadvantaged insects, and will ignore even the naturals that have made a clean break and are ready to take off, in favor of them.

The fly shops are full of Antron and Antron-like products. There are lots of colors available, including white, or translucent.

True Yarns

This term doesn't necessarily refer to wool yarns; it is intended to describe the *texture* of the material, not what it's made out of. Yarns have long been a commonly used material in fly tying, dating back to the earliest writings. Then, all yarns were made of some sort of wool. The modern era has brought us synthetics, which have brought us to where we are today.

While wool has been somewhat disparaged as a dry-fly material, I have to say that I do miss one product. Years ago, we could buy cards of a fine yarn used in mending. It was sold under the brand name of Bernat, and I still have a few cards of it in my yarn drawer. It was just the right thickness for the most common hook sizes, and could be reduced further by untwisting it and separating the strands. It came in a multitude of colors, and accepted dyes very well. Also, it was quite smooth; not as smooth as poly, but more so than the heavier yarns used in knitting.

Perhaps, somewhere in the world, Bernat mending yarn still exists. However, I haven't seen it in the fabric and knitting shops (which I haunt) for a long time. And besides, I don't think many people today would know how to mend a knitted garment if they had to. We live in a throwaway society.

You can go into any knitting/sewing/fabric shop and see an array of yarns that will dazzle you. Most of the contemporary ones are synthetic, but there's still lots of wool out there. A wide assortment of colors is available, some of which are not flat, or solid colors, but are a composite. Deniers also run the gamut, but you probably won't find any really fine stuff unless you get into embroidery material.

True yarns are typically composed of two or three strands. I refer to the main strands, not the individual fibers. One can always use less than the entire bunch to adapt diameter to hook size. However, this may create problems. The reason that yarn is multi-stranded is to give it strength, and to keep it from pulling apart. Often, reducing it to a single strand results in easy break-age. I wouldn't say *never* to follow this practice, as I sometimes indulge in it myself. I do, however, advise caution. It's better to find a material that can be used in its original form, if possible.

An assortment of good yarns is usually available in better fly shops. They are generally more adaptable to fly-tying applications than knitting products. Let's examine several that differ, but typify what's available.

Gordon Griffith offers a fluorescent wool. It is two-stranded, and of medium denier, meaning that one can dress average-size salmon and streamer flies with it as it comes off the spool. It is tough stuff, and doesn't break readily when a single strand is used. It will cover well enough with one layer, working back to front, but two layers, working front-back-front, produce a better result. Plenty of attractive colors are available.

Uni-Yarn, a Uni-Thread product, is also two-stranded, but is much finer in denier than the Gordon Griffith. It does not adapt well to being separated. In fact, trying to do so is roughly the equivalent of picking fly excrement out of pepper. But Uni-Yarn packs so nicely that you won't have to worry about untwisting it. I don't know whether it is wool or some sort of synthetic; some-times it's hard to tell. It will accommodate smaller flies of various types: Soft-Hackle or standard wet flies, streamers, salmon flies, even dry flies. Lots of pretty colors are available, including the most brilliant red I've ever seen.

Danville offers a product labeled Depth Ray Nylon Wool. This is some-what of a misnomer though, because wool usually refers to organic materials. Nylon yarn would be more descriptive. It's a two-stranded yarn, slightly finer and somewhat fuzzier than Uni-Yarn. It's good and strong in its original form, but does not hold up well when broken down into single strands. As the term *Depth Ray* implies, the colors are fluorescent.

All of these yarns, and practically any yarn you'll encounter, is more-or-less fuzzy. The only yarn I know of that isn't fuzzy is polypropylene. The amount of fuzz varies considerably, and affects what sort of body will result. Thus, one must assess the material in terms of the desired application.

It's possible to reduce the fuzziness by giving the finished body a trim job. It's also possible to increase fuzziness by teasing out the fibers. For this task, there's nothing like my Velcro teaser, which is nothing more than a piece of fine-toothed "male" Velcro stuck onto a slim piece of wood, or something similar. The best ones I've made so far are constructed of an emery board cut in half lengthwise, with the Velcro glued to the smoother side with Zap-A-Gap.

Quills

Quills of various types have long been popular for making bodies, especially on dry flies. They produce a neat, smooth effect, and a realistic segmentation. Several important hatch-matching flies incorporate the word in their pattern names: Quill Gordon, Red Quill, Blue Quill.

Today, the two most commonly used quills are:

- Stripped peacock eye
- Stripped hackle stem

During my early years at the vise, condor quill was very popular. These quills were actually individual barbs from the great bird's wing feathers. If used as they came from the feather, unstripped, they rendered a fuzzy sort of segmented body, the fuzz being the barbules along the edges of the quills. Stripping, which involved the use of Clorox and was quite tricky, removed this fuzz; thus, the quills produced a light/dark segmentation, similar to stripped peacock. However, condor was thicker and heavier, and the dark edge had a distinct ridge. Many veteran fly tyers loved this effect, including J. Edson Leonard, whose excellent book *Flies* was one of my main sources of information in my formative years.

Condor took dye nicely, and could be purchased in many colors. Particular favorites of mine were dark olive and dark bluish gray, for imitating *Baetis vagans* and *Paraleptophlebia adoptiva*, respectively.

Condor is absolutely illegal today. The law prohibits the use of even a molted feather from a zoo-kept bird—in fact the zookeeper is supposed to destroy these feathers. The purpose of this regulation, which also applies to a number of other birds on the CITES Treaty endangered list, is to prevent any dealing whatever in this plumage. It would be nice for tyers to be able to get even a small supply of such commodities as condor, scarlet ibis, golden bird of paradise, and other such rare feathers, but if the rules were relaxed to allow the distribution of molted feathers, or those from birds which had died, you can bet that molting and expiration would soon be accelerated by human intervention.

So much for condor. Peacock quills from the eyed portion of a tail feather make lovely segmented bodies. It is necessary to know how to remove the fuzz, which is much more tenacious in the eyed area than down on the tail proper. Here are two effective techniques:

METHOD 1. Use the ink-eraser end of one of those double-ended erasers kids use in school. Lay an individual quill on a piece of cardboard and rub it until all of the flue is gone. Usually, you'll have to rub both sides to get it perfectly clean.

METHOD 2. In a small saucepan, boil some water. Drop in a piece of paraffin about the size of a large gumdrop. After the paraffin has thoroughly melted, remove the pan from the stove, and let it stand for a minute or two. Then immerse an entire eye, and withdraw it slowly, over the course of several seconds. A coating of paraffin will adhere to the feather. Set it aside for a couple of minutes and allow it to cool. Now, you can remove individual quills and strip off the fuzz with your thumbnail.

When buying peacock tails expressly with quill bodies in mind, you can tell which ones have the most contrast by squeezing the eyed part and observing the back sides. The better ones flash the lightest. Usually, the larger, the better.

When tying with these quills, best results are obtained by tying them in with the dark edge to the rear. Looking at an eye from the front, the quills to the left side of center have the dark on the opposite side of those from the right of center. No problem—you simply tie those from the left side in by the skinny ends, and those from the right side by the butt ends. Spacing is controlled by overlapping, or not overlapping, the wraps. Given a choice, I prefer those from the right side, because there is better contrast and more quill strength nearest the butt end.

Now for stripped hackle quills. These produce a somewhat different sort of segmented body—thicker, and with a distinct coloration. They are obtained by stripping the barbs off large hackles from a rooster cape or saddle. Ginger and brown feathers are most commonly used. The idea is to select those which have quills of the shade you want, and proper thickness, or width. They should not be so thick that they create tying problems, and not so fine as to not yield the desired segmentation. It should be mentioned that these quills can be dyed to different colors, if so desired. A.K. Best is an advocate of this.

It is possible to strip these feathers in quantity with a strong Clorox-and-water mixture, but I don't recommend it. A slight mistake in timing or in strength of the mix results in the ruination of the quills. I prefer to simply pull off the barbs by hand.

In the past one could buy stripped quills in bound bundles from fly shops. I haven't seen them lately but I'm informed that a West Coast importer by the name of Swaleff still carries them. I hope the shops will start stocking them again. True, they aren't a big profit item, but they are certainly a great convenience to the tyer.

These quills work much better when thoroughly moistened. The best method is to make a mixture of about 25% hair conditioner and 75% water in a small jar, and simply leave the quills in there. When you want to use one, just grab it with tweezers and wipe it on a paper towel. If you want to get fancy, you can flatten it by running a metal object over it, such as the closed blades of your tying scissors. This makes for less bulk in the tie-off area, and aids in hackling.

Reinforcement

Both of these types of quills are prone to breakage during use. To protect them, apply a coat of Zap-A-Gap to the finished body. Better yet, apply a thin layer of Zap-A-Gap just prior to wrapping the quill, and also a finish coat. Rub off any excess with a toothpick. If the quill you're about to reinforce is still moist from the water and hair conditioner, set the fly aside and allow it to dry before applying the adhesive.

Substitutes

I have seen simulations of the quill effect obtained by wrapping different colors of floss or thread spiral-fashion. I don't like them as much as I do the natural materials.

A very high-contrast segmentation can be effected by using moose mane. These hairs are mostly dark brown in color, but some swatches also contain white or pale cream hairs. Wrapping one of each together, or perhaps two darks with a light, produces a striking result. You should be forewarned that moose mane is brittle, and will break even during wrapping. Soaking in a conditioner mix, as previously described, helps somewhat. The before-and-after Zap-A-Gap procedure is a must.

Chenille

This is French for "caterpillar," and it is a most appropriate analogy. Chenille is an older material and still a very good one for making fuzzy-bodied flies. The infamous Woolly Bugger has a chenille body, as does the Montana Nymph, the Girdle Bug, and the much-maligned San Juan Worm.

Chenille is composed of fuzzy material locked in by a multi-strand thread core. It is pretty tough, and will survive typical angling encounters very well. It comes in a variety of thicknesses, and a wide range of colors, including fluorescents. The idea is, as always, to pick the size that suits the task at hand.

Chenille is one of the easiest materials to use, and one of the most forgiving, in that it covers virtually anything. Lead wire, bumpy underbodies, tie-offs and trims—all disappear beneath chenille. It also has other nice features. For example, hackle wrapped palmer-style sinks into its fibers, and is thus protected from breakage.

About the only times when one might get into a little trouble working with chenille is when tying it on and tying it off. It is bulky material, and if you tie it on *en toto*, you may create an ugly lump. The solution is to strip off about one-fourth-inch of the fuzz, and tie on by the thread core alone.

When tying off at the front, take care not to crowd the eye. In fact, if you want to get cute, do this: when you are in position to make the final wrap, cut the chenille to about ¼ inch and strip off the fuzz, as you did when tying on. This allows you to tie off just the core, and results in much less bulk and clutter.

In recent years, some new types of chenille have emerged. One type is made of flashy plastic, and for this reason I also included it in Chapter 9, on Glitz. Another is a fine, soft chenille that is made by sticking fuzz to a tough synthetic thread core. I don't know how this is done—some sort of electromagnetic process, I've heard—but it sure works. You won't be stripping this stuff off for tying on.

I see this material sold under the names of Ultra-Chenille and Vernille. There may be some minute difference between the two, but after the closest examination, I can't find any. It is fine in diameter, and the fuzz is densely packed. Lots of colors are available.

The classic San Juan Worm is made of this material. The exterior is some sort of synthetic, and the Western worm mavens singe the ends, which contributes to aesthetics and strength as well. I notice that the resident gurus on the great tailrace rivers switch colors from time to time, because the fish become suspicious. Last autumn the killer color on the San Juan was lavender!

Incidentally, I can't understand the big squawk about this pattern. There *absolutely is* a natural San Juan Worm, which lives in the weeds and bottom detritus in cold streams. It looks just like a little night crawler. That makes this fly an imitator. Thinking back in time, I don't recall hearing any complaints about leaf rollers, artificial hellgrammites, Japanese beetle patterns, and other imitators. So, what's the beef? Maybe having the word *worm* in the name is the problem.

Plastic

How many of you remember that famous line from the opening scene in that 1968 film classic, *The Graduate*? The older, obviously affluent gentleman took Dustin Hoffman aside and whispered in his ear the Meaning of Life. In a word: "Plastics!" Turns out he was clairvoyant.

As you may have deduced by now, I have no qualms about tying with synthetics. My only concern is *what works*, from both a tying and fishing standpoint. When it comes to stuff for wrapping bodies, some of the new materials work very well, others less so. Let's look at a particular type that I feel has positive attributes.

Larva Lace

This unique material is actually narrow-diameter, soft, hollow plastic tubing. It stretches easily, which renders it much more tyer-friendly than some earlier materials that were stiff and not a pleasure to tie with. Currently two diameters are available: regular, which ties down to perhaps a size 14, and midge, which ties at least several sizes smaller. An array of colors is available, including several fluorescents. It also comes in clear, which is very nice for making glassy-bodied crustaceans and such, and also for over-wrapping colored underbodies.

Okay, so what can one do with this stuff? A lot! It can be wrapped around a hook, tied along a hook laterally, or woven, using the macramé process. A hook can be inserted inside the regular-diameter material by threading it around the bend and along the shank. This makes the neatest little S-J-Ws! You can run a strand of Krystal Flash or something similar inside the tubing, and make bodies that glitter a little. You can also inject colored liquid inside it (this technique is covered in Phil Camera's book, *Fly Tying with Synthetics*).

A similar product from this supplier is called Nymph Rib. It's solid, rather than hollow, and is rounded on one side and flat on the other, so that the cross section is semicircular. This makes for ease of wrapping. Like Larva Lace, it comes in clear, plus a slew of colors, including (are you ready for this?) Maggot Ivory! I once found a bunch of trout that were very selective to maggots, because a rotting deer carcass was lying in the riffle above. If only I'd had my Larva Lace Maggot Ivory, what an article I could have written: *Upstream Maggoting for Selective Trout!*

Nymph Rib is about the same thickness as the standard Larva Lace tubing. It can be skinnied down somewhat by stretching while running hot water on it, or simply by rubbing it between your fingers, building up some heat in the process. But I still wish it came in a narrower width. I should mention that a similar product is also marketed by the Orvis Company under the name of Body Glass.

One of the most important uses of this type of material in contemporary fly tying is to protect the bodies of saltwater flies from the lethal teeth with which they will hopefully be making contact. This applies to such flies as the Crazy Charley series, the Joe Brooks Blond series, and the Glass Minnow.

There are other plastic products available for making fly bodies. Because of their nature, I've chosen to cover them in Chapter 9.

Glitz

The influx of glittery stuff into the fly-tying marketplace has steadily acceler-ated over the past two decades, and shows no sign of slowing—in fact, quite the contrary.

Each year we have our Fly Tackle Dealer show. Everyone goes to find out what's going on in the business and to make their deals for the following year. It's now reached a point where one must wear dark glasses when walking the aisles, such is the array of shiny stuff glowing away in the booths. Apparently, anything that glitters can be repackaged and offered as fly-tying material. Probably fish can't tell one type of glitz from the next, but there are other con-siderations, and those are what we'll examine here.

Traditional Tinsel

Tinsel has been with us for many generations. It comes in the following con-figurations:

- Flat—for forming bodies and ribbing. Various widths available
- Oval—mainly for ribbing. Various diameters available
- Twist—no longer common. Used by Atlantic salmon-fly traditionalists
- Round—ditto Twist
- Embossed—mainly for bodies where a diffused effect is desired
- Wire—just what the name implies. Various thicknesses available

The most popular color is silver, because so many salmon-fly and streamer dressings call for it. Gold is next, and then copper, which has come on strong in recent years as ribbing for nymphs and other subsurface flies. All of these vary a bit in shade, copper more than the others. This is primarily a factor of the material type.

In the old days, the problem with silver tinsel was that it tarnished. This is why many ancient flies in collections look as though the tinsel is made of pewter. In modern materials, that problem has been corrected through the use of alloys and coatings.

The salmon-fly traditionalists still tend to favor real tinsel. It has a classic look about it, and also performs several functions relative to that school of tying better than the contemporary Mylar substitute. A prime example is the protection of body hackle, where a combination of flat and either oval or round tinsel is used to shield the quill. The thicker tinsel works better here than the filmy Mylar. The downside is that it's bulkier and will also cut the thread of the careless tyer.

As for quality points, the main things to consider are resistance to tarnishing, handling characteristics, and durability. The latter is of particular importance with oval and round tinsels. They are built around a thread core and have a tendency to peel when being wrapped, some brands more so than others. A gentle hand helps compensate for this, but I also recommend attention to quality when purchasing.

Mylar

This space-age material has become extremely popular, and with good reason. It is far more forgiving and easier to handle than real tinsel, and stays bright for eternity. The flat type is the most widely used, its most popular version being the double-sided variety, which is silver on one side and gold on the other.

Other configurations similar to those listed for regular tinsel are also offered. They may differ slightly from the old stuff, due to the nature of Mylar. One must be careful of the types that have a thread core, since they are at least as prone to peeling as tinsel. Also, I've noticed that embossed Mylar doesn't hold the impressions very well. It's lovely stuff to handle, as compared to the cranky, saw-edged traditional tinsel, but under the moderate tension of wrapping, the impressions are all but wiped out.

A problem with Mylar is that it's not awfully strong. I've had quite a lot of breakage of ribbing on my salmon flies, particularly in Russia, where the action can be fast and furious. I've also noticed a lot of breakage when I employ the contemporary technique for tip/tag construction—under-wrapping with Mylar at the bend of the hook, then covering with floss or the equivalent. To combat this, I now rub a small droplet of Zap-A-Gap over the Mylar.

At this writing, the most widely used flat Mylar comes in four widths: 10, 12, 14, and 16/18. I guess these numbers are supposed relate to hook sizes, but there is little direct relevance. The tyer must simply select width based on function; for example, choose a size 10 when covering large hooks, and so on down the line. The 16/18 is intended mainly for ribbing small wet flies, but I prefer to use oval or wire instead, for reasons of durability.

Contemporary Glitz

There is no limit to the glittery products one can buy on spools or cards. All of it represents either an alternative to some other material, or an opportunity to innovate. That's great, except that there is so much of this stuff, and the similarities are so close, that making well-considered selections becomes confusing.

Being in the business, I get to see and play with materials far more than the average tyer. My approach to this sort of glitz is this: once I'm past the visual part—in other words if I like the looks of something—I make my selection based on function. This means how it ties, and how durable it is. Such a strategy isn't always convenient for the typical tyer, who may be shopping by mail, or is limited to what his local shop has decided to carry. Some shops are staffed with talented tyers who know what to stock. Others are less circumspect in that regard. I can only say this: if you buy some stuff and it comes apart in your fingers as you wrap it, or is miserable to work with, return it, and be sure to tell the people you bought it from why you're returning it. If enough tyers do this, we can get a lot of the junk that's out there off the market, and begin to whittle the glitz problem down to manageable proportions.

The materials you'll see on spools or cards run the gamut. Every conceivable color or shade is available, including mixed, or braided shades. Practically every conceivable width and texture is also available. Thus, one can use these materials for virtually any application, from highlighting and ribbing to full body construction. Of course you have to apply the judgment factor, and the fish will let you know how you did.

For example, years ago Poul Jorgensen designed a pattern called the Blue Rat. He used a particular shade of bright blue floss that was dyed up specially for that fly. It was never generally available in the shops, and people who wanted to dress the Blue Rat authentically were at a loss.

A few years ago, I came upon some spooled glitz—some kind of plastic tinsel substitute—that was the perfect color. I used it, and it worked. I caught plenty of salmon in Russia on those flies. I told others about it, and some were delighted, while others were rather negative—not because of the color, but because it wasn't the "real thing." Some people get quite exercised about departures from tradition, such as putting plastic on an Atlantic salmon fly. I can relate to their feelings, but that's strictly what they are—personal feelings, convictions, and preferences. The fish don't care, believe me.

At this writing, here are some of the more popular stranded glitzy products, and their primary applications:

- Krystal Flash. For highlighting streamer wings, Woolly Bugger tails, and like flies. This material is also widely employed in tying flies for Alaskan salmon fishing, where the criterion seems to be: the better the fish sees the fly, the more apt it is to take it. Many successful patterns used for silver salmon, or cohos, are made entirely of this type of material, mixing various colors.

- Flashabou. Ditto the above for applications. Flashabou yields a somewhat different effect than Krystal Flash, because it is more fluttery in the water. This product is available in a heavier version for large saltwater-fly tying

- Axxel. This is a product of the Uni-Thread Company, which offers many wonderful threads. This is a sort of twist, with variegated coloration. It can be used in place of traditional body materials, such as tinsel and floss, or in strands, as with Krystal Flash

- Lite-Brite. This is for enhancing saltwater flies, Alaska flies, baitfish imitations, and other large patterns. It is a fine, hairlike material, similar in texture to the hair on a Barbie doll. It can be tied on in bunches or cut up and mixed with dubbing. With regard to the latter process, I suggest using a method other than blenderizing, since the blender beats up on the Lite-Brite fibers badly. Try the following: put the materials to be mixed in a bowl of lukewarm water with a few drops of dish detergent added. Stir it around until total blending is achieved, and then dump the mixture into a sieve and rinse out the detergent. Lay the dubbing on a bed of paper toweling and press out as much water as you can. Then, let the stuff air-dry

- Krystal Chenille. A material like Krystal Flash, but in chenille form. Perfect for garish bodies, if that's what you want

- Tubing. Mylar and pearlescent. This comes in a number of diameters, and is generally sold by the foot or yard. It has a fiber filler that is easily removed. The gold and silver Mylar tubing can be used for bodies. The popular Zonker keel-style body is made of such tubing, and it is capable of expanding, like a snake eating its meal. This expansion accommodates the large metallic underbody. The pearlescent tubing is translucent, and one can underlay it with various colors to obtain different effects

- Corsair. This is a type of tubing, but with more strength and different behavioral characteristics than regular tubing. Jack Gartside discovered it and originated the first pattern designs and techniques that employ it. He also distributes it. Please refer to Chapter 12 for more information on Jack and his tying methods. Corsair is pearlescent in its basic form, but it can be given color, either by inserting materials inside it, or with a waterproof marker. One can also change the form of the material simply by compressing or extending it in the tying process. This is illustrated in the photos of Jack's flies

- Mylar sheets or tape. The material I examined while working on this chapter is put out by a company named Witchcraft. Undoubtedly there will be others by the time this book makes the shelves. This material was originally intended for lure-making, but since a lot of flies are actually lures these days, the adaptation came naturally. It is available in many colors, and usually has some sort of pattern impressed into it, giving it an almost holographic appearance.

I have treated these materials in a highly generic fashion since I have no way of knowing what will happen while this book is in production, and in the ensuing years. I can safely promise you that lots of similar materials will be put into the marketplace. Some are already here. For example, there is a product called Fire Fly that is somewhat of a cross between Krystal Flash and Flashabou. It would be ridiculous for me to try to catalog all such materials. The only viable approach is to describe the characteristics and applications of the most prevalent ones, which hopefully will assist you, the tyer, in coping with substitutions and future evolutions.

Having said that, I might observe that the criteria for choosing what particular glitz you want to use will be driven by fly-tying practicalities. Obviously, those materials that seem similar on the display rack will be so in the water too. However, certain ones may be better to tie with than others, and that's what I recommend you base your decision on. You will find that some of this stuff is not at all pleasant to work with, and all things being equal, the practical thing to do is to use one that ties the easiest.

And there's also the matter of how much flash one wants in a given fly. Can fish be put off by too much flash? I have seen trout in a quiet spring creek spooked by the sun reflecting off of a brightly finished reel at a distance of fifty feet, or put down by a shiny line being false-cast over their backs. For most types of civilized trout fishing, glitz should be used to effect a highlight and nothing more. However, in other circumstances, such as with Alaska salmon, maybe there's no such thing as too much glitz. Who knows? I do notice that while a lot of this shiny stuff appears on saltwater flies, most patterns incorporate other sorts of materials that are less reflective, and balance out the dressing.

Hackle, Wet and Dry

Much has been written about feathers for hackling flies in recent years, some of it by Yours Truly. What's left to be said? Perhaps some reiterations, refinements, and updates would be of value.

Dry-Fly Hackle

We all know that hackles for floating flies must possess certain qualities—stiff, web-free barbs, and all that good stuff. Here's a list of what I feel is important:

- A fine, flexible quill
- Uniform length of barbs throughout the usable length of the feather
- High barb count—i.e., lots of barbs per wrap
- Strong barbs, all the way out to the tips
- Straightness of barbs, or at least, relatively so
- Absence of significant web
- Rich coloration—an attractive "sheen"

Let's take the last first. Most healthy birds that have the quality points listed above will also have a lustrous coat of feathers, just as a healthy dog or cat has lustrous fur. At this point in time, I really don't care very much whether the color is natural or obtained by a *properly done* dye job, since modern techniques produce marvelous results without damaging feathers in the least.

One thing to remember about color: the backs of feathers will almost always be somewhat lighter than the fronts. This is true even of dyed necks, or capes, and saddles, except for black. So you'll normally get a composite when you wrap. In other words, the back side shade will be a little lighter than that of the front side of the cape or saddle.

Jumping back to the top of the list, the more I tie, the more strongly I feel that the quill is the most important of all considerations. Here's my rationale: given a very narrow quill that wraps true, you can compensate for other attributes that are less than optimum. For example, if barb count isn't very high, you can use more turns and pack the wraps more densely. This also compensates to a degree for barbs that aren't quite as strong as you might wish. The results are pleasurable tying and dry flies that perform well astream.

The Matter of Color

Much has been made of this topic over the years. I've seen tyers agonize over the subtle, almost imperceptible differences between two capes, as though the success and failure of their entire angling lives depended upon making just the right choice. Well, we all love beautiful colors, and we all have our own perceptions of what fits the standard descriptions found in books and catalogs. One man's ginger is another man's light brown, and so forth. And when it comes to that elusive shade known as dun—well, few tyers agree completely on exactly what dun is.

There are also marked or patterned feathers. Here's a list of the most commonly used:

- Grizzly. Originally grizzle (British name). White and gray or black-barred feathers. Also known as Plymouth Rock or Barred Rock
- Badger. A white or pale feather with a dark center stripe
- Furnace. Originally Furness, named after a town in Scotland. A brown feather with a dark center stripe
- Cochy-Bondhu. One of several accepted spellings. Also called List. Furnace with dark edges
- Barred Ginger. Grizzly-marked cream/ginger feathers
- Cree. Mixed barring of grizzly, with ginger and brown pigmentation. Rare and coveted

Minor variations are practically infinite. I think I can best serve you by referring you to the captioned color page of hackles included in this book. These are my perceptions; others may take exception. As mentioned previously, I have no problem with dyed colors, given an expert dye job.

Capes, or Necks

While saddles have advanced a couple of light years over the past few decades, capes are still the most popular, mainly because they offer a wider range of sizes, and have additional applications, such as tailing and winging dry flies, and possibly, streamer flies. In addition to the items on the preceding list, here are a few more attributes to look for when buying capes:

- Lots of feathers *in the size range you want to tie in*
- Usable feather length—that is, long "sweet spots"

- Tailing material, which is getting to be a scarce commodity
- A well-prepared cape, without a lot of body fat or grease

That last item is a particular bugaboo of mine. There's nothing I dislike more than a cape or saddle that hasn't been properly scraped and treated. It is most distasteful to have to handle a pelt that oozes fat all over one's hands. This is simply a matter of the grower and/or his employees doing the right kind of job, and there's no excuse for them doing anything less.

If you should happen to obtain such a pelt, here's what to do: first, wash it in lukewarm water and dish detergent, and allow it to dry. Next, take a stiff-bladed knife and scrape away as much fat as you can without damaging the skin. Then spread a mixture of salt and borax onto a pad of paper towels, lay the pelt on it skin-side-down, and put a book or some other fairly heavy object on it. You may have to refresh the salt/borax mixture at some point. In a day or so, you'll have a much cleaner pelt. Brush off the excess mixture, and store the pelt in a plastic bag with a cardboard and perhaps a folded-up paper towel over the skin side.

As for tailing material, decades of breeding for shorter-barbed feathers in the main part of the cape has resulted in truncation of the throat or "spade" hackles along the sides. This is particularly true of grizzly, or barred-rock breeds. To accommodate tyers, some shops carry packaged tailing hackles, but this is not common. Some tyers substitute Microfibbets. These are fine for realistic tails on spent patterns, where the body and wings float the fly, but not so good for traditional dry flies.

By the time this book is published, there may be lots of excellent tailing feathers available. It's in the works, and that's about all I can tell you at this time. Meanwhile, covet what good tailing feathers you may find on your capes. Without compromising by using the softer stuff lower on the quill, get as many tails per feather as you can. A good spade hackle, properly handled, will yield at least two and often three tailing bunches. Here's the procedure:

- Remove the feather from the pelt and strip off all the soft barbs, working towards the tip
- Grip the butt end of the quill with your hackle pliers. Hold these with the bottom two fingers of your hand—the pinkie and the one next to it. It doesn't matter which hand you use—whichever is most comfortable for you. This leaves the thumb and forefinger free to work on the barbs.
- Stroke the barbs to a 90-degree angle from the quill and check to see that they are uniform in length on each side
- If they are uniform, take the feather by the tip with the thumb and forefinger of the other hand—the one that's not holding the hackle pliers. Then, with the thumb and forefinger of the hand that *is* holding the hackle pliers, stroke the barbs from both sides so that they come together with the tips even, 90 degrees from the quill.
- If the barbs are not of uniform length, work on one side of the feather at a time

- Hold them in this position with the fingers that did the stroking. Then grab them by the tips and either cut or pull from the quill enough to make a tail. If there are more usable barbs remaining on the feather, save it

I call this procedure barb-gathering. It is one of the least-emphasized techniques in the fly-tying instructional literature, yet one of the most important and least understood. This procedure is used in many essential tying functions in addition to gathering tailing barbs. For instance, it is also used in folding hackles for wrapping collars, palmering wet flies, bass flies, and Woolly Buggers, and making "true" beards. It would serve all tyers to become adept at this technique.

A final word. Top-quality capes are somewhat pricey; thus, there is a temptation among tyers to try to use as much of a feather as they possibly can. The mindset seems to be: "I paid for this stuff, and I'm going to use every last barb of it."

This practice will cause you much grief. In every class I teach, I see people not stripping their feathers back to the sweet spot. They tie them on, and have to cope with the thicker portion of the quill while deploying less-than-optimum-quality barbs. This stuff eats up all the available space, so there is no room for the quality material nearer the tip end of the feather.

My friends, please don't do this to yourselves! Get rid of everything that's less than the best material that the feather has to offer. Even the finest cape hackle, in the more popular size ranges, will have real quality in less than half its length. Except in the rarest of cases, I find that I can cut a feather in half first-off, discard the butt end, then strip back to the sweet spot, where the quill is fine, the barbs uniform in length, and the web minimal or entirely absent. Admittedly this is a bit drastic. And as I've already told you, small hackles tend to have a longer sweet spot proportionately, so keep that in mind.

Saddles

As mentioned, saddles are coming on strong. The incredible saddle pelts from the Hoffman Supergrizzly flock, which is now owned by Dr. Tom Whiting, who holds a PhD in poultry genetics, are generally available in better fly shops and are causing quite a stir. The Hebert roosters, owned by Ted Hebert of Laingsburg, Michigan, are known more for their wonderful cape hackles, but Ted is also producing some fine saddles these days. The Hoffmans tie quite small, while Ted's stuff runs larger, so between them, they cover a wide range of sizes.

And size range is one of the main differences between capes and saddles. A good cape will have seven, eight, or perhaps even nine sizes on it, whereas a saddle rarely possesses more than three, and may often have only two.

When I started tying in 1959, saddles were considered little better than throwaways. Today, top-grade saddle hackle compares favorably in quality with cape hackle. In some respects, it may be even better; the barb count tends to be high, and the quills are usually thread-fine and wrapable. The sweet spots are also quite long. In fact, on a top-grade Hoffman, almost the entire feather is a sweet spot. Typically, dry-fly quality begins within an inch or two of the butt end of the feather, and runs throughout its length. This allows the dressing of a number of flies from a single feather.

Saddle hackles do have a few idiosyncrasies. Interestingly, a single feather may have barbs that run to two, or even three sizes. I recall some samples sent to me by Henry Hoffman, the founder and developer of the flock that bears his name. He wanted some feedback. My response was to send him a half dozen Pale Morning Duns tied from a single feather. There were three 16's, two 18's, and a 14!

Another most interesting characteristic of these feathers is that sometimes the barbs get longer, rather than shorter, nearer the tips. This is something to look for when purchasing saddles. If you size-grade by checking the barb length in the tip area alone, you may not get a true picture of what the feathers on the pelt will tie. So I suggest you examine barb length throughout the entire usable portion of the feathers.

Saddle hackles have a tendency towards cupping, meaning that the barbs don't protrude straight out from each side of the quill, as they do on capes. This causes the feather to look strange, but unless the barbs themselves are overly curved, it won't matter from a functional standpoint.

The tyer can minimize the effect of cupping by following two rules:

- When tying in a feather, leave the tiniest bit of bare quill exposed at the tie-in point. This will allow the quill to roll into winding position before any barbs peel off. This helps prevent the first series of barbs from laying back over the shank of the hook.
- Tie in the hackles with the outside, or pretty side, of the feather towards you, so that it will be in front during wrapping. This mitigates against cupped feathers leaning forward as the hackling process progresses.

Saddle feathers may also show a tendency to toe outwards. Again, this usually isn't the problem it appears to be. However, I have run into feathers with outward curvature that wanted to flare off in various directions when being wrapped, so be aware that this can happen. I think that any reputable dealer would take back such a pelt with no questions asked.

Grading

Both capes and saddles are graded by the grower before being sent to the retail store. That's the basis for how much the shop pays, and subsequently, how much you'll pay as a customer.

Birds vary considerably from flock to flock, and each grader must take into account the quality of the other growers' birds, as well as relative quality within his own flock. Growers' criteria tend to vary somewhat, since they naturally wish to emphasize the points of quality in which their chickens are strongest. For example, one grower might rate barb strength and stiffness very high, with quill diameter and flexibility secondary, whereas the next one would do just the opposite.

However, everyone is in agreement that the quality considerations already mentioned, along with the quantity of material on a given pelt, determines grade. Most growers grade on a 1-2-3 scale, with 1 the highest. Occasionally, you may see some "off-grade" pelts offered for sale at reduced prices. If they are from a reputable grower, look them over carefully; you may be pleasantly surprised. Sometimes these are pelts that were damaged in preparation, or have one particular negative characteristic—odd color, for example—that renders them less than optimal from a marketing standpoint. Perhaps they may not have as many feathers on them as a high-grade pelt. However, they may be quite good in other respects, and a real steal.

What about color? Is it a legitimate factor in grading? The answer is both yes and no. Here's what that means: certain colors, or strains, of chickens don't produce as good a grade of hackle as others. This is simply a matter of genetics. They can be improved, to an extent, by selective breeding, optimal care, and such, but still, they will fall somewhat short of another strain that is genetically superior, from a hackle standpoint.

A prime example is the Hoffman flock. The browns have been carefully infused with the fantastic grizzly bloodline over a long period of time, but they still aren't quite a match for the pure barred strain. I should state that the people at the farm are very careful to take this into consideration when grading, in order to be fair to the consumer.

So yes, I have no problem with a magnificent natural dun being graded up a half-grade over, say, a cream that tends to breed more consistently for quality. But no, I wouldn't agree that pretty color alone should justify rating a pelt highly, when its other quality attributes are not so good.

Another criterion that graders often apply is range of size. Capes that tie over a very wide range—let's say from 12 to 26—are likely candidates for high rating. The message is that if you don't care about small hackle, why pay the price for it? In such cases a grade 2 or 3 may be just fine for your purposes, at a substantially reduced price.

What does grading mean to you, the end user? Well, it's a helpful guideline, and a good starting point, but not an absolute. Don't get stuck on insisting on #1s. They are not so common and probably less than ten percent of even the top-quality flocks turn out to be legitimate 1's. Learn how to evaluate capes and saddles yourself, in terms of what you will be tying from them. You'll save money, and you'll be happy, because you'll be able to find what you need without sitting around for months on end waiting for Superneck to arrive. The growers and dealers will also love you.

It occurs to me that I've used the names of Hoffman and Hebert almost generically. I do this because in my opinion they represent the state of the art at this time, and thus set the standard. However, it should be noted that there are other growers out there, producing feathers that are at least acceptable.

Certainly, no dissertation on hackle would be complete without acknowledging Buck Metz of Bellville, Pennsylvania. Buck was responsible for the first major movement towards developing genetic hackle grown just for fly tying. He made a big contribution to the field, both because of his work in feather culture and because he was instrumental in developing an awareness, and thus, a market, for genetic hackle. At this writing, he is still producing large amounts of fair-to-good hackle in a complete range of colors.

Several growers of recent vintage include Chanticleer, Colorado Quality Hackle (CQH), Grasmick, and Keough. I'm not sure of the status of these growers at this time. I'm particularly concerned that Keough seems to have disappeared from the scene, since they had good-quality grizzlies that were suitable for larger flies.

In western New York State, Charley Collins of Collins Hackle Farm has a moderate-sized flock of very nice birds, in a wide range of useful shades. He raises nice grizzlies and specializes in breeding towards barred shades, such as cree, barred ginger, and barred dun. I've always loved such feathers; they're very fishy.

Al Brighenti, of Al's Grizzly Farm, and Spencer Hackles turn out some nice grizzly pelts, although I do find that I must regrade them sometimes, since they are not consistently the same dry-fly quality as the market leaders.

Wet-Fly Hackle

In this category I will include hackles for various types of subsurface flies, including nymphs and Atlantic salmon flies.

Not counting the creation of realistic legs on flies, which falls at least as much into the model-making category as that of fly-tying, there are two basic methods for applying wet-fly hackle: you can simply tie a bunch of it in place beard-style, or you can wrap it. There are things to be said for both.

The beard technique is quick and easy, and allows larger feathers to be used on smaller flies, length being under the control of the tyer. A skilled fly dresser can fashion a most attractive and effective hackle via this method.

Wrapped hackle requires that the feather match the fly in size. In some cases, this isn't quite so precise a discipline. For example, the collar on a soft-hackled wet fly needn't be as right-on in terms of barb length as the hackle on a traditional dry fly. However, a precisely sized nymph should have an accurately sized collar or beard, in order that the components balance out with each other.

More and more, hen capes are being used by the nymph tyer; they offer the desired texture, wrapping properties, and range of sizes. A most attractive hackle can be formed by stroking back the barbs, folding the feather as it is wrapped, exactly as the salmon-fly tyer makes the collar on, say, a Rusty Rat. Then, if desired, it can be fashioned into a beard by stroking down the barbs around the sides and pruning out those that want to stay on top. This is the method I prefer, for reasons of both appearance and function. I find that this sort of hackle on a nymph or wet fly holds its form better, and has superior action in the water.

Obtaining hen capes of good quality has until recently been virtually impossible. The reason is economic. Hen hackle is a by-product. Tyers simply won't pay even a fraction of the price of a good dry-fly cape for a hen pelt. On a hackle ranch, the job of the hens is to make more chickens. Then, if they happen to have a usable coat, they are treated to a noble demise, and an afterlife in the tying cabinet of some arcane character like me.

Even as a by-product though, the profitability of hen hackle is questionable. Someone has to skin the bird and prepare the pelt. Then there's packaging. And for all this, a top-quality entire hen skin will bring less than $20 retail. It's almost cheaper for the growers to throw them away, which is exactly what they have done in the past. Some still do.

Fortunately, several of the leading growers, notably Hoffman, are packaging hen pelts for sale. They are not very costly, and have other uses besides hackle, such as winging dry flies, streamers and matuka patterns. I should mention that hen body feathers also make great matukas, and sometimes are suitable for hackling larger wet flies, particularly salmon flies. Many shops now offer these feathers in both natural and dyed colors.

Which brings up another matter. Tyers of Atlantic salmon flies, steelhead flies, and streamers are constantly in search of dyed feathers in various colors for making hackles. In order for the dyed colors—especially the lighter ones—to be bright and attractive, the feathers have to be truly white to begin with, or at least very nearly so; the closer, the better. I'm having a tough time, at this writing, finding white hen pelts, because they are not common in flocks of birds raised for fly tying. We can get pale grays and creams, but pure white is a scarce item.

Perhaps there's an opportunity for some enterprising chicken-grower out there. Pure white strains of chickens, such as the white leghorn, are common. It would be no trick at all to raise these birds, and thus satisfy a market that's going begging right now. Or maybe the simple thing would be to make a deal with one of the egg-and-meat farms to take white pelts off their hands. Properly skinned and manicured, these feathers would be worth a lot more than the carcasses themselves.

Feathers from birds other than chickens are commonly used in wet-fly and nymph work, and are quite valuable in certain applications. Pheasants, grouse, and various other game birds have usable feathers. Best of all is the Hungarian partridge. These pelts feature a wealth of small feathers with beautiful speckled markings. They are great for all wet-fly and nymph hackles, and are particularly excellent for hackling the popular soft-hackled wet fly, of which there are many pattern variations. These pelts are not terribly costly, and you'll get many hundreds of flies from each one. Feathers from the saddle, neck, and shoulders lend themselves to both the wrapping and bearding techniques.

Up until this point, I've discussed primarily hen feathers for wet-fly work, and they are my preference. However, rooster feathers can, in some cases, be quite suitable, especially for salmon and steelhead flies. They tend to produce a different effect than hen feathers. The barbs, whether natural or dyed, are glossier, and considerably stiffer. This is often desirable, particularly on salmon flies, which are frequently fished on a tight line in faster currents. The stiffer hackles hold their shape better in such an environment.

Exotics

Perusal of older pattern books tells us that over the years, a myriad of types of feathers have been used in hackling subsurface flies. In his seminal work on the subject, *The Art of Tying the Wet Fly*, James E. Leisenring, the wizard of the Brodheads, mentioned coot, grouse, jackdaw, land rail, partridge, plover, snipe, starling, and woodcock. These, just for his particular school of trout-fly tying! Old salmon-fly books list many more species, including various herons, waterfowl, and tropical birds.

Much of this plumage is now off-limits to the fly tyer. Laws and treaties, notably the CITES treaty, protect many species of birds and animals, both domestic and foreign. Whether the regulations make sense or not (some do, some don't), they are the law, and should be heeded. For example, even though the great blue heron has overpopulated, and has become at best a nuisance and at worst a lethal threat to fish populations, it's still illegal to use the plumage. The federal government sometimes issues permits to proprietors of fish hatcheries and such to kill herons, but they must destroy the feathers immediately. Much as salmon-fly tyers crave the body feathers for spey-fly hackles, they are a no-no, and it's a federal offense to possess them.

However, there a quite a few birds that are perfectly legal, and quite useful. I've mentioned grouse, partridge, and pheasant. The woodcock also has beautiful little feathers for making soft hackles. They are somewhat similar to those of the Hun, but differently marked. There are also waterfowl, such as the coot, which has gorgeous blue-gray body feathers. These are game birds, and their plumage may be obtained through shops or from hunters.

Certain non-game birds are also legal, such as starlings, crows, and pigeons. I don't know that I'd go out and knock off one of them to obtain its feathers, but there's nothing wrong with grabbing a road-kill. I used to get lots of starling every fall, because the birds would fly down my chimney, and not be able to get out. They would soon perish, and I'd simply open the flue and pick them out of the fireplace.

Chickabou and CDC

The last first. CDC stands for Cul de Canard. These are rump feathers from ducks. Some, but not all of them, can be wrapped to form a type of hackle. In my opinion, this is not their main utility. CDC is covered in detail in Chapter 16.

Chickabou is a registered trade name of Whiting Farms, Inc., where Hoffman hackle is raised. It is, simply, chicken marabou. These soft feathers are found around the rear and rump areas of the birds, and between their legs. Those with more distinct barbs can be wrapped to form soft hackles. They are very fishy, as they tend to trap air bubbles in the water, and undulate in life-suggestive fashion. Those feathers that do not lend themselves to being wrapped can be used as mini-marabou. A great New Zealand pattern, the Cockabully, calls for marabou from a Barred Rock.

These feathers have only recently become available in fly shops. I strongly suggest that you give them a try.

Wish List

With all the wonderful hackle that's available today, perhaps I'm being overly audacious in wishing for something more. However, I do see a few windows of opportunity in the field of hackle culture. Briefly, I offer these for consideration:

- Larger dry-fly hackles. In the old days, the problem was finding hackles small enough. Now it's just the opposite. I'd love to see capes that have quality hackles in sizes 8 to 12, or perhaps 14, and that also have plenty of spade hackles for tailing and variant-style tying. Badger and furnace would be particularly valuable shades, as several of the universally popular Wulff patterns call for them.

- Very fine-barred grizzly. These are desirable for winging the Adams, as well as for the effect they yield when wrapped. For winging, grizzly hen would be ideal, if only the markings looked more like those of the rooster.

- Cree in quantity. By way of definition, cree is a barred feather that contains brown and/or ginger shades, as well as grizzly. In the old Herter catalogs, it was referred to as multi-variant. Buck Metz calls it the single-feather Adams. By any name, it's wonderful stuff. Unfortunately, cree is an aberration, and does not breed true. I hope breeders are able to solve this problem at some point.

- Feathers for streamers. This isn't actually a hackle consideration, and in some parts of the country it might not mean a great deal. However, here in the Northeast, we love our streamers. In order to properly dress them, we need very large rooster hackles that aren't too skinny, have lots of web, and rounded tips. In addition to such naturals as grizzly, badger, gray, and furnace, we desperately need pure white, for dyeing. These would also be of great value to the salmon-fly tyer. Birds bred for dry-fly hackle seldom yield good streamer material in either the capes or the saddles. True, streamer capes wouldn't command the price that dry-fly capes do, but then, they don't require all that excruciating care and breeding either.

- White hen pelts. Salmon, steelhead, panfish, and saltwater tyers are starving for dyeable hen hackle. The market is seriously under-supplied, and the pelts that are available are often not truly white. This gives the dyer fits, since light, bright colors simply don't take to pale gray, cream, or beige feathers. This forces us to resort to bleaching, which is costly and a pain in the neck. Except for jungle cock, I can think of few commodities that would be more welcome than good-quality, snowy-white hen pelts.

From the pre-publication feedback I've received, it appears that most, if not all, of my wish-list items will come to pass. Maybe I should be writing a book about sex.

Materials for Wings

Historically, wings for wet and dry flies have been made from two materials: feathers and hair. A few synthetics have come on the scene in recent years, but surprisingly, the natural materials still predominate. Let's examine them.

Dry-Fly Wing Feathers

With a few exceptions, dry-fly wings made of feathers are formed in one of three ways:

- Clumps of material, divided and gathered by thread. Example: wings made of waterfowl flank feathers, such as wood duck, teal, or mallard
- Matched pairs of individual feathers. Example: the Adams wing, fashioned out of grizzly tippets
- Sections from quills. Many old traditional patterns employed this type of wing. A contemporary example is the No-Hackle family

The Quill Section Wing

Addressing the last type first, I have to confess that it's not my favorite, from either a tying or fishing standpoint. My primary complaint is that it does not produce a very durable wing, even with some sort of adhesive supplement. Also the technique, although not complex, is a bit cumbersome. This is due to the nature of the material.

The traditional method involves taking two narrow sections from opposing feathers, such as the wing quills from a duck or goose, pairing them back-to-back, so that they flare away from each other, tying them atop the hook, and positioning them with discreet thread wraps. Skillfully done, this makes nice-looking wings, but they don't stay that way for many casts. Improved durability can be achieved by running tiny amounts of adhesive along the edges of the wing sections, in order to prevent the fibers from separating. Zap-A-Gap and Dave's Flexament both work well for this.

The no-hackle wing, while similar in appearance to the traditional type, is remarkably different from a functional standpoint. In addition to representing a wing image, it also plays an essential role in balancing the fly on the water. The technique for tying this wing is at considerable variance from the standard method. It is described in *The Fly Tyer's Almanac* by Robert H. Boyle and Dave Whitlock, and also in my own *Versatile Fly Tyer*.

If you decide to try this winging method, the key is to select feathers that are thin and pliable. Wing quills from the various ducks work well. I particularly recommend the smaller birds, such as wood duck and teal. Canada goose is okay, provided you choose the softer portions of the secondary and tertial flight quills. Feathers from other sorts of birds are also usable, such as pigeon and starling. They are nice for smaller flies.

One caution: don't try to tie a large fly with quill section wings; they are too heavy for that and cause tying as well as fishing problems. Even a size 12 is pushing it.

The Hackle Tippet Wing

This type of wing is typified in the ever-popular Adams, and is called for on quite a few popular patterns. It involves simply selecting two matched feath-

Left: *hen hackle tippet wing, shaped with wing-burner.* Center: *wood-duck flank feather wing.* Right: *waterfowl quill section wing.*

ers and tying them into position, back-to-back. These wings are much more durable than quill section ones, because they have a center stem, or quill. They also have better aerodynamics, which results in easier casting.

The key is feather selection. In the case of the Adams, which specifies grizzly hackle tippets, the trick is to find those with the following characteristics:

- Rounded tips
- Adequate width
- Density, or opaqueness
- Fine barring
- Quills that won't roll

Usually, the top-quality hackles found on prime dry-fly capes, such as those from Hoffman, aren't the best for wings, which is good, because you don't want to tear up your best dry-fly hackle for wings, anyway. If you do want to use such capes for winging, choose feathers from well down into the cape, away from those precious 12's, 14's, and 16's. Use just the tips; they have a better shape, and won't slim down to nothing when wet.

Years ago, there used to be a lot of soft, webby grizzly around, and they produced great winging material. We don't see much of those any more, but if you tie a lot of Adams, and happen to find an inexpensive cape with good barring and feather shape, take it home.

Hen Tippets

Grizzly hen capes are now commonly available, and they have all but one of the attributes mentioned above, sometimes to an extreme. They are almost solid web, and produce a very opaque silhouette. However, the coloration and marking is quite different from that of rooster hackles, and your Adams will look different. If that's okay with you, go to it. You may find that some of these tippets are so wide that they need to be trimmed and shaped a bit, with scissors or wing burner.

In some cases, hen saddle feathers can be used for winging. However, you'll often find that they create tying problems, since the quills tend to be out of round and insist on twisting. The quills are generally very soft and don't stay in position as well as cape quills do. Also, these feathers are often webby to an extreme. They offer a lot of wind resistance during casting. Unless the wings are aligned perfectly, your leader will look like a Slinky after a few casts.

Aside from the Adams, and a few lesser dressings that call for grizzly wings, the most useful color is gray. Many of our important aquatic insects have gray wings, ranging in shade from pale watery to almost black. These are effectively imitated by hen hackle tippets.

While it's okay to use these feathers as they come off the pelt, a favorite technique is to pick the larger ones from the middle and rear sections of the cape and cut or burn them to shape. This results in a distinctive, highly visible silhouette. If care is taken during tying to fix both wings in straight align-

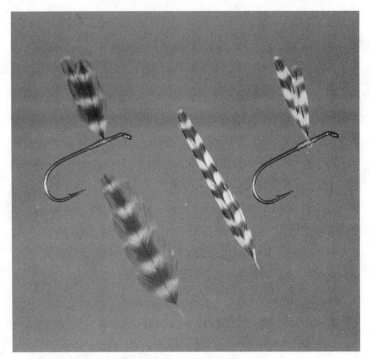

The Adams-type wing. Left: grizzly hen. Right: grizzly cock.

ment, leader twisting is kept to manageable proportions. Even so, size is limited, and a #10 is about as large as is feasible, even with the best tying technique.

During the 1960's, when I was making rapid progress as a tyer, I tried a lot of things. Some of the larger Eastern mayflies, notably the March Brown and the fabled Green Drake, were sources of great excitement, and I wanted to imitate them closely. I was very much influenced by Vincent C. Marinaro's brilliant work, A *Modern Dry Fly Code*, in which the author emphasized the importance of the wing silhouette, in terms of the trout's window, and refractive phenomena. Thus, I tried a number of feathers that had the color, markings, and shape of the wings of the naturals. These included grouse and pheasant saddle feathers, various flank feathers, and large hackles from mottled hen capes and saddles.

To say that I encountered problems with leader twisting would be a gross understatement—some of those Green Drakes actually twisted my fly line, and for all I know may have even torqued the rod itself! I abandoned them for more forgiving materials, predominantly hairs. Lee Wulff knew what he was doing when he designed the first of the series of flies that now bear his name, back around the time I was born. More about that a bit later.

Flank Feather Wings: Wood Duck

The ongoing popularity of this type of wing is remarkable, considering that it doesn't really look very much like the wings of many of the naturals it's supposed to replicate, and the most desirable feather—that of the drake wood duck—is, as the Russians would say, *oh*-chin dor-ah-*goy*: very expensive.

But what a thing of beauty a well-tied wood-duck wing is! Those golden feathers, flecked with gray, gently flaring, delicate and alar, quicken the pulse of tyers everywhere. This was Theodore Gordon's choice for the wings on what is now known as the Gordon Quill. They also adorn several other timeless classics, such as the Hendrickson, the Red Quill, and the Cahills, light and dark.

For a time, it was feared that we would lose this bird, as stocks were seriously depleted. Strict federal bag limits effectively controlled hunting mortality. This, combined with pesticide abatement and habitat protection that came mainly through the efforts of Ducks Unlimited and the Nature Conservancy, resulted in a resurgence, particularly in the Missouri flyway. There are plenty of wood ducks now. The shame of it is that the vast majority of them are wasted, insofar as the feathers are concerned.

If you know someone who hunts wood ducks, or if you hunt them yourself, here's what I suggest. Take some Ziploc bags along, stapled together in pairs. When a drake is killed, strip off all of the flank feathers, including those with black and white tips, from each side. Be sure to keep them separated by depositing them in the paired bags; left sides in one, rights in the other. That's about all you need to do, unless you want to manicure them by stripping off the fluff around the bottoms and pruning the quill butts. The ones with the black and white tips are treasured by salmon-fly and streamer-fly tyers. They should be paired as closely as possible, and kept that way. The plain lemon-barred feathers can be mixed together once the others are sorted out.

As a matter of fact, I recommend following this procedure even with full pelts purchased through shops. Duck skins are not easy to prepare, and many of them aren't properly cleansed of grease and oils. Removing and bagging the flank feathers will keep them unsoiled and prime for tying. If you intend to use the wings, cut them off at the base, or simply take what feathers you want and bag them discreetly, as with the barred feathers.

If you do decide to take an entire duck skin—and this goes for any species, not just wood duck—you must clean all of the fat off the skin, a delicate and tedious chore. You should also clean off any blood that has gotten onto the feathers ASAP; simply rinse it off with cold water, pat dry with paper toweling, then blow-dry the feathers with a hair dryer. Treat the skin with borax, exactly as recommended for an animal pelt, per instructions in Chapter 7.

There are several methods for forming wings from wood-duck flanks. To a large degree, the size and shape of the feathers will determine which method you choose. The legendary Catskill tyers, notably the Darbees and the Dettes, preferred to use sections from opposing feathers, or from the sides of one large feather, holding them convex-to-convex, and positioning them with thread. The rationale was that this minimized bulk behind the wing tie-on point by doing away with the quills. True, without doubt—but what about feathers that weren't suitable for this method? Nobody throws away wood duck, myself in particular. So, we simply use alternative methods, such as:

- Using one good-sized feather by tying it in as a bunch, and using thread techniques to fashion the bunch into wings
- Using two smaller feathers, positioning them convex-to-convex, crushing them onto the hook with thread, then dividing and positioning them with crisscross and figure-eight wraps

These techniques appear in many magazine articles and books, including my own *Mastering The Art of Fly Tying* and *The Versatile Fly Tyer*, both of which offer detailed photographic sequences of the respective methods.

The British writers referred to this bird as "summer duck." This might have been due to its penchant for early migration—it's the first duck to head south in autumn—or for when the feathers were prime. Actually, as far as the American wood duck is concerned, there are two periods of prime plumage annually: fall, when the bird is getting ready to migrate and spring, when breeding takes place. It would be unthinkable, as well as highly illegal, to kill them during mating season, so fall birds are what we get.

There was a time when a great many mandarin ducks were being imported from China. They are so similar to wood duck as to be considered interchangeable. The supply has been cut off though, or at least greatly reduced, since the Chinese probably felt that the ducks were being overharvested. In any case, the days of $5 mandarin skins are now a fading memory.

Other Flank Feathers

While not the equal of wood duck, flank feathers from several other ducks can be used to make passable dry-fly wings. Of these, my two favorites are teal and widgeon. The former is widely sold in bags in fly shops; the latter is available only through hunting sources, in limited quantities.

Teal flanks are distinctly barred in dark gray or black and white. They are similar to wood duck, and are handled in exactly the same manner, but don't have quite as nice a texture. Their coloration is also quite different, although with care, they can be dyed to closely simulate wood duck. As a matter of fact, for beginning tyers I strongly suggest substituting them until competence is attained. They can also be dyed gray, and substituted for quill wings.

One use for teal flanks that I very much like is as a substitute for grizzly tippets in the Adams wing. This does alter the design of the fly a bit, but the result is most pleasing. Also, it obviates the need for locating suitable grizzly hackles and laying out a lot of money for them. Bagged teal is a real bargain.

Widgeon flanks, like wood duck, are barred, but darker in shade, running to a medium brown. They are not quite the same in size, shape, and texture, but are close enough that the same tying techniques can be used. They yield an attractive effect on patterns that call for darker, mottled wings, such as the March Brown, the big Michigan *Hexagenia* and *Litobrancha*, the *Callibaetis* family, and several others. They also make great tent-style wings for caddis.

Another very common barred flank feather is mallard. It's similar to teal, but in my opinion, not quite as good from a texture standpoint. Like teal, it can be dyed to imitate wood duck. For wet flies, it's fine, and it's also useful for practicing technique. Availability is almost universal.

You may find that some teal and mallard flank feathers have raggy tips that appear to have been damaged. This is the result of constant preening by the birds, the molting process, and long migratory flights. These feathers are so inexpensive that I usually just discard such a feather, and reach for another one. However, if you get a bag where a large percentage of the feathers are badly beat up, return it.

The tips on mallard and teal, even when not damaged, are usually not as even as wood duck. When trying to fashion them into a well-shaped wing, it is often necessary to play games with them during the gathering, or bunching, process. If the feather is held at an angle, it is often possible to bring the tip ends of the fibers into alignment.

Church Windows

Another most valuable feather for making a specific type of wing is found on cock-pheasant saddles. It's commonly called the church window, because of its resemblance to the stained-glass windows so common in houses of worship. Its primary use is for making grasshopper wings, which it definitely resembles. However, it will require some sort of adhesive coating, e.g., Tuffilm, Dave's Flexament, or perhaps Pliobond.

Storage

The two major enemies of this type of feather are wetness and infestation by insects, mainly moths. Storage in tight-lidded plastic boxes or Ziploc bags, in a dry place, with moth repellent, is all that's necessary to properly preserve them.

If you have the time and patience, strip off the fuzz at the base of each feather, and prune the butt end of the quill. This will reduce storage space requirements considerably.

Before leaving this discussion of flank feathers, I should state that in addition to accommodating the classic upright-and-divided dry-fly wing, they may also be used for flat wings, such as those found on many caddis patterns. Simply substitute them for the hair that's usually specified for these dressings.

Hair for Wings

The use of hair for winging dry flies is credited, and I think accurately, to Lee Wulff, circa 1931, when he first tied the White Wulff to imitate the Coffin Fly spinner falls on the Esopus Creek in the Catskill Mountains.

The Esopus, where it all began for me in 1955, is a rough-water river, with innumerable swirls, eddies, and frothy pockets. One can easily understand how Lee, the ultimate practical fly fisher, would become frustrated with the performance of conventional flies, and would come up with something better. Few innovations have enjoyed the enduring success of Lee's hairwings—

Classic hair wings. Left: Wulff style, using deer tail. Center: parachute post, using deer hair. Right: Wulff style, using calf tail.

which, by the way, he did not name after himself. Dan Bailey dubbed them Wulffs several years later.

Today, we use several hairs for wings, including deer tail, calf tail, woodchuck tail, and various body hairs. Let's look at tails first.

Deer Tail

Often called bucktail, regardless of the animal's gender, deer tail reportedly was Lee's original material. At first glance, one might not believe a neat wing can be fashioned from such material. The keys are:

- Choosing fine, rather than coarse, tails
- Cleaning and "stacking" the bunches
- Strict attention to quantity—not one hair more than is needed

Deer tails vary enormously. For winging material, seek out the smallest ones you can find, with the finest hair. You can use the white portion for the many flies that call for white, and the brown portion for other patterns.

If people give you tails from animals they have shot, or if you find that those you have purchased aren't properly cleaned, wash them in lukewarm water with a mild soap, such as Ivory. Rinse, squeeze out as much water as you can, and set them aside to dry.

When using these tails, be sure to clean out all shorties and underfur, either with fingers or a fine-toothed comb. Then use a stacker to even up the tips. This is *very* important—you can't really tell how much usable material you have until the tips are even. Also, avoid using more than is necessary to make a clearly visible wing. Any more than that simply contributes to tying problems, and unbalances the fly.

Deer tail hair is also good for tying the upright post wing frequently used in parachute fly tying. It also makes excellent tails on larger flies.

Calf Tail

This is probably the most widely used material for making Wulff-type wings—as a matter of fact, it eventually became Lee's choice. In the old Herter catalogs, these were called kip tails, and occasionally we still hear that term today.

This hair produces a different effect than deer tail, because it's much more kinky and curly. This attribute makes it a little tricky to work with, but understanding how to handle the stuff renders it quite feasible. Here are the essentials:

- Select those tails with at least fairly straight hair
- After buying a tail, comb the whole thing with a fine-toothed comb—this removes any junk and loose stuff
- As with deer tail, be very discreet in terms of quantity, thoroughly clean out all short and aberrant hairs, and run the bunch through a stacker

Which reminds me of an amusing anecdote. One of my books, *The Versatile Fly Tyer*, was published in 1990, and shortly thereafter, was reviewed in the various fly-fishing periodicals. One reviewer gave it a particularly positive write-up, which very much pleased me. In the same issue, he wrote an article about wing materials. In it, he stated that the problem with calf tail was that you couldn't use a hair stacker to even up the tips. I guess he skipped over Chapter 11 of my book!

"Stacked" calf tail hair, using large-diameter tube.

Here's the drill: Before cutting the bunch from the tail, comb it well, unlocking the kinks as best you can. Cut off an appropriate amount and comb towards the butt ends, getting rid of all aberrant hairs. Then, comb towards the tip ends a couple of times, and proceed with stacking.

I must also tell you this: the most important thing about stacking this or any sort of hair is to use a stacking tool with sufficient *inside* diameter! I see all these cute little stackers in the shops, and they certainly have eye appeal, but the smaller ones, meaning those with the narrower tubes, are impractical, except for evening small bunches of relatively straight hair. Some are deceptive, because the outside diameter appears adequate, but the thickness of the metal in the tube greatly reduces the inside diameter. There's one that looks like an un-Sanforized spittoon that is the epitome of this.

At this writing, my choice is the Renzetti stacker. It is available in a jumbo size, which is great for the task at hand. There's more about this in Chapter 2.

Calf tails come in three natural colors: white, black, and brown. There are several shades of each. They are also available in an array of dyed colors.

Woodchuck Tails

This material might be categorized as a sleeper, because it seldom appears in shops or catalogs. However, it is most useful for both winging and tailing.

Woodchucks are a plentiful, if regional, animal. They are also a damn nuisance, as any gardener or farmer will tell you. They dig holes that pose a danger to grazing livestock, and they can scarf up a vegetable garden in the blink of an eye.

Some tails, such as squirrel, can simply be cut off and laid aside in a cool, dry place to cure. There's not much there except for hair and cartilage. Woodchucks, however, have a little fat and gristle in the tail, and thus require some cleaning.

This is not difficult. Take a scalpel or razor blade and make an incision the full length of the tail on the bottom side. Gently spread the cut, and use the blade to separate the skin from the tail cartilage, removing as much gristly stuff as possible. Then, apply a layer of salt–borax mix, and tack the tail onto a board, so it doesn't shrivel up while curing.

Woodchuck tail hair makes excellent wings on flies such as the Black Wulff. It responds nicely to stacking, and is much easier to work with than the brittle, slippery moose body hair commonly used for this application. It also makes great tails.

These tails range in color from rich chocolate to very dark brown to almost black. Some of them are flecked with gray, which I find attractive. They are excellent for imitating the wings on the huge *Pteronarcys* stoneflies that Westerners call salmon flies.

Left: woodchuck tail, Wulff style. Center: deer body hair, Humpy-style. Right: moose body hair, Wulff style.

Body Hairs

With these materials, life becomes somewhat more complicated. Tail hairs have certain similarities, the main one being that they are harder materials, and don't flare much, if at all. The three tails mentioned earlier each have different characteristics, but in respect to texture they all handle about the same.

Body hairs, especially those of the deer family, run the gamut. These hairs are commonly used in tying spun-and-clipped bodies and heads, such as those found on bass bugs and sculpin patterns. Generally speaking, hairs that are suitable for spinning are no good for winging, as they tend to flare all over the place. There are some sneaky tricks that enable the tyer to manage such hairs, but it's much easier to simply choose the right stuff in the first place.

So, what is the right stuff? That depends on the type of wing being tied. Considerations about species and all that complicated stuff will be discussed in Chapter 13. However, for our purposes here, all we need to be concerned with is the texture of the hair, and how it behaves when the thread intersects it. For example, Wulff-style wings of the type we've considered up to this point require a hard-textured hair that flares little, if at all. This also applies to post-type wings for parachutes. On the other hand, Comparadun wings, Humpy-style wing/bodies, and "down" wings, i.e., the type tied flat along the top of the body, are best accommodated by slightly softer hair that flares just a little under thread pressure. This type of hair also compresses more readily than hard hair, which makes life easier for the tyer, who's trying to get the stuff to stay securely in place and perhaps smooth it down for subsequent hackling.

Here are a few hairs that lend themselves to Wulff-style tying:

- Calf body hair
- Moose body hair
- Elk hock hair
- Deer's mask hair

Left: elk hock, Comparadun style. Right: blond elk, Troth Caddis style.

Calf body hair can be very nice, provided it's long enough. Those which are harvested in cold weather are by far the best in this respect. Moose body hair is coarse and somewhat of a challenge to work with, but it makes a pretty decent wing, after manicuring and stacking. Elk hock hair is more like true body hair, in that it flares a little, but one can still make a set of wings out of it. Ditto for deer's mask. These hairs are handled in the same way as tail hairs. You may find them to be a bit on the coarse side, especially the mask.

Please understand—there will be variations in all of this stuff, depending upon the age and size of the animal, what time of year it was killed, and exactly where on the body the hair came from. It's impossible to generalize. Again, you have to look the material over and evaluate it in terms of what you'll be using it for.

It's important to understand that body hairs are much softer and pithier near the butt ends. So, for down-wings, Comparaduns, and Humpies, look for hair that's long enough to allow you to work with the outer portion, towards the tip ends, where the texture is harder. You must also determine that the hair matches up with the size fly you're tying, in terms of thickness; the smaller the fly, the finer hair you'll want.

There's one exception to this that comes to mind. Al Troth, the legendary angler/guide of the Beaverhead, designed a caddis imitation that uses blond elk. This hair comes from the light-colored patch that's the last thing you see as the elk goes over the hill. The hair does flare quite a bit. In Al's basic design, there's no hackle, and the fly depends on the wing and the short trimmed bunch that sticks out the front for buoyancy. This makes the tying a challenge. But you just have to grit your teeth and wrestle the hair two falls out of three!

Synthetic Wing Materials

Despite the onslaught of technology and a great deal of hype and promotion, synthetics have been slow to replace natural materials for wings. There are some reasons for this, above and beyond the innate tendency of fly tyers to resist change. I've found that while many of us are innovators, we tend to express this by developing improved techniques, and finding better ways to work with the same old materials, rather than jumping onto all the new stuff as it comes out.

Like anything else, the way to judge new fly tying materials is: Does this stuff work better than what I've been using up to now? This should be an objective, rather than an emotional evaluation. If the answer is an honest "Yes," then you can decide whether or not you want to use it. I know people who simply won't tie with certain types of materials. That's up to them. Aesthete and traditionalist that I am, I also like to catch fish, and if something comes along that will enhance my ability to do that, I'm going to jump on it.

When evaluating synthetic wing materials, keep this in mind; the one thing that all of the natural materials previously described have in common is that air passes between their fibers. The one partial exception to that is the larger cut wing, which I classified as a potential leader-twister. Air does not pass through plastic, and this must be weighed against the rather obvious eye appeal some synthetics have, at least to humans. Wings have to do more than look realistic—they have to be tieable and facilitate fishing.

John Betts might be called the father of synthetic wing materials. He wasn't the first to use synthetics; I remember seeing several types of wing materials listed in the Herter catalogs of the 1950's. I also recall a guy who fished the Catskill rivers with spent flies that employed cellophane from cigarette packs as wings. I'm sorry that I can't remember his name.

But John has been a perennial advocate of synthetics, and is recognized as one of their leading exponents. He has developed materials which are marketed under his name, and he has worked out dressings and tying methods for them. For this, he deserves recognition. I'm sure these flies work well for him.

In evaluating synthetics for wings, I played with several materials. The first one is a translucent, virtually clear sheeting that is used to make spent wings. It's pretty tough stuff; you can tear it lengthwise, but it doesn't break easily crosswise, and thus it makes a wing of acceptable durability.

To form a set of spent wings, I folded the material double and cut a wing-like shape, so as to achieve symmetry. I then figure-eighted the wings onto the thorax area of a spent-style fly. It helps to wrap a little dubbing in the area before tying on the wings. In place, they look very realistic—more so than the more impressionistic effect obtained by using hackle to make spent wings.

I tried casting these flies and they didn't twist my leader more than I could put up with. I think this is because the material is very pliable, and perhaps folds back during casting. I fished a spinner fall with this dressing one evening; I referred to it in the Introduction. The fly produced. However, it didn't float as well as my hackle-winged spents, and I did have a couple of wings break off.

Another material I tried out is a ribbon-like plastic that comes wrapped around little cards. There are a number of colors available. I used a light tan, with mottlings, to create a caddis-style wing. I found this material to be less than pleasant to work with. When I folded it over to facilitate cutting out a symmetrical set of wings, it stuck to itself, and I had a devilish time separating it again. Following directions and a sketch on the package, I tried using a wing burner on it. Disaster! Burning a folded piece to obtain a symmetrical set of wings resulted in a fused hunk of plastic. Burning one wing at a time didn't work much better. If you're going to use this type of material, count on cutting out the wings with scissors. And whatever you do, don't lose the tag end on the card, because it's very difficult to find and get going again when you want the next piece.

I spent two evenings fishing caddis patterns with wings made of this material. They worked, but so did my hair-winged and teal-winged flies. They cast okay, and held up well enough. I would say it's up to you tyers out there to experiment further. It is possible that similar materials will come onto the market that aren't as unpleasant to work with as the one I tried. They could be there now, for all I know.

I played at the vise with one more synthetic wing material, named Microweb. It is a fabric somewhat similar to the organza that bridal veils are made of. It comes in the usual array of colors, from black to white. The batch I experimented with had a lot of tiny pearlescent spangles stuck to the fabric. Most of these came off during handling, and some more disappeared during casting.

Even so, the material is no problem to work with, and I was able to shape it into nicely formed, attractive-looking caddis wings. In that form, the flies cast without twisting the leader. I didn't try making mayfly wings from it, so I have nothing to report about that.

Finally, I tied up some spent dressings using several types of synthetic yarn. These included polypropylene, Antron, Polyfluff, and Z-Lon. This was, to some extent, a revisitation, as I had done quite a lot of fishing with spent flies that had poly yarn wings back when it first came out.

Not a lot has changed in respect to the manner in which the material behaves, both at the vise and astream. I do like the latter three of the materials mentioned above better than poly yarn, because they are a bit less supple, and have a little more glitter, which I like in a spent wing. The texture is slightly more coarse, so one can use less material and still obtain the desired silhouette. The tying method is very simple—you just figure-eight them into position, then cover the thread wraps with a little dubbing, preferably both top and bottom.

The problem I find with all of these materials is that they don't hold their form very well. I've even tried putting small droplets of adhesive at the bases of the wings, but that helps only marginally. Unquestionably, they take fish when they are fresh, before they get beat up, but that happens too quickly for my liking. I should mention that this problem lessens with diminution, and from a size 18 down, it becomes progressively less of a hindrance. In fact,

George Kesel reports good results using such materials for conventional divided wings and posts for parachute dressings on smaller flies.

In summary, I will say that yarn wings are certainly a cinch to tie, and in no way inhibit casting or leader health. The material is also relatively inexpensive. They have not proven to me that they offer any advantage over the spents I tie with hackle wings, and also they don't float as well. However, some disagree, and I won't debate the matter. It's up to you. I would advise that you try several materials, since they all have subtle but distinctive differences in texture.

I think the recommended approach to these newer materials should be something like this; if it looks good to you, buy a small package and give it a try. The important thing is that it should meet a set of simple criteria:

- Be reasonably user-friendly
- Be reasonably durable
- Not twist leaders
- Not make the fly sink

As far as attractiveness to fish is concerned, they'll have to speak for themselves. I do well enough with the hairs and feathers I've been using up until now and so I don't feel a strong inclination to do a lot of experimenting with synthetics. But that's me. I'm sure John Betts and his cohorts wouldn't be fishing with this stuff if they weren't catching anything. Certainly, there's lots more stuff coming out in the future, and some of it might well convert me in a New York minute.

Wet-Fly Wings

I cut my teeth, so to speak, on traditional Northeastern wet flies. Hardly anyone fishes them any more. These days, we are all so preoccupied with being scientifically accurate that we have embraced the contemporary nymph and emerger designs and forsaken the historic and seductive patterns that enabled Grandaddy to fill his wicker creel in that idyllic time before no-kill and political correctness.

Considering that my subject was somewhat archaic, I was amazed at the amount of positive feedback I received from my column in *American Angler*, March/April, 1994. In the same issue there was also an article by Tom Travis about fishing with these flies, which made for a nice article-marriage. Judging by the comments I got, it appears that folks were glad to rediscover winged wet flies, and were eager for information about tying them. So, from a materials standpoint, here goes.

Feathers for the Quill-Section Wing

This is the penultimate wet-fly wing that appears in silhouette form in so many angling graphics, including my own logo. Some tyers groan when con-

Left: waterfowl flank feather. Center: waterfowl wing quill sections. Right: mottled turkey sections.

fronted with having to tie this wing, but it's not at all difficult, given optimal materials.

The most commonly used feathers are those from waterfowl wings, mainly ducks and geese. The first few flight quills on the leading edges of these wings are called primaries. A little further in are the secondaries, followed by a succession of interior feathers that are called tertials.

What one seeks in such feathers is softness and pliability. Trying to use the coarse, thick, stiff material near the outer portion of a flight quill will only validate the tyer's fears. However, the softer, finer material towards the mid-section and base of such a feather will tie to perfection.

The secondaries generally produce the best winging materials, but don't overlook the lower portions of primaries—they can be very nice indeed. The tertials embody the softness and pliability we desire, but are sometimes poorly shaped and curled at the edges. This can be partially corrected by steaming and ironing with a steam iron, but this technique isn't a cure-all. Given the wide availability and low cost of this type of feather, one is better off choosing those which are optimal, and chucking the rest.

Almost any set of duck wings will yield good wet-fly material. For the best results, use feathers taken from a pair of wings from the same bird, and match them as closely as possible. Except for white domestic ducks, the feathers are invariably gray. Shades will vary widely, from dark slate to pale-pearly. Black ducks—and I refer to the species, not a black dye job—produce wonderful quills of a leaden shade. Mallard wings are somewhat lighter, and wood duck paler still. Feathers from smaller ducks, such as wood duck and teal, may tie nicely, but are limited as to size.

Canada goose wings are also excellent. One should have no qualms about using these feathers, since this bird has seriously overpopulated and needs to be thinned out. The feathers are larger but other than that they are similar to duck, and are used in the same manner.

While on the subject of geese, I should mention that feathers from domestic geese are widely used in tying Atlantic salmon flies. However, the most desirable ones are not wing quills. Rather they are from the shoulder area of the bird's body. They are dyed in a wide range of colors, and are used as a substitute for swan in married and built wings. Actually, they are much more pleasant to work with than swan, which tends to be quite coarse. The only problem the full-dress tyer has to contend with is the difference in thickness and texture between the goose shoulders and some of the other types of feathers that go into a married wing. The assortment of bustards, turkeys, pheasants, and such generally have thicker feathers, and when sections of them are married-in as the upper layers of a wing, they can overpower and crush the softer goose strips. Refinements of technique and strict attention to quantity help overcome this.

Before moving on, I should mention that this book doesn't address the subject of materials for Atlantic salmon flies, other than in a tangential manner. That's because salmon flies are in a class by themselves—a whole different ball game—and should be dealt with in a separate book.

Another feather often used for this type of wing is cinnamon or oak turkey wing quill. Once practically a giveaway, these feathers are now in short supply and have become rather pricey—$5 for a prime pair is just about the going rate at this writing. This makes the Muddler tyer blanch. Years ago, when I was cranking out wet flies commercially, you could buy a dozen matched pairs for less than that. Then, all of a sudden, American housewives decided they liked white turkeys, and there went our beautiful quills!

In addition to the Muddler, mottled feathers such as turkey are used for winging certain wet flies, such as the March Brown, the alder, and a number of caddis patterns. There are quite a few other feathers that have similar markings, such as various grouse, partridges, pheasants, and even domestic chickens. The problem is that they don't tie so well. An excellent substitute is peacock wing, which can be purchased from suppliers who serve the salmon-fly market. Usually, they carry two grades: average, and extra-select. For wets and Muddlers, the average ones are perfectly suitable. Leave the others for the salmon tyers.

At one time, we were able to buy feathers from the capercaillie, also known as the Auerhahn. This is an enormous grouse that at one time was plentiful in the British Isles and Western Europe. The feathers were beautifully mottled in browns and cinnamons, and were a delight to the wet-fly tyer.

War, pollution, and overhunting almost rendered the species extinct. Careful husbanding programs have reestablished viable populations in Scotland and Germany, but I very much doubt that we shall ever see these feathers in fly shops again. They allow hunting for Auerhahn in certain parts of Germany. The limit is one per lifetime.

The Flank Feather Wet-Fly Wing

Flank feathers, which were discussed earlier in the section on dry-fly winging materials, are also used for wet-fly wings. Tying techniques are, of course, different, and in some respects, so are the criteria for choosing feathers. For example, mallard and teal flanks make better wet-fly wings than wood duck.

Hence, we save the real thing for our dry flies, and use dyed mallard or teal for our Dark Cahills and such.

Selecting a flank feather that will work on a wet fly is closely tied to the method one intends to use for making the wing. I use a simple technique, which actually amounts to nothing more than gathering or bunching the fibers in a controlled manner, and tying them in place. This works best with feathers that have symmetrical tips and more-or-less centered quills. Strip off the junky stuff from the sides, bunch the tips, and tie it on. Often it is necessary to snip out the quill near the tip, so that it doesn't interfere with the tying process.

Fuzzy Feathers for Bodies and Special Effects

Certain feathers have been traditionally and not so traditionally employed in making highly effective fly bodies and other components. Let's have a look at the most interesting of them.

Peacock Herl

This is one of the most widely used body materials of all time, and one of the best. It is more popular for wets than drys, because of its texture and poor floating qualities, but even so, it appears prominently on perhaps the all-time greatest dry fly, the Royal Wulff.

Before examining this material in detail, I'd like to pass along an observation from many years of fishing peacock-herl flies. While it works on all kinds of fish, it seems to be particularly alluring to rainbow trout. I well recall my fledgling days on the Esopus Creek in New York's Catskills. This is one of the few self-sustaining rainbow fisheries in the Northeast. The hottest fly in my very limited arsenal at that time was the Leadwinged Coachman. If it hadn't been for the inherent deadliness of that pattern, I might well be a golfer today. It was also the first wet fly I learned to tie.

The tail is the most common form in which we purchase peacock. We recognize it by those large plumes with the iridescent "eye" at the tip. These are quite plentiful and low-cost, since they are shed by the birds periodically. The eyed portion is used for making two-tone quill bodies, as outlined in Chapter 8. The fronds on the tail proper are used mainly for making wrapped bodies, and also for embellishments to streamer wings on quite a number of patterns.

The herl on tails varies considerably in thickness, or density. This has to do with the size of the bird and the condition the feathers were in when molted. The thicker ones are suitable for large flies, but overdress small ones. They also tend to have heavier quills, which can interfere with wrapping. The fronds near the eye tend to be most prone to that. As a rule, the nicest herl comes from well down the feather.

We can also purchase peacock in bundles, with the butt ends strung together. This is very interesting stuff. It isn't true tail herl; rather, it is material that is molted from around the bird's body. The fronds, or individual fibers, are longer than those from the tail, sometimes reaching a foot in length. The herl sometimes tends to be much shorter. In fact one must take care when buying bundled peacock to make sure the fronds carry a sufficient amount of herl for making a fly body. Keep in mind that these are molted feathers, and sometimes there's not much material left when they drop off.

Bundled peacock, if it is good quality, is an inexpensive way to buy this material. Also, the finely herled fronds accommodate smaller flies, for which the fronds from tails would be too thick. Handle it the same as tail herl, but with more gentleness, because the quills are not as strong.

There are several methods for applying peacock herl, the most simple being to tie on a few fronds and wrap away. That will work, but reinforcement of some kind is needed if the fly is to endure an encounter with a trout's teeth. The method I was taught initially was to reverse-rib with fine copper wire; that still works pretty well, and also contributes a bit of coppery glint. However, the technique I prefer is this:

1. Tie in a bunch of fronds by the tip ends. Why the tip ends? Because the quills are thinner there, and also the herl itself is usually a bit shorter, which results in a body that tapers gradually from a slimmer rear to a heavier front.

2. With the thread at the rear, where the herl is tied in, pull a quantity of thread from the bobbin that is approximately twice the length of the herl.

3. Form a loop by holding the thread with the left forefinger at the bottom ends of the fronds and passing the bobbin over the tie-in point, just as though you were making a spinning loop.

4. After making sure both sides of the thread loop are secure by taking a few wraps rearward, cut off one side so that a single strand of thread hangs down among the peacock. Cut it to length. Then wrap the working thread forward to where the body will end.

5. Twist the thread and the herl together, forming a virtual chenille. Don't twist too tightly at first, since this may cause the thread to break the herl. About six or seven twists are sufficient.

6. Begin to wrap the body. Once the first one-and-a-half wraps are in place, twist almost to your heart's content. If you have trouble twisting because of the flatness of the quills, use an electronics clip, as depicted.

I use this method in making the two bumps of herl on Coachman bodies, as well as for full herl bodies. The result is not only a strong herl body, but a sightly one as well, because the herl comes out nice and dense.

Sometimes in a catalog or pattern book you will see a reference to bronze peacock. It is a fact that some peacock herl has a distinct bronze, al-

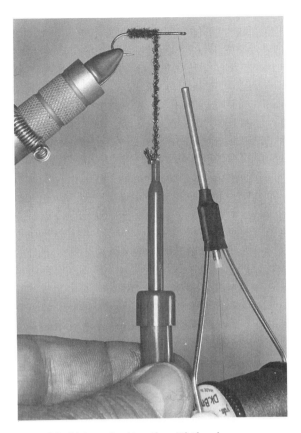

Peacock herl being twisted together with thread.

most purple cast. This occurs in tails in particular. I'm not one hundred percent sure what causes this, but I have found that it can be created by laying the herl in a window where it gets a lot of sun, and leaving it there for a long period of time. This amount of time necessary will vary; sometimes it takes months.

There is another type of peacock feather that can be used in fly tying. This is the sword and it extends along the flank of the bird. The herls out towards the tip ends are iridescent greenish blue in color, and very beautiful. Mostly, they are called for in salmon-fly dressings as highlights. One pattern, the Alexandra, utilizes a bunch of sword herls for the entire wing.

I must caution you that working with the fronds from near the tip of a sword feather is less than pure joy. The quills are flat, the feathers usually twisted, and they go more-or-less wherever they please. I recall my frustration at trying to get the Alexandra to look like the one in Bergman's *Trout*. The problem was that I was copying a painted rendition of the fly, and the artist's brush can solve any fly-tying problem. If you should ever want to tie this old pattern, just do the best you can, and let it go at that, because when the fly is in the water, it all comes out okay. Of course, if you're looking for cosmetic effect, that's something else again. In such cases, I improvise.

If you are a mini-fly tyer, you might be interested in the lower part of the peacock sword. Here the fronds are very tiny of quill, and the herl is minuscule. This facilitates making very small fly bodies. I use this herl on my Griffith Gnats from size 20 on down.

A wide range of sizes is possible with peacock herl.

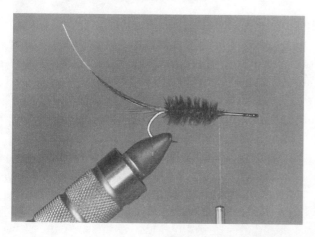 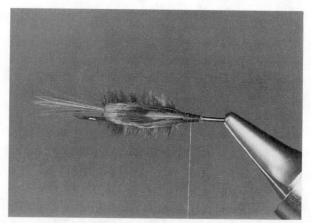

Ostrich herl used to produce gilled effect on a nymph.

When working this small, you won't want to use the thread/twist method of reinforcement. In fact, you may well be working with a single frond. If you wish to enhance the durability of these tiny flies, try this: rub a fine layer of Zap-A-Gap around the hook shank, then wrap the feather right over it while it's still wet. Be discreet with quantity; too much glue will mess things up.

Ostrich Herl

Possibly your first viewing of ostrich herl was similar to mine. I was a little kid, maybe three or four years old, and I was watching my maternal grandmother, who lived with us at that time, do the dusting. The implement she used consisted of a bunch of ostrich feathers. In fact, there's a fly pattern by that name, the Feather Duster. The body is, of course, ostrich herl.

While mainly of interest to the classic salmon-fly tyer, ostrich has other uses. Sometimes we wish to create large mayfly nymphs with a lot of fluff along the sides, which imitates the pronounced gill structure of the big, burrowing nymphs. Ostrich herl fills the bill. It also makes a nice thorax on larger stonefly nymphs, for the same reason; it looks and behaves like gills, which on a stonefly are located in the thoracic area, rather than along the sides of the abdomen.

Any time you want a fuzzy effect that comes alive in the water, you might consider ostrich. For example, it makes a beautiful hellgrammite imitation by simulating the many short, centipede-like legs those creatures have. The natural color is gray, with the shades varying somewhat. It is also available in an assortment of dyed colors, including the omnipresent pink that seems to be so popular with the dancing girls in Las Vegas!

Ostrich is used on a number of saltwater patterns in place of marabou. It has a higher density than that material and holds its shape better when wet. It is also longer, and better accommodates larger flies.

There is a wide variance in size between ostrich plumes, and commensurately, in the length of the herl. Look for those that suit what you're tying. Mostly, fly tyers use the smaller feathers, and leave the large plumes to the girls from Caesar's Palace.

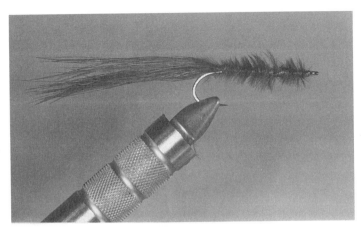

The marabou leech.

Marabou

This material is used for a number of things. It is given detailed coverage in the streamer-wing section (Chapter 14), since that, along with tailing the Woolly Bugger, is marabou's prevalent application. However, it should also be noted that marabou wrapped around the hook shank makes very attractive bodies on Leech and Damsel Fly nymph patterns. As mentioned, it can also be used for gilling fuzzy nymphs, and can be wrapped like hackle to obtain a unique effect. Jack Gartside's Soft-Hackle Streamer is tied in that manner.

Aftershaft Feathers

In the early 1980's, one Peter Lazlo wrote an article for United Fly Tyer's magazine, *Roundtable*, about the inimitable and irrepressible Jack Gartside. It was entitled, *Filo-Au-Go-Go*, and it extolled the properties of a little-known feather, the filo plume, which Jack had incorporated into his fly-tying repertoire. It turned out to be a matter of misidentification, a fact which several ornithologically-astute persons pointed out in letters to the magazine. The proper name for the feather is aftershaft. This prompted Gartside's comment, "You see; there *is* life aftershaft!"

If you fluff up the saddle portion of a grouse or pheasant skin, you'll see some soft, gray plumes that look something like individual marabou fronds. These are aftershafts; the Latin taxonomy is *Hypor hachis*. They occur on many kinds of birds and vary considerably, depending on the size and type of bird, and the climate in which it lives. They are very densely herled, and the material is extremely soft. When the birds need to stay warm in winter weather, they fluff their feathers a bit, and the aftershafts act as down.

These feathers really come alive in the water, and in my opinion, make better nymph gills than ostrich. Gartside, who likes to tie flies with what comes out of used vacuum cleaner bags, has designed several deadly dressings that utilize aftershafts, notably the Sparrow and the Evening Star. These, and other novel dressings, are described in a booklet he publishes and dis-

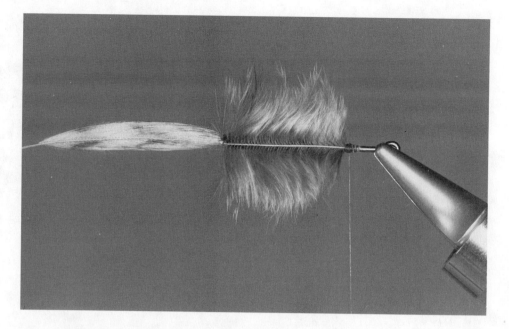

Aftershaft feather used to produce gilled effect on a nymph.

tributes himself, *Fly Patterns for the Adventurous Tyer*, which can be obtained by writing as follows:

Jack Gartside
10 Sachem St.
Boston, MA 02120

Jack has also written another book, entitled *Flies for the 21st Century*, which can likewise be ordered from him. It deals with some new patterns that utilize Corsair, a most interesting material that is covered in this book in Chapter 16.

Aftershaft feathers can either be wrapped like peacock, or tied in lengthwise. A typical application of the latter technique involves bordering each side of the rear portion of a nymph, thus creating a gilled effect. In order to sup-

A fly tied by Jack Gartside that uses an aftershaft feather for the body, and chicken rump for the hackle.

plement the strength of the delicate quills, ribbing of some sort is recommended. If it appears that the dense barbules of an aftershaft feather will overdress a nymph, take a pair of scissors and trim the barbs off one side.

In addition to gilling mayfly nymphs and making soft bodies, aftershaft feathers can be used for making emerger-type wing cases, soft alternative heads on Muddlers, and creative dressings, such as Gartside's Sparrow and Evening Star. Certainly, there are other uses yet undiscovered. Maybe you'll be the designer of the next killing pattern!

I might mention that individual marabou fibers can be used in place of either ostrich or aftershaft feathers. However, I think you'll find that the two described here work better.

I predict that aftershaft feathers are a material that will become more widely used in the future. Besides their inherent value, they are really a bargain—you buy a grouse or pheasant pelt for the other feathers it yields, and you get the aftershafts for free.

Wing Feathers and Such

In the section on wings for wet flies (Chapter 14), we examined feathers from the wings of large birds, such as goose and turkey. It is also possible to use individual barbs from these feathers to make moderately fuzzy bodies. The barbules will produce a fuzzy effect, similar to the shorter gills on active nymphs, such as the swimmers of the family *Baetidae*.

The procedure is as follows: Tie in a bunch of five or six barbs by the tip ends, along with a piece of very fine thread, such as Spiderweb. Then, simply twist and wrap, as described for peacock herl. Length is limited to about ¼ inch (6 mm), but if you need more, simply tie in an additional bunch and piece of thread and keep on going; the "splice" is not noticeable.

Bodies constructed in this manner are fairly rugged, in and of themselves. Additional durability and a bit of glint can be obtained by reverse-ribbing with fine wire, either copper or gold. And by the way, you are not limited to just wing feathers—any large body feather that has fuzzy barbs will work.

Pheasant Tail

This ubiquitous material is so popular for tying nymphs that an entire family of flies bear its name. The Pheasant Tail, or PT series is possibly the most universally effective group of nymphs in existence. They seem to work wherever they are fished.

A classic example of this is the incredibly simple dressing of Mr. William Lunn, the fabled river keeper of the Test. It consisted of pheasant tail fibers twisted together with copper wire. That's all there was to it, and according to accounts in John Waller Hill's wonderful book, *The River Keeper*, that's about all Mr. Lunn needed to deceive the Test's discriminating brown trout, of which he was such a devoted custodian.

The best of this material comes from the longer tail feathers of an mature, wild cock ringneck pheasant. Why do I stipulate "wild"? Because pen-raised birds not only don't grow as pretty a set of plumage as do wild ones; the feathers are often damaged by crowding, and the neurosis that accompanies it. Once you've seen a truly prime tail feather from a large, wild cock bird, you'll never be happy with anything less. The coloration is coppery brown, often with iridescent overtones. Unfortunately, such birds are rare these days, particularly here in the Northeast.

Barbs from a prime feather may be as long as two-and-a-quarter inches, which yields the dressing of quite a sizeable nymph body. A popular method, and one that I particularly like, is to tie in a bunch of perhaps six barbs in such

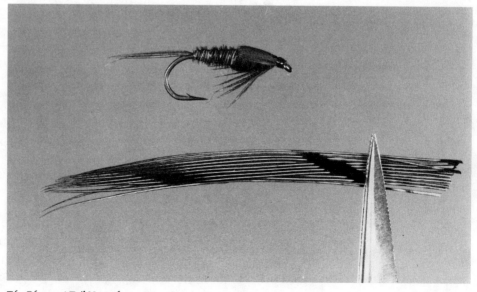

The Pheasant Tail Nymph.

The Sparrow, tied by Jack Gartside. The hackle is pheasant rump, fronted by aftershaft.

a manner that the tips form the tails of the nymph. Tie in a piece of thin copper wire and then make an underbody out of fine yarn, or something similar, to the desired shape. Wrap the barbs over this, then reverse-wrap with the wire. You can then finish the fly with whatever type of thorax, wing case, and hackle you prefer. In fact, a second bunch of barbs can be tied in and fashioned into these components.

Pheasant Saddle Rumps

On a cock ringneck pheasant pelt, in the lower portion of the saddle, there are some very beautiful feathers. The barbs are long and exquisitely colored, running to iridescent blues, greens, and rusts, and also to shades of gray. This is yet another feather that I think has more potential than has yet been realized.

Perhaps the most popular use for these feathers is as a substitute for the forbidden heron on spey-type salmon flies. True, they aren't nearly as large as heron, but for moderately sized flies, they are adequate. Gartside's Sparrow is hackled with a turn or so of pheasant rump.

Rump Marabou, or "Chickabou"

These feathers have been overlooked by fly tyers for eons, but are now beginning to gain the recognition they deserve. In the past, people who prepared chicken pelts for packaging trimmed this stuff off and threw it away. Now that its value has been realized, it is either left on the skin at the rear of the saddle, or sold separately. Grizzly or Plymouth Rock chickens seem to produce superior rump marabou feathers. Hence the name "Chickabou," which is

A midge pattern, tied by Gartside, using chicken rump hackle.

A wet fly, tied by Gartside, using chicken marabou for the wing.

a trademark of the Hoffman line grown by Whiting Farms, Inc., who have been instrumental in popularizing this material.

Like the more common turkey marabou, chicken marabou varies, depending on exactly where on the bird it is located. Some of it resembles the true soft marabou we all know and love. Other feathers are less fuzzy and have more definition. Because of this, they are used differently. The super-soft ones are tied on in bunched fashion, and make excellent tails for smaller Woolly Buggers and such.

Feathers with more distinct barbs can be wrapped the same way that so many other feathers are, and used for making soft-hackled flies that have marvelous character and effectiveness. The barbs have a capacity for trapping air bubbles, and despite their softness, float quite well. Thus, the fibers can also be tied on in bunches for emerger wings, and even for wings on certain types of adult-fly imitations.

While the natural grizzly is nicely marked and very useful in that form, dyed feathers of this type should not be overlooked. They are great for tying the same sorts of flies we have traditionally used regular marabou for, but in smaller sizes.

Hair

In several other chapters we have examined different sorts of hair that are used for wings, and in some cases tails, on various kinds of flies. Here, we will deal with the kinds of hair that are used for spinning and trimming operations. This is another distinctly American technique, and it gave birth to several major schools and styles of fly tying. This innovation gave us hair-bodied bass bugs, hair-bodied dry flies, such as the Rat-Faced McDougall, and the hair-collar-with-trimmed-head style, as epitomized by the Muddler Minnow.

I refer to this type of hair as "soft"; George Kesel, a true hair maven, refers to it as being "pithy." This defines it as opposed to the "hard" hair used for, let's say, a streamer wing. There are varying degrees of softness, and they suit various applications. For example, extremely soft or pithy hair flares, spins, and floats well. The main problem with it is that its softness detracts from durability. Also flies tied from it may lose their form. Intermediate, or less-soft hair works best for making sculpin heads, and such.

The old books referred to the very soft, coarse hairs as hollow hair. Some of it is, to a degree, hollow, but not in the same manner that a drinking straw is hollow. Rather, it is sort of honeycombed, and contains many air pockets. If you are interested in seeing what this looks like close-up, I refer you to Darrel Martin's well-researched book, *Fly-Tying Methods*, which features several photos of hollow hairs, taken with the aid of a microscope.

Honeycombing imbues such hairs with a low weight-to-bulk ratio, which helps them float. It also makes them soft in texture, which enhances flaring and spinning. This characteristic will vary greatly with the age and size of the animal, the part of the body on which the hair is found, and the time of year the animal is killed. Most deer and other hair-bearing animals are killed by hunters in fall or early winter, when the hair is prime, or close to it. Usually, the larger the animal, the more hollow the hair.

Animals that have hair suitable for spinning include:

- Deer; various domestic
- Reindeer
- Antelope
- Elk
- Caribou
- Big-horn sheep

Hair from the common *white-tailed* and *mule deers* that are native to the North American continent are generously honeycombed. This, plus their low cost and general availability, makes them the most widely used types for spinning. Natural colors range from tan to various shades of gray, which predominates closer to the butt ends. Some coastal deer run to almost a creamish tan.

Another beneficial attribute is the presence of a generous amount of white hair, from the inside portions of the legs, and around the perimeter of the belly area. Hair from the belly proper gets beat up from the animal lying on it, and is often unsuitable for tying. White hair lends itself to easy and effective dyeing, which accounts for the bright colors we use on bass bugs and trimmed Atlantic salmon flies, such as the Bomber series.

This hair varies remarkably with respect to the geography of its origin. Warm-climate deer, such as *Florida Keys deer*, and particularly *Texas coastal deer*, produce extremely short, soft, fine-textured hair. It is great for making smaller fly bodies and mini-Muddlers.

It is of great importance to understand that the spinability of hair varies not only with respect to the anatomy of the animal, but also with respect to the position on the hair where the thread intersects it. This is particularly true with deer and elk hair. Consider, for example, a bunch of typical deer hair one and a half inches long. Near the butt ends the hair will flare and spin admirably. But near the tips, this is much harder to do.

This phenomenon has a distinct bearing on the selection of hair for applications such as making Muddler heads and collars, where some of the hair is trimmed, and some isn't. If you select the optimum-length hair for the size fly you're tying, you'll be able to make an integrated assembly, where the tips are left untrimmed to form the collar, and the rest is trimmed to form the head. If you choose hair that is too long, it won't flare properly, and you'll have trouble forming the head. Conversely, hair that is too short will produce a poorly formed collar.

Reindeer hair is sometimes found in fly shops. I think that eventually it will become more widely available, since these animals are raised domestically for meat. The hair is very spinnable, and quite fine in texture for such a large animal. It is darker in color than our native American deer, running to a rich gray at the base.

Antelope hair is the most honeycombed of all, and can be so coarse and large in diameter that it is suitable only for bass bugs and very large flies. In some cases, it is also quite brittle, and can easily be cut in half by modern "super-threads," under severe tension. Color ranges from cinnamon brown to white and off-white. Dyed colors are also available.

Elk hair is, as one might expect, more coarse than deer hair, on the average. There is plenty of good spinning hair to be found on an elk, provided one is selective. Younger animals yield much finer hair than older ones. Color is about the same as a northeastern whitetail. The blond hair from the rump patch spins reasonably well, and is also useful for making wings on certain dry flies, such as the Troth Elkhair Caddis.

Caribou hair is the joy of the small-fly tyer. It is much finer than any of the other large members of the deer family, and spins into neatly packed bodies. The natural color is pale gray. For Irresistibles, small bass flies, and those New Brunswick salmon flies the locals call wet bugs, there's nothing better.

Big-Horn Sheep are included in the list, even though most tyers will never be able to find this hair. I have a couple of pieces given to me by a very lucky fellow who drew a permit to hunt big-horns in the Wyoming lottery, and then actually shot one. The hair is medium gray and reminds one of caribou. Nice stuff, if you can locate some.

Comparadun Hair

The Comparadun style of fly was introduced by Al Caucci and Bob Nastasi, and the name is copyrighted by them, although it is now used generically. These flies are characterized by a distinctive upright hair wing, which is tied on in a single clump, and fashioned into a wide "V," or semicircular shape. Hackle may be added, but the typical Comparadun is hackle-free, and depends on its wing for flotation as well as silhouette.

The problem with Comparadun tying is that the hair that floats the best ties the worst. Hollow or honeycombed hairs are very frustrating for the tyer to work with, as they want to flare and spin all over the place, rather than conform readily into the desired wing shape. This is exacerbated by the fact that Comparaduns are tied in medium to small sizes. A twelve is actually a big one, and out West, they are tied as small as size 24.

What this all means is that the Comparadun tyer must compromise and walk a tightrope between too soft and too hard a hair. Too soft, and it's tough to handle; too hard, and it doesn't float well. *Elk hock*, or ankle hair, is highly favored, particularly from a young animal. *Deer's mask* is also quite useful, as it is harder than body hair, and resists spinning and flaring. These hairs are also well-suited to caddis, stonefly, and terrestrial patterns, which are tied down-wing style.

For very small Comparaduns, look for the finest hair, but not necessarily the shortest. Some coastal deer hair is only about a half-inch in length. The problem here is that you'll be working in the middle portion, and flaring will be a problem. With hair that runs a little longer, you'll be working more into the outer ends, and the result will be better control, and neater wings.

In addition to considering bulk and spinability, there's also the matter of durability. The softer the hair, the better it flares, true enough; however, durability is compromised. This may matter little, if at all. Small flies, where the hair is clipped close to the hook shank, aren't a problem. However, with large flies, such as bass bugs, you may find that they soon tend to become misshapen, and your diligent and tedious trimming efforts are lost. For this reason, many hair-bug experts use really tough threads, and spin harder hair than the average tyer might be able to deal with.

George, my chief hair consultant, tells me that he looks for medium-textured hair that has a nice "squish" to it. He has learned to tell by squeezing how the hair will behave. This would be a valuable skill to acquire, if you plan on doing a lot of this type of tying.

About Deer Skins

Probably more than any other fly-tying commodity, deer from hunting sources and the like are appropriated by tyers. It is not a difficult material to properly prepare.

Deer do not have fatty tissue in the meat itself, as beef cattle do. Instead, they have a layer of tallow that lies between the skin and the body proper. When preparing a deer carcass for use as food, the first operation is to hang the animal upside-down and skin it. This is really quite easy—once the proper incisions have been made, you can virtually pull the skin off the carcass, with a little discreet knife work here and there. Most of the tallow adheres to the skin. That which sticks to the meat is carefully removed because it tastes terrible.

When the head is reached, the going gets tougher. The hunter or butcher, who is concerned only with meat, will simply cut off the head and throw it away. The fly tyer, in most cases, will want the mask; thus, assiduous skinning techniques are required. If you have no experience in this sort of undertaking, and don't know anyone who can help you, go to the public library and get a book on the subject. There are quite a few available.

The most important thing is to thoroughly scrape off all traces of tallow from the skin. Having done that, apply some borax, or a mixture of borax and salt, per the instructions in Chapter 7. Allow the skin to cure in a dry place.

In the case of an entire deer skin, you'd be well advised to cut it into storable-sized pieces while it's still fresh. Once the skin has cured, cutting becomes quite a chore. In the case of larger animals, such as elk and caribou, a saw is required to cut untanned hide, once it's cured.

With such a large animal, you might opt for having the hide tanned. This is not cheap. A tanner will charge about $150 to do a large skin from a typical deer or bear. Elk and caribou will cost more, based on size. However, the result is a beautiful hide that will last a lifetime, and the tanning process eliminates any possibility of bringing unwelcome infestations into your tying room. Pre-tanning procedures are the same as for curing.

The procedures for preparing deer generally apply to other members of the deer family. The main difference, as far as the carcass in its entirety is concerned, is size. Any hunter who has shot a moose, elk, or caribou will tell you that the thrill and fun of the hunt ends when the animal hits the ground. It's all work from then on. A large elk is about three to four times the size of a large deer. A team effort is required, along with a large helping of assistance from a pickup truck or similar vehicle, and a block and tackle.

Materials for Streamer Wings

It's appropriate that I preface this section by clearing up some confusion in terminology. Streamers don't really have wings—we use the term for convenience in describing components and materials that are placed in a similar position to the wings on flies that imitate bugs. Actually, streamers are lures fished with fly tackle, but so what? It's fly fishing, and a very exhilarating form of it at that.

Streamers comprise a large and growing group of flies in angling today. A distinctly American contribution, they originated in the Northeast about a century ago. At that time, wild brook trout and landlocked salmon were large, abundant, relatively naive, and usually hungry. Small fish were a very important dietary item. As fly fishing extended to bass, pike, pickerel, and eventually, to the salt, tying flies that appealed to predatory fish became all the more important.

While some streamers are intended to be imitative, most fall into the attractor category, which is a lot of fun, in that it allows for a wide range of creativity. In fact, there are few rules. Thus, we see many materials being incorporated in streamer wings, both natural and synthetic. We shall begin with the more traditional.

Feather-Wing Streamer Materials

These are the true classics; the flies of Carrie Stevens, Herb Welch, Bert Gulline, Dr. J.H. Sanborn, Lew Oatman, Joe Stickney, and others whose names have been lost in antiquity. While some contemporary streamers, such as the Clouser Minnow, the Woolly Bugger, and the many versions of the Muddler Minnow may be generally more effective, these old flies still work, and they are gorgeous when skillfully tied.

The main challenge is finding feathers that are suitable for wings on these flies. The early tyers had at their disposal lots of feathers from big chickens that were grown for meat and egg production. Some were domestic, others came in from places like China. The feathers at the rear of rooster capes, and in some cases, saddles, are shaped very much like a little fish. They were rather wide and had lots of opaque web in the center. These feathers became the main components of the streamer. Some possessed markings that resembled small baitfish, such as the furnace and badger striped feathers. These were selected on that basis, and used "au naturel." Dyed feathers in gaudy colors were also very widely employed.

Chicken growing has changed, and so have the feathers. We don't see much of the large, densely webbed stuff of years ago. The birds grown for the dry-fly market seldom produce ideal streamer material. Scientific methods and automation have essentially cancelled out by-product feathers from the food industry. Mostly, the streamer tyer relies on what trickles in from overseas, and these feathers are not what they once were.

Capes, Saddles, and Bundles

What streamer hackles we do find as a fallout from the genetic hackle growers almost invariably come from capes, rather than saddles. Generally speaking, cape feathers are more likely to have the desired properties for streamers than saddles, for the following reasons:

- They are wider and webbier, and hold their form better when wet
- The quills are usually more amenable to tying. Saddle hackles tend to have very fine quills, and under thread pressure, they are liable to roll into any position except the one we want
- Saddle hackles often have reverse curvature, which results in a messy-looking wing

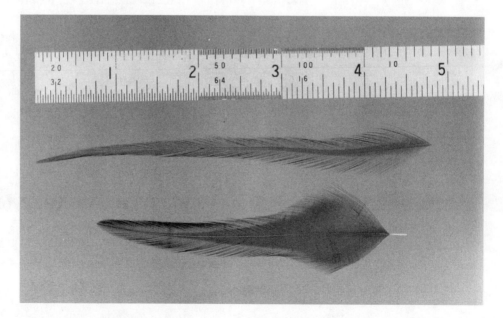

Top: saddle feather. Bottom: cape feather.

I'm speaking of typical freshwater streamers. With saltwater patterns, such as the Lefty's Deceiver, substantial bunches of saddle feathers are used, with less regard as to whether they have a picture-book silhouette or not.

Capes, or necks, for streamer tying can be purchased as is, or in bundles, strung together by thread. Saddle feathers intended for streamer use are almost always sold in bundles. In either case, you get a lot of feathers for not much money. The question is how suitable they are. The bundles are assembled overseas by people who haven't a clue as to how they'll be used. Sometimes, bundled feathers are twisted, and not usable at all. Often, a moderate number of nice feathers are bundled with a larger number of ratty ones. Even with good bundles, count on a certain amount of waste.

If you care about symmetry and eye appeal in your streamers, I suggest that you find the best capes available, and buy those. It's far easier to select well-matched feathers from a cape, where they are lying neatly alongside one another, than from a bundle.

Marabou

Before we get to the tying qualities of this stuff, let's learn a bit about the name. Many years ago, fly tyers used the fluffy feathers from a huge, ungainly African bird called the Marabou Stork. If this creature delivered babies, I'm sure they would be traumatized for life, it's that ugly! As for the feathers, I can't comment, because they were off the market long before my tying career began.

What we now call marabou is actually turkey down, or underfeathers. To the uninitiated, they look more like pillow stuffing than fly-tying material. However, their appearance when dry belies their behavior when wet. In the water they slim down, take on a minnow-like shape, and virtually come alive.

Marabou has become a highly popular material, and rightly so. Its two main applications are making streamer wings and tails for Woolly Buggers. It can be used wherever softness and action in the water are the primary considerations.

Marabou is sold in bundles, similar to streamer feathers. You'll see them described as marabou bloods, or shorts. This is to differentiate them from the large, virtually useless, ostrich-like feathers some dealers used to offer.

Here's where one has to be careful. The feathers in some of these bundles are indeed short. They may be okay for making tails on Woolly Buggers, but for streamer work they are not of sufficient length. If you are shopping in person, look the bunches over carefully to ascertain that you're getting adequate length. When catalog shopping, be sure to let the dealer know what sort of marabou you want.

When tying streamer wings with marabou, what you're trying to do is to obtain a certain shape and effect. You must remember that marabou looks radically different in water than when dry. It slims down a great deal, and sometimes what looks like a lot of material isn't very much at all. To get an idea of what your wing will look like to the fish, wet it while the fly is in the vise. You may find that you want to add some more material.

Marabou applied Gartside-style.

The most common method for using marabou streamer-style is to pick a plume that fits the fly you're working on and tie the entire feather on in one operation. To prepare the feather, strip off the wild-looking stuff around the butt end. Also, if the quill runs out near the tip, snip it off somewhere in the middle, so that it doesn't interfere with the softness of the plumage. However, not all marabou feathers lend themselves to this method of handling. Some have too thick a quill, or aren't of the proper shape. But these feathers may still yield good plumage. Simply stroke the fronds out to the sides, cut them off at the base, and tie them on in bunches.

Jack Gartside, one of fly tying's leading talents and enjoyable eccentrics, does a special fly with marabou called the Soft-Hackle Streamer. The basic technique is wrapping marabou hackle-style, stroking it rearward in the process. An ingenious innovation; these are very effective flies. When selecting marabou for such tying, look for neat feathers with thin quills.

Like just about everything, marabou comes in a plethora of colors, including some fluorescents. One thing to watch out for though: when these feathers are dyed in bundles, sometimes the dye doesn't penetrate to the innermost plumes.

Hairs for Streamer Wings

It wasn't long after the initiation of the feather-winged streamer that hair-winged versions were developed. They soon became known as bucktails, because deer tail (not necessarily from a male deer) was the main component. While perhaps not as artsy as the feather-wing, hairwinged flies were easy to tie, utilized a readily available material, and caught fish like crazy. This is true to this day.

Numerous hairs are, or have been used in streamer tying, such as:

- Deer tail—still the most common
- Skunk tail
- Squirrel tails of various kinds
- Bear hair—black and brown
- Monga ringtail, also known as cacomistle
- Calf tail, also known as kip tail
- Yak hair
- Sheep and goat hairs of various kinds
- Polar bear hair
- Arctic fox tail
- Woodchuck tail
- Badger underfur

As far as I know, all of these are still legal, though not always available.

Bucktails, or Deer Tails

Deer tail is mainly a by-product of hunting. Tails from all over the United States are offered by the dealers, and they differ dramatically. For example, those from large northern white-tailed deer have long, stiff, relatively coarse hair, where smaller southern deer tails have much softer, finer hair. The big ones are fine for saltwater streamers and such, but for the smaller flies we use for trout and other freshwater species, the fine-haired tails are much preferred.

Deer tail hair varies in straightness as well as in texture. Again, hair that's somewhat crinkly is okay for rough work, but for smaller streamers, where neatness counts, the straighter the hair, the better.

Deer tails are predominantly white in color—or at least those from the species known as white-tailed deer are. They also have some darker hair on them, and in some cases, this can be very useful. Many popular bucktail-type streamers call for brown hair over the backs. It's not always easy to find tails that have hair of suitable length, texture, and color for this application. If you intend to tie these patterns, don't pass up any chance to buy tails with good-quality brown hair on the back sides. You have to be careful here though; brown hair down near the butt end of the tail, where it connects to the deer, may be long enough for streamer work, but the texture may not be suitable, because it's actually almost body hair, and will flare.

If you are a deer hunter, or are offered tails by hunters, be advised that they must be properly and promptly cared for. Deer tails aren't like squirrel tails; they have to be deboned and cured. The time to do this is as soon as possible. If you can't work on a tail immediately, refrigerate it, or for long-term storage, freeze it. If a tail has already begun to decompose, don't bother with it.

To debone a deer tail, lay it on its back and make an incision the full length of the cartilage. Then, gently begin to peel off the skin around the cartilage, using a scalpel or very sharp knife to separate it from the connective tissue, and laying it to the sides. Don't get impatient and try to yank the cartilage out by brute force, as you'll rip the skin.

Once the bony matter is removed, scrape off all remaining flesh and fatty material. Then, tack the tail to a board, exposing the cleaned area. Apply a thick layer of salt, or better yet, a mixture of borax and salt, per the instructions already given in Chapter 7. Pat it a little, so that it makes good contact and begins to absorb. Set the tail aside in a dry place. After a couple of days, check to see how the curing process is coming. You'll probably want to brush off the skinned area and apply another helping of the borax/salt mixture.

Squirrel Tails

Larger types of squirrels, notably the common gray squirrel and the fox squirrel, have fairly long hair in their tails that is often used in streamers. Gray squirrel tails are a mixture of grays, tans, and white. Fox squirrel tails are a mixture of tans and reddish browns, with black barring. There is also a black squirrel; I'm not sure whether it's a separate species, or a melanistic phase of the gray squirrel. In any case, natural black squirrel isn't really black; it's a very, very dark brown. This is nice, but when true black is desired, use dyed squirrel tails.

Texture is the same for both: hard and slippery! While it yields very nice results, squirrel tail is no joy to work with. It's solid protein, and compresses almost not at all. Because of this, it's best to apply squirrel-tail hair in small quantities, building up to the desired amount in stages, with lots of thread wraps securing each layer. I also suggest a droplet of adhesive between each layer. Dave's Flexament is good for this.

Squirrel tail is also very popular for tying hairwing Atlantic salmon flies. Gray squirrel has enough white and pale gray coloration in it so that it can be dyed successfully to simulate the bright shades called for in salmon flies. The hair can be tied on in layers, reestablishing a thread base between each layer to maintain separation. For example, the hairwing simulation of the Silver Doctor has red, blue, and yellow layers, topped off by a bunch of natural fox squirrel. The latter simulates the mixture of mottled and speckled feathers that are married into the wings of the classic dressing.

Black-dyed squirrel tail is great for making the stripe on a Black-Nosed Dace streamer, as the hair is very straight and neat. The technique is exactly the same for the layered salmon-fly wing. First, a bunch of white hair is tied on. A generous amount of thread is used to recreate a base. The black squirrel is then tied onto this thread base, which inhibits it from mixing with the white. Another thread base is established and finally a layer of brown hair goes on top to finish off the fly.

If you indulge in collecting road kills and the like, squirrel tail is one of the easiest. Just cut the tail off and set it aside in a dry place. It isn't necessary to debone these tails, as you must with deer.

Skunk

Here's a road kill you'll want to stay away from. I've checked around, and so far have found no one who has a method for de-scenting skunk. Old-time bird hunters talked about washing their dogs in tomato juice after confrontations with skunks, but from what I can gather, that process has little effect on a skunk carcass.

I wish that skunk pelts were readily available, because they have beautiful black-and-white hairs. Sometimes we see a few tails. These have long, lustrous, black hairs that lend themselves to streamer tying nicely. They can be used for contrasting stripes, as described above for the black squirrel.

Bear Hair

This material is used for making wings on both streamer and salmon flies. The eastern black bear is the most common variety available. The hair isn't really jet black; it varies from soft black to very dark brown. Length and texture vary widely, depending on the age and size of the bear, the condition of its coat at the time it was killed, and where on its anatomy the hair comes from.

Bear hairs in various shades of brown are also generally available in fly shops. These may come from grizzly bears, or from Western black bears, which have many color phases, and are seldom as dark as the Eastern strain.

Bear hair makes pretty decent wings. It's softer near the base, and easier to work with than squirrel. However, it doesn't lie quite as neatly. It's a matter of what effect you're aiming for.

If you're a hunter, or if you have friends who hunt, and you anticipate the possibility of acquiring some bear skin from such a source, be aware that it must be properly and promptly cared for. The process is the same as for curing a deer hide, which is set forth in Chapter 13. However, I can tell you from personal experience that skinning a deer is child's play compared to skinning a bear.

Monga Ringtail

These tails come from a southwestern animal similar to a raccoon. The tails feature alternating segments of white and very dark brown. The hair is soft, manageable, and of sufficient length for tying smaller streamers. The white hair is excellent for the lower wing layer on many popular bucktails, including the Black-Nosed Dace.

Monga tails can be dyed, in which case the white segments take the color of the dye, while the brown remains virtually the same. If they were to be dyed black, that would be a different story, but I've never seen them dyed black.

The only nettlesome problem with monga is that the white hairs often have dark tips. This still shows when they are dyed. From a fishing standpoint that probably means nothing, but visually it bothers people.

Monga ringtail.

Calf Tail

This material is more commonly used for wings on dry flies, and this process is fully described in Chapter 11. However, sometimes we come across tails with longer, straighter hair. These not only make passable streamer wings, but salmon-fly wings as well.

Natural colors are white, black, and shades of brown. The white ones take dye very well. Just keep in mind that the only ones that make good streamers are those with the longest, least-crinkly hair.

Yak Hair

This material is most popular in Scandinavia, where tyers make elver patterns for salmon fishing. The most well-known is a tube fly named the Sun-Ray Shadow.

Yak hair is very long, sometimes running six inches. The natural color is brown, and it is commonly dyed black. Availability is quite limited in the U.S.A., although I have encountered it in a few shops that cater to salmon tyers.

Sheep and Goat

Sheep hair is packaged under several brand names. One of the most popular is Sea Hair. This is quite accurate, since the hair has a usable length of about six to nine inches. This is long enough for most saltwater flies. A nice array of colors is available, but as of yet, I haven't seen black. This is unfortunate, because many patterns call for it.

This hair is quite soft, ties well, and comes alive when wet. It has an attractive sheen, and, in bunches, is quite translucent. When gauging quanti-

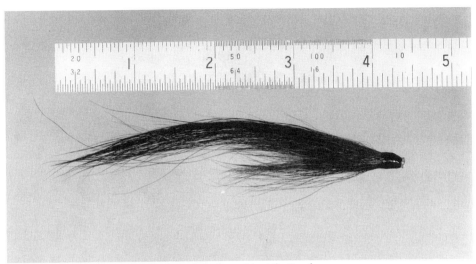

Yak hair. The fly is the Sunray Shadow, a tube fly used for Atlantic salmon.

ties, keep in mind that it slims down considerably when wet. In addition to its obvious application in larger saltwater patterns, this hair also makes excellent tube flies. In case that term is new to you, this is a type of Atlantic salmon fly whereby the material is tied around a plastic or metal tube. The leader is passed through the tube, and a hook tied on, which hangs off the rear. This allows the angler to fish a large fly with a small hook, positioned appropriately for optimal engagement.

Goat hair, of the type found in fly shops, is considerably shorter than sheep, having a usable length of one and a half to three inches. It is also straighter and slightly more coarse, though not objectionably so. Its natural color is white. It takes dyes quite well, provided the proper type of dye and process is used.

Provided supplies are dependable, and given a wide assortment of colors, goat hair will soon become an enormously popular material, not only for streamers, but for salmon, steelhead, bass and saltwater flies as well. It is a much more tyer-friendly material than those presently being used, especially squirrel and calf tail, and the effects obtained on the finished flies are most attractive.

Polar Bear Hair

This material was quite popular years ago. Tyers used the longer hair for all sorts of things, and the underfur was used as dubbing on salmon flies, in place of seal.

Polar bear was illegal for a while, and hunting the animal was banned. They soon overpopulated, and ate a few folks in arctic outposts. Hunting on a tightly controlled basis was reinstituted, and soon one could buy polar bear hair again. At this writing there is a limited though legal supply, but I'm quite sure that will vary periodically, as bear-hunting regulations change.

I don't much care for polar bear. It's about the most slippery and recalcitrant material one can find. True, its natural gleam and translucency are remarkable, but there are now synthetics that are at least as attractive, and much easier to use. And we'll learn more about these subsequently.

Arctic Fox Tail

If you like softer hairs for your streamers, this material will greatly please you. It is snowy white, and long enough for most freshwater streamers. The hair has an attractive glint to it, and is very easy to work with. It also has a lively action in the water.

This is another limited-availability item, but it does show up in shops from time to time.

Woodchuck Tail

This material was also mentioned in Chapter 11. It is straight and ties neatly, but is limited in length. If you want to acquire some chuck tails, you'll probably have to scavenge, or shoot a chuck yourself, as they are rarely seen in fly shops. Too bad.

I have found that it is essential to remove the cartilage from these tails, or they will quickly spoil and be ruined. This isn't difficult; just follow the procedure in the section that covers caring for animal skins in Chapter 7.

Synthetic Hairs

Synthetic hairs are also used in streamer tying—more so all the time. Frequently, they are substituted for natural hairs, tradition not being observed in such cases. My opinion is simply this: if it looks and performs like the natural, go ahead and use it.

In some respects, synthetic hairs have it all over natural hairs. There are virtually no practical limitations as to length, texture, or color, and technically, man can make any kind of stuff he wants. This flexibility, as well as their toughness, makes synthetic hairs ideal for saltwater flies. They are also fairly inexpensive, usually costing less than real hairs. And, they can be freely substituted for natural materials, thus taking the pressure off the demand for hairs from animals that may be in a precarious state.

Synthetic hairs have been around for a while, but are just coming into their own. My first encounter with such a material was in a craft store, where I saw some squares of shiny stuff lying in a bin. It's called "craft fur." People use it to make doll's hair, little animals, and all sorts of caricatures. Those alluring, overpriced creatures you see people hurriedly buying in airport gift shops as they race for their flights are usually adorned with craft fur.

No way can the literature manage to keep current on products of this type; even trade magazines are having trouble doing that. What I can do, though, is take a snapshot in time of the types of hairs that predominate at present, and address their attributes and peculiarities.

Craft Fur

Having made reference to it, let's begin with craft fur. This is a softer type of material, with lots of glisten. It comes in mats with cloth backing. Like many natural hairs, it has underfur that must be cleaned out, either with fingers or by combing.

Within the last couple of years, craft fur is at last showing up in fly shops, packaged under such names as Fly Fur and Fish Fuzz. It's more expensive than in craft shops, but there are some unique colors available that the craft stores don't have. Also, the hair is of suitable length for streamer tying. Some of the stuff found in craft stores is too short to be of much use.

Craft fur, by whatever name, is one of the materials that can be substituted for polar bear. In fact, I think it's better than polar bear. It has comparable translucency, more action in the water, and is infinitely easier to tie with. It's also very reasonable in price.

There's one more application for craft fur that's worth mentioning. It makes very nice Crazy Charleys and MacVay's Gotchas, which are killer bonefish flies.

Super Hair, Ultra Hair, Bozo Hair, Fishair, and Others

I lump these together because their similarities are much more apparent than their differences. I hope no supplier will take offense at this. I have no intention of denigrating anyone's product; quite the contrary. If it wasn't a good product, I would simply have said nothing about it at all.

The hairs mentioned by name above come from three different suppliers. They are all packaged in a similar manner, in elongated plastic bags. The quantities per dollar are reasonably close. They all have adequate length for even the largest saltwater flies, with the hairs running from eight to twelve inches in usable length. They are all somewhat crinkly and somewhat slippery. All are rather translucent, except that Ultra Hair offers an opaque version in a few colors. All come in a wide array of colors, with Ultra Hair having the largest selection.

Are there any meaningful differences? A few, and they are subtle. Bozo Hair is slightly finer and more crinkly than Super Hair, which is slightly finer and more crinkly than Ultra Hair. Bozo Hair is a little softer and more tractable from a tying standpoint, but not to the exclusion of the others. It's also a little more crinkly, and has a similarity to Sea Hair, which is a type of sheep hair.

There is another commonality in all of these hairs: they are hard, and resist being compressed. You'll need a very strong thread—perhaps the monofilament threads have an application here. Unless only a slender bunch is being used, tie these hairs on in layers, with lots of thread in between. Some adhesive is also a good idea. You may want to stagger them a bit, since the tips aren't tapered as natural hairs and some synthetics are. Unless you offset them, you'll end up with a distinctly chopped-off effect.

Since the predominant use for these products is on saltwater flies, often the epoxy type of head is employed. This is good, because it locks the hairs in place and effectively protects the thread. When monofilament thread is used, epoxy will cause the heads to turn translucent, in varying degrees. My saltwater connections inform me that Ultra Hair has more of a penchant for this than others they've used, reason unknown.

Just as I was finishing up this book, I came across a product named Polar Aire. It's very bright and glitzy, and reminds me somewhat of craft fur, except that it doesn't come attached to little rugs, and is quite long. It is soft, pliant, and easy to work with. I believe it could be used as either a highlight or a stand-alone. This is a product worth examining. See the color plates for a photo.

Lite-Brite

I'll mention one more product here: Lite-Brite. It is described in Chapter 9, and appropriately so, I believe. However, it's closer to being a hair than a dubbing, or any other type of material, and is usually used in streamer-fly tying of some type. It doesn't appear to be a stand-alone but rather a highlighting material for adding brilliance and texture. It comes in a variety of color blends.

What else can be said? Without doubt, there will be more synthetic hairs appearing on the market. One hopes they will address the needs of the fly-tying fraternity/sorority, and be functionally oriented. Let's face it; technically, anything's possible. Man could make a wide variety of synthetic hairs that would all but eclipse the natural ones we've depended upon for so long. I hope that's how things will shake out. As for the present, it's up to the tyer to select what best matches his or her needs.

Eyes

The past quarter-century of angling experience in Alaska and various salt-water venues has confirmed what many of us suspected and what some of the old-timers apparently knew—eyes make certain types of flies more effective. Experimentation indicates that the presence of a conspicuous eye on streamers and flies of similar design triggers strikes from larger predatory gamefish.

The Jungle Cock Eye

Past generations of fly designers made frequent use of the unique eyelike feathers from the neck of the gray jungle fowl, *Gallus sonerati*, commonly known as jungle cock (JC). In the late 1960s, the Department of the Interior (D.O.I.) shut down the import of this bird. Eventually, import control of this and many other species was incorporated under the CITES Treaty, which was signed by a large number of countries. Basically, CITES sets up lists categorizing various species: endangered, controlled, and so forth. It also sets quotas that allow for limited distribution of all but the most threatened species on the lists.

Each year, a conference is held to reevaluate the lists. Species may be moved up or down, depending on their welfare, and quotas can be adjusted. The last copy of CITES I saw, which is now several years old, listed certain species as endangered (List 1), which means that no traffic whatsoever is allowed, and possession of such feathers or pelts without express licensing from D.O.I. is illegal. Conspicuous on List 1 were the condor and the florican bustard, *Otis tarda. Gallus sonerati* was not on that list; it was on List 2, which allows for limited import under quota.

Jungle cock cape.

Good-quality jungle cock, dark and light phases.

At this writing, jungle cock is being imported legally in packets, and less commonly, in pelts. Apparently, D.O.I. allows this because a British grower of birds has developed a quasi-domesticated bloodline of jungle cock, along with several other exotic fowl. The feathers in the packets are currently priced at fifty to sixty cents apiece, and buying an entire pelt doesn't reduce the price all that much. But at least they're available on a decriminalized basis. I have also heard, but have not yet been able to confirm, that a couple of other sources are now licensed.

There are several substitutes for jungle cock that are perfectly acceptable from a fishing standpoint, and may in fact produce a more effective fly than the real thing. We'll examine them a bit further along. However, those who dress classics such as the incomparable Atlantic salmon patterns and the beautiful streamers of the golden age of the brook trout and landlocked salmon require real jungle cock to maintain the integrity and aesthetics of these dressings. Perhaps it would be appropriate for the practical tyers to concentrate on substitutes and options, and leave the limited and very costly supply of jungle cock to the collector-fly contingent.

Jungle Cock: Reinforcement and Protection

The jungle cock situation being what it is, it's important to protect these valuable feathers. This implies two things: storage and usage. Storage is simply a matter of keeping the pests away. For some reason, jungle cock is a great favorite of moths and the like. For many years I used conventional moth repellents, but having been convinced by a friend in the medical field that there may be a health hazard associated with prolonged use of that stuff, I now use the herbal sachets that can be purchased almost anywhere. They seem to work on bugs, but I doubt they'd be an effective deterrent to mice. I don't have a mouse problem, but for those who do, I'd suggest those tough, lock-sealing plastic boxes marketed by Rubbermaid and other companies, although I can't absolutely guarantee they'd stop a determined rodent either.

Various adhesives can be used to reinforce individual "nails," as the eyed feathers are commonly called. An important consideration is that whichever one you choose doesn't discolor or disfigure the feather—please refer to Chapter 3 for further information. This is a matter of discreet application, as well as selection. Many adhesives shrink a great deal in the drying process, and will thus cause a feather to bend or curl. A good example is the ubiquitous Shoe Goo or Goop. In my running days, I always had a tube of that stuff around, and I tried encasing jungle cock feathers in it. They curled up. For encasing an entire nail, a much better choice is silicone rubber cement, which is a colorless adhesive that dries tough, but with a rubbery consistency. It causes little, if any, curling. The downside is that it takes a very long time to dry.

There are several adhesives that do a fine job of reinforcing jungle cock if applied in very conservative amounts to the back side of a nail. They also enable the tyer to make preassemblies by sticking a nail to another feather. A classic example of this is the cheek/shoulder assembly of the famous Gray Ghost streamer, where a nail is glued to a silver pheasant saddle feather. The originator of the pattern, Carrie Stevens, also glued these to a pair of large neck or saddle hackles, thus forming the entire wing assembly for one side. However, I don't recommend this.

My two favorite adhesives for this sort of work are Pliobond and Zap-A-Gap. Each must be applied with care and discretion. Pliobond is amber in color, and will discolor feathers if not confined to a very small area. Zap-A-Gap, while clear, can turn a feather into a crusty mess, and will cause curling.

With both of these compounds, the trick is to apply a very conservative amount to the back side of the nail. I recommend a toothpick for an applicator/spreader. In the case of Zap-A-Gap, rubbing with the toothpick accelerates drying. The nails can then be either set aside on waxed paper to dry or joined with another feather while still tacky.

The Gray Ghost assembly.

The eyes on the left and right need healing.

The same eyes, after repair.

Forming assemblies must be done carefully. Be sure to get the feathers lined up exactly as you wish before pressing them together, especially if you're using Zap-A-Gap. Use tiny amounts of glue, so that the excess doesn't run out into the other feather in the assembly, or leak through to discolor the nail. Allow the assembly to dry thoroughly before handling.

Here's another neat trick for when you're using Zap-A-Gap to form assemblies. After sticking a jungle cock feather to a larger feather that will form the base of the assembly, turn the assembly over and locate the area covered by the nail. This is no problem in most cases because one can see through to the other feather. If necessary, hold the assembly up to the light. Then, take your toothpick and apply a tiny amount of Zap-A-Gap to this area. It will bleed right through the feather and onto the back of the nail. Lay the assembly on waxed paper and rub until dry. This trick can also be used with other types of eyes, as we shall see further on.

Adhesives can be used to heal splits in nails, which are very common. One method is to select a small, webby feather from a hen cape or saddle and trim it to a shape similar to but very slightly smaller than the nail to be healed. Hold them spoon-fashion and slightly separated. With a toothpick, apply a tiny amount of either Zap-A-Gap (my choice) or Pliobond to the back side of the nail. Then gently stroke the two feathers together. A pain in the neck? Absolutely. But the result is a strong, well-restored nail.

With moderately-split jungle cock nails, you can dispense with the reinforcing feather and simply stroke a small amount of adhesive to the back side of the nail. This takes considerable care—you don't want the glue to soak through onto the good side. If you've decided to encase the nail in silicone cement, you can stroke the feather into conformity and stick it to a piece of waxed paper, back-side-down. This will keep everything together during the long drying process.

The plastic jungle cock eye; a poor replacement.

Whichever adhesive you choose, I suggest using thin vinyl gloves to keep the stuff off of your fingers. If you opt not to use gloves, you'll want to clean off your fingers afterwards. A small amount of acetone on a paper towel will do the job, but use as little as possible, and do it in a well-ventilated area. Those fumes are wicked.

Substitutions

In lieu of jungle cock, you can either use a feather that bears some resemblance to a nail, or you can go with a completely different sort of eye. I must tell you that there is really nothing else in nature that closely resembles a jungle cock nail. Now and then you may run across a pelt from a grouse, pheasant, or some other fowl that has feathers with eyelike markings. It's necessary to trim them down to obtain a jungle cock effect.

While it doesn't compare aesthetically, you can easily fashion a more than acceptable eye out of common guinea fowl. The body feathers on this bird come in two configurations: single-dotted and double-dotted. The latter are used for hackle on some of the most famous Atlantic salmon flies, including the hallowed Jock Scott and a great favorite of mine, the Sir Richard. The single-dotted type lends itself to the present application. Believe me, you'll have no trouble distinguishing one from the other, even the first time you see them.

You will notice that many single-dotted guinea feathers have a nice white dot centered on the quill, well out towards the tip. You trim around this,

Single-dotted and double-dotted guinea.

Simulation of jungle cock eye.

forming a shape that is roughly jungle cock-like. Go easy—you can always trim off more, but once it's gone, you can't put it back.

The nice thing about this substitute, along with its availability and low cost, is that it has a quill down the center that makes for strength. The only little hiccough in tying on a guinea feather is that the quill has a tendency to roll, which skews the feather. This is solved by catching a tiny bit of the feather itself with the tying thread, rather than only the quill. This will keep everything flat against whatever the wing is composed of. I use guinea on my Hornbergs,

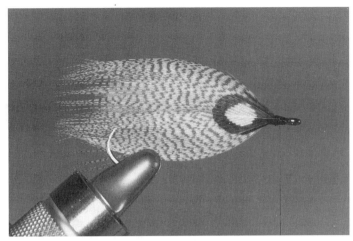

Substitute eye in place on what is about to become a Hornberg.

and they seem to catch just as many fish as did those adorned with jungle cock, back in the good old days of Herter's and legal jungle cock necks for $5 or $6.

Synthetic Eyes

By synthetic, I refer to all techniques for making eyes from other than a natural feather, including paint jobs and manufactured products. There are quite a few such items. Some are made expressly for fly tying, some are a spin-off from lure making, and several are borrowed from the non-angling world. They produce remarkably different effects. Several, notably the "dumbbell" eye and the bead chain, also contribute weight in varying amounts.

Let's begin with a few techniques for making painted eyes. This is quite simple. All that's needed is some paint or lacquer in two different colors, a device for applying it, and some adhesives to assist the process. Here, we shall employ two of the substances mentioned in the adhesives section in Chapter 3: a protective spray, such as Tuffilm, and epoxy.

The Painted Eye

First, we shall make painted eyes on the head of a streamer. For the photos, I've chosen that garish and improbable attractor, the Mickey Finn, but it could just as well be any pattern. Because it utilizes three layers of hair, this streamer, by its very nature, has a bulky head. We build this up even further with layers of thread. When sufficient size is obtained, we coat the head with a layer or two of either clear or black cement, allowing thorough drying. This is essential, in that it enables the paint that will be used for the eye to go on smoothly.

When the final coat is dry, make the larger part of the eye by applying a drop of light-colored paint—yellow, white, gold, whatever—to the head. For this, a round applicator is required. The best I've found is the back end of a

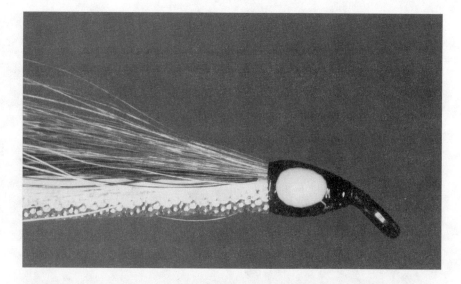

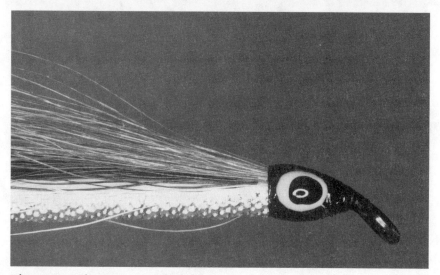

The two steps in dotting on a painted eye.

drill bit, a neat trick I picked up from the "Tying Tips" column in *American Angler Magazine*. Select a bit with a diameter appropriate for the size head. Use a sufficient amount of paint to cover most of the head area, as shown. Do both sides, and allow the paint to dry completely. Then, form the pupil with a drop of black paint, using a slightly smaller drill bit, or similar round object. Again, let it dry thoroughly. Don't worry if thread ridges show through the paint; the epoxy is self-leveling, and will take care of that.

For the final step, mix up a batch of epoxy. You can use the so-called five-minute type, but at best you'll be able to do only a few flies before it becomes too viscous. I would recommend the two-hour type. You can apply it with a toothpick if you wish, but a small brush works better. You can use a disposable brush, or a good one, with epoxy thinner handy to clean it.

Be ready to work fast. Put a fly in your vise, or otherwise secure it in an upright position, and apply a generous droplet of epoxy to the top and sides

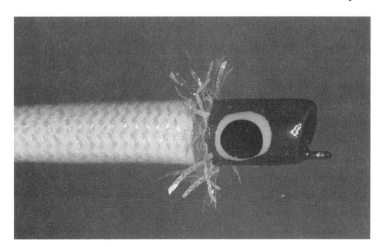

A painted eye on a saltwater popper.

of the head. Help it flow over the head on all sides. If any excess runs to the bottom, remove it. Then, set the fly aside. Once the epoxy sets up, you'll have a beautifully decorated, indestructible head.

This is a long, involved process, and as a matter of practicality, I suggest you have at least a half-dozen flies ready for treatment. The number you can epoxy with one batch relates to the drying speed of the glue. With the five-minute type, if you get everything ready to roll and work fast, you can do just a few heads per batch. With the slower-drying type, you can do a dozen or more.

While on the subject of thinners, I might mention a word of advice from George Kesel of Hunter's Angling Supplies, who helped a great deal with the preparation of this book. George ties a lot of flies with painted eyes. He has found that sometimes, even after the first droplet has dried completely, the application of the second droplet for the center of the eye cause an interaction. For this reason, George uses lacquers that have dissimilar thinners, thus avoiding runny eyes. An interesting observation.

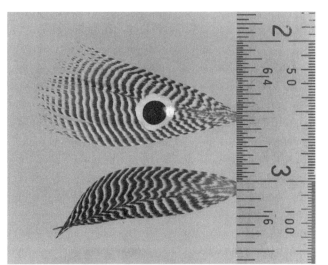

A painted eye on a flank feather that has been lightly coated with Tuffilm spray. Bottom: what happens to a feather that has been sprayed too much.

Painted Eyes on Feathers

Now let's combine the use of two adhesives to allow the application of a painted eye to a softer, more absorbent sort of material: a feather. Many saltwater, and a few freshwater streamer patterns call for an eye painted on a cheeking feather, such as teal or mallard.

Try this method: spray-coat the exposed side of the feather with Tuffilm or something similar, using two coats, and allowing thorough drying both between coats and after the second one. Then create the eye as described for the Mickey Finn, leaving out the epoxy process. For added durability, lightly spray again, after the eye is dry.

The Mylar Sheet Eye

Of course, the process just described changes the texture of the feather. In most cases, I'm very happy about that, but there are times when we want the feather to remain soft, for action's sake. For this, I recommend the use of the Mylar synthetic eyes. These are available in a wide variety of sizes and colors; they are actually intended for use on lures. For the fly tyer, the most valuable are the smaller sizes, either yellow or white with a black pupil.

The eyes are sold in sheets, to which they are stuck via an adhesive backing. They can be lifted off with tweezers and stuck onto the fly or lure. On a hard, high-gloss surface, such as a casting plug, the glue on the back of the eye is probably sufficient. However, getting them to stick to a feather and endure fishing conditions requires a supplemental step.

Here's my recommended method: Before tying on the cheeking feather, stick the eye in place, being careful to get it exactly where you want it. Then, turn the feather over, and with a toothpick, rub a small drop of Zap-A-Gap into *only that area covered by the eye.* You'll be able to see the eye, since the feathers used for cheeking are somewhat transparent. If you're brave, you can mount the cheek/eye assembly while the glue is still wet. But you'd better get it right the first time, because you won't get a second chance. Or, you can rub until the glue is dry, and proceed with your tying. This is similar to the process for making assemblies with jungle cock nails.

Mylar eyes have many wonderful applications. For example, if you prefer, you can use them in place of painted eyes on streamer heads. They go on quickly, and are very handsome. All you have to do is to stick them in place, and then follow the previously described epoxy procedure. They are particularly attractive on Thunder Creek streamers.

There may be others, but at this writing, the leading supplier for these eyes is the Witchcraft Company. They also have a number of other Mylar items, some of which are used in fly tying.

At this writing, I'm not altogether certain that Witchcraft is aware of the fly-fishing market. Of course, we're not yet as large as the lure market, but what with all the innovation that's going on, we're getting there. I hope that by the time you read this, these products are readily available in your favorite fly shop. And wouldn't it be great if some company started making a jungle cock substitute, using this technology? They wouldn't be at all suitable for "classic" applications, but for fishing flies, such as Hornbergs, streamers and such, why not?

Bead Chain

For years, tyers have been making attractive and effective eyes out of plain old bead chain, either silver or gold, and more recently, pearlescent. This is the

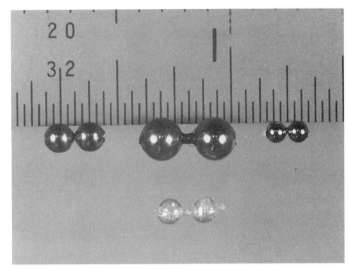

An assortment of bead-chain eyes.

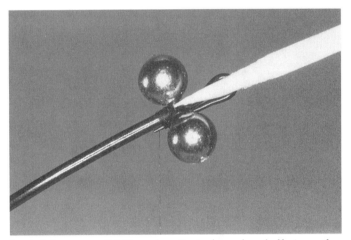

Bead-chain eye mounted. It's good practice to place a drop of adhesive on the thread wraps, as indicated.

same stuff lamp-light pull-chains are made of (except the pearlescent). It comes in several sizes, and is available in hardware stores as well as many fly shops.

This is also an easy material to work with. Simply cut off a two-bead length with a pair of small wire cutters. Create a thread base, then lay the beads atop the hook, one on either side, and figure-eight them in place. You'll find that a looped-eye hook offers a distinct advantage in this instance. After doing the figure-eights, take a few snug wraps laterally around the base of the wraps themselves, above the hook shank. This helps tighten the figure-eights and helps set the eyes in place. Finally, apply a tiny bit of Zap-A-Gap to the thread wraps.

If you wish, you can paint these eyes, but you'll need a type of paint that adheres to a very slick surface, because the bead chain is plated with a compound of some sort to make it shiny and stain-resistant. I haven't enjoyed much success with painting them, and so I use them as is.

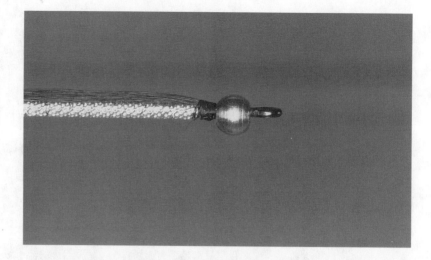

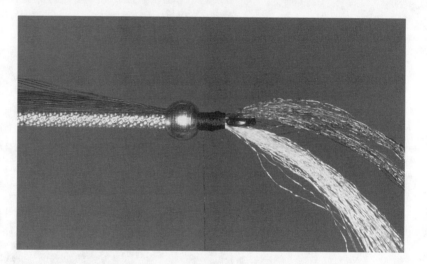

The steps in making a single-bead eye assembly.

The Single Bead

This technique was introduced in my book, *Mastering the Art of Fly Tying*. It was shown to me by the late Matt Vinciguerra, the wonderful photographer and fly tyer who worked with me on that book. I added a chapter about one of Matty's originals, the Beadyeye, to showcase this type of eye.

Matt Vinciguerra wasn't a writer and in fact was most reluctant to blow his own horn. For this reason, Matty's many innovative contributions to fly tying have not been publicized, or properly credited to him. For example, I got the idea for two of my favorite nymphs, the Perla Stonefly and the Isonychia, from prototypes developed by Matty. In addition to his tying and photography, he was a very hard worker for the environment. His passing was as unexpected as it was untimely, and we all miss the guy a lot.

Recently beads became available with holes drilled through the centers. At this writing, they are offered in several sizes and metallic colors, such as gold, silver, copper, and black. I wish Matty were around to enjoy these products, since they are just the thing for his beloved Beadyeyes.

A good-sized bead is required for this procedure. Slide it over the point of a debarbed hook, work it around the bend, and secure it in place near the eye of the hook with thread and perhaps some Zap-A-Gap. The remaining components are then tied in and folded back Thunder Creek style, top and bottom. Then, the head area is epoxied. A painted or mylar eye may be added prior to applying the epoxy, or the bead may be left plain.

Beads have become quite an item these days. We now see them as heads on many nymphs, Woolly Buggers, and similar flies, and it seems to enhance their effectiveness. I believe this is due to the jig-like action caused by the bead, which has always rendered otherwise sagacious fish quite vulnerable.

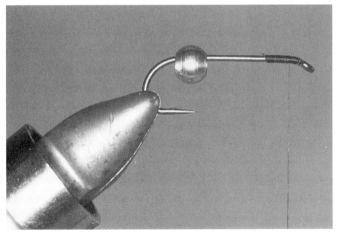

Bead about to be slid forward over thread base.

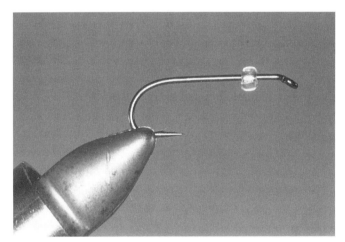

A glass bead.

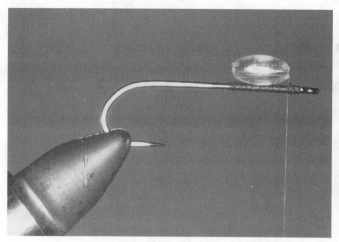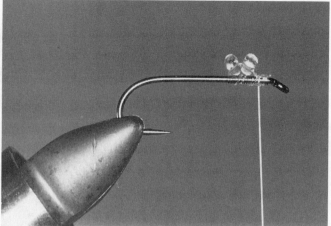

Methods for mounting various glass beads.

Dumbbells

These are a specialty item, created expressly for the fly-tying market, and sold in fly shops. They produce an effect rather similar to bead chain, but are considerably heavier because they are made of a lead-based compound. They come in several sizes and take paint nicely, except for the chrome-plated version. The method for tying them in place is the same as for bead chain.

Painting these things is, frankly, a pain in the neck. I'll relate my method but first, a message to the manufacturers: why not, as an option, offer dumbbells pre-painted? It shouldn't be difficult, in a processing facility, to paint these things by the thousands in white, yellow, gold, and maybe another shade or two. The small cost could be passed on to the consumer. Speaking for myself, I'd be delighted to pay a little extra for pre-painted dumbbells. Then, all one would have to do is dot on the pupils, which can be done when the dumbbell is in place on the fly. Who knows? By the time this book is out, this may be a reality.

Dumbbells can be easily painted after they are mounted on the hook. On some patterns, where the area around the head is clear, painting may be left until after the fly is completed. For durability, I recommend a finish coat of some hard-drying clear lacquer that uses a thinner that won't affect the paint. Epoxy is also great.

You may prefer to gang-paint dumbbells. My former method was this: I prepared a piece of thin cardboard by cutting a series of wedge-shaped slots in the edge. Into these, I inserted the dumbbells. I then painted on the base coat—white, yellow, or whatever—and let it dry thoroughly. Then I added the pupils, using the painted-eye dotting technique. Then I noticed an item in the "Tying Tips" section of *American Angler Magazine*. Some smart guy simply inserted the dumbbells between the teeth of a comb. Why couldn't I have thought of that? Incidentally, if you prefer, you can wait and add the dot after tying the dumbbell in place.

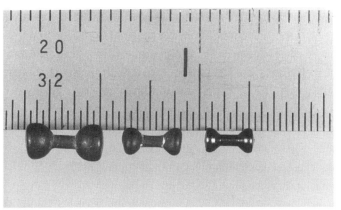

Lead dumbbells.

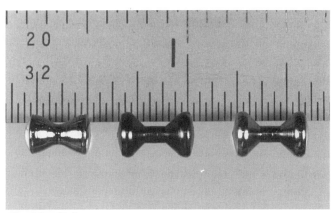

Plated dumbbells.

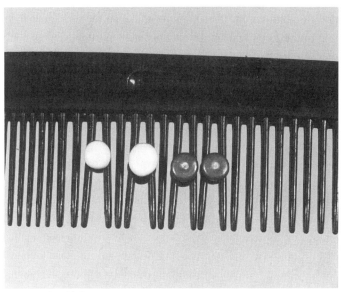

Painting dumbbells.

Whichever method you use, if the dumbbells are lead, you should soak them in vinegar before painting. This removes the casting resin, and is one more thing the manufacturers could easily do for us, if they so desired.

Be aware that dumbbells have a tendency to make flies turn over and ride upside-down. Bead chains do too, but not to such an extent. This isn't automatic—it depends on the construction of the rest of the fly. Also, dumbbells and beads will change the balance point of a fly, and may create a virtual jig. This can be great; the jigging action has been deadly for centuries.

At this writing a miniature variation of the dumbbell has made an appearance. These mini barbells are named Joe's Nymph Eyes, and are currently available in four sizes: large, medium, small, and extra-small. They are sold in packets, and are a bit pricey for what they are. However, I can see that there's a lot of nit-picky work involved in making them, and this, along with their usefulness, justifies the price.

These eyes are handled just like dumbbells or bead chain in that they are set in place with crisscross wraps of thread. A drop of adhesive on the thread wraps is a good idea. A coating of black lacquer turns them into things of beauty. I prefer to wait until the end to paint them, so that I don't have to deal with suspending them somehow until the paint dries. A tiny brush will do the trick.

A painted dumbbell eye.

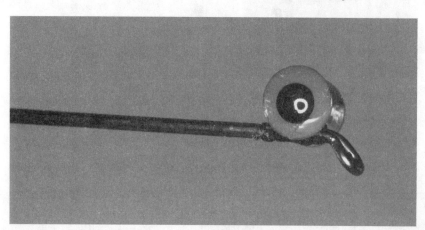

Problem with painted eyes on plated dumbbells: the paint can be easily scraped off.

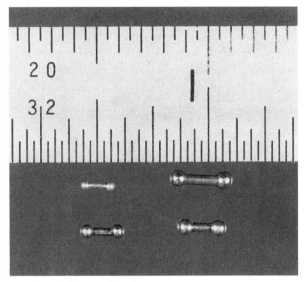

Joe's Nymph Eyes, various sizes.

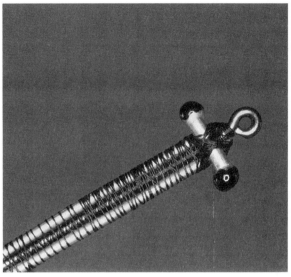

Joe's Nymph Eye in place, painted.

The Stemmed-Glass Eye

This very attractive and stylish eye is a bit pricey, but boy, what an effect! I don't see this item in a lot of catalogs, and that's probably due to their cost, which is a little beyond what the typical tyer is willing to pay.

The manner in which this eye is attached is simply this: The wire "stem" is bent to a right angle, and is then bound to the hook shank. Care must be taken to prepare and tie on both eyes in a near-identical manner, so that symmetry is achieved. The wrappings should then be coated with Zap-A-Gap.

The position at which the eyes are affixed depends on what sort of head is being created. For example, if a wool head is to be used, adequate space must be allocated behind the eyes, and in front. Other types of heads, such as the collar-and-yarn type shown in the photos, may require different positioning.

Stemmed glass eyes, mounted.

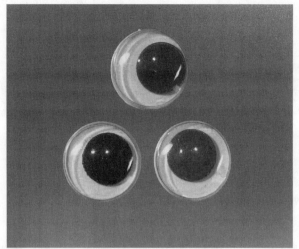

Doll eyes.

Doll eye on popper.

Doll eye on post.

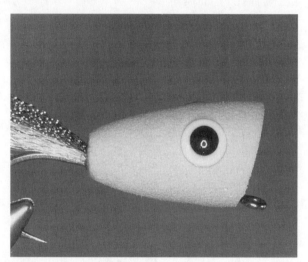

Doll eye mounted, with post inserted into popper material.

Doll Eyes

These are literally what the name implies—eyes that are used in making dolls and little souvenir-type animals, caricatures, toys, and what-have-you. They come in a wide range of sizes. Some have fixed pupils, others have free-floating ones that roll around inside the casing. How do fish react to being ogled at by rolling eyeballs? WHO KNOWS?!

Basically, the method for attaching these eyes is to simply glue them in place. They can be glued to a number of surfaces or materials, including clipped-hair heads and wool heads. A very powerful adhesive is required. A few of the best are Goop, or Shoe-Goo, Dow Corning's Urethane Bond, and five-minute epoxy. Contact cement and barge cement are also excellent, but require a very long drying process, up to two days, if you follow the instructions to the letter.

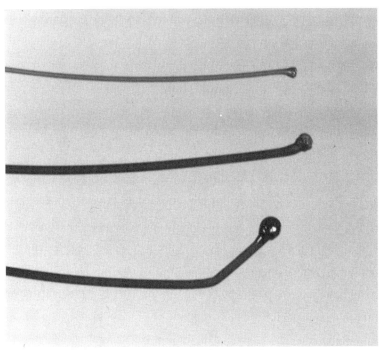

Singed monofilament eyes. The larger one has been painted.

The main thing is to do some testing to ascertain whether the adhesive will stick to the type of material in question. With natural materials, balsa wood, and most plastics, there is no incompatibility; but certain synthetics, and vinyl compounds in particular, will not bond with anything but very special adhesives, applied in a particular manner. You may have already learned this from trying to replace felts on vinyl wading shoes. It isn't simply a matter of obtaining vinyl cement. You must be able to duplicate the heat-and-pressure process used by the manufacturer—which didn't produce such a dependable result, either.

Melted Monofilament Eyes

These eyes look great, and are easy to make. One simply singes or burns the end of a piece of monofilament with a lighter, or other heat source. Almost instantly, a nice little ball forms. Remove the flame, blow out anything that's still burning, and in a few seconds, you have an eye. You can even control its shape and positioning to some extent by the angle at which you hold the mono while doing the melt job. If you hold it straight up and down, you'll get a perfectly round ball that is centered on the mono.

You can vary size to some extent by controlling how much you melt the material, but essentially the size of the eye is dictated by the diameter of the mono. You can make some very sizeable ones out of heavy shock tippet material in the sixty- to one hundred-pound class.

There are two methods for preparing a pair of eyes:

- Burn two pieces of mono, and tie them on separately, one on each side
- Burn both ends of a short piece, and tie it on as though it were a dumbbell eye

The first method requires that you bend the mono just behind the eyes, so that they stick out a bit. A pair of fine-nosed pliers will do the trick. The second method requires strict attention to controlling the burning process, so that the length of the mono between the eyes is just right for what you're tying. When tying these on, it helps to flatten out the mono in the middle with a firm pinch from the pliers.

You can color these eyes by dipping the round balls into some sort of lacquer and letting them dry. Black looks fantastic. Another very attractive effect is obtained by using the "traditional" dark Maxima material, not the new green stuff. This produces a shiny dark brown eye.

Novel and Interesting Materials

Possibly, by the time you read this, the products I'm about to describe will be old hat, obsolete, or replaced by others. But they are new now, or at least relatively so. They represent alternatives and facilitate innovation. For these reasons, they are worthy of our attention.

There is no direct relationship between these materials. I have chosen them because of their utility, and I will present them individually and independently.

Bugskin

This material is, simply, very finely sliced leather. It was discovered by Chuck Furimsky, noted fly-fishing-show entrepreneur, angler, fly tyer, and bon vivant. Chuck owns a leather goods shop at the Seven Springs Resort in Champion, Pennsylvania, where he began his series of fly-fishing symposiums. He noticed that the sample patches the leather goods salesmen brought in had very attractive markings and coloration, and appeared to be adaptable to certain fly-tying applications.

Chuck began to experiment with this material around 1991. Within a short period of time, he had created some remarkably realistic-looking patterns, including various nymphs, scuds, and crayfish. At first glance I was intrigued, but not 100% convinced. There were so many innovations taking place at the time that I was actually a bit put off by anything novel.

Then Chuck took me fishing on Spruce Creek. It was early season, and the hatches hadn't started yet. I was fooling around with an assortment of nymphs and gross-looking attractor patterns, and rolling the occasional fish. Meanwhile, thirty yards upstream, Chuck was sticking trout left and right—and big ones at that. I waved a white flag, and walked up to see what he had on. It was a little Bugskin crayfish, so small it didn't even hang over the edges of a quarter. That sold me.

Bugskin comes in small square pieces in plastic bags, with instructions and descriptive material. It is invariably thin, but does vary in that respect from piece to piece, and such variation can define its application. For instance, the thicker material is perfect for crayfish because it lends itself to making cutouts of the claws, and is the proper texture for forming the head, carapace, shell, and tail. The very thin stuff is great for making nymph wing cases and backs, scud shells, and other small components, for which the thicker material is a little too bulky. You'll need to consider this when buying Bugskin.

Bugskin has a finished side and a dull, soft side. Colors and shades run the gamut from black to light tans and beiges. Many are quite suggestive of insects, both in shade and texture. Others are brighter hued and some even have a chromed finish. These can be used to create novel patterns.

The examples shown here aren't even the tip of the iceberg. Bugskin has an enormous amount of potential, and as creative tyers begin to play with it, some astounding innovations are bound to occur. Surely the saltwater contingent will make many contributions in this area.

Cul de Canard (CDC)

I chose Russian, rather than French, for a second language, but I do know that "canard" is duck, "de" is a preposition meaning "of," and "cul" is something's rear end.

These feathers come from the backsides of ducks, from the area adjacent to the gland from which the birds obtain an oily secretion that they preen themselves with. Allegedly this substance gives feathers remarkable flotation properties. In fact, it is now being bottled and sold as a fly floatant. Thus, the rationale for using cul de canard feathers is that they will float a fly, even though they are very soft and pliable. A number of recent fly designs are based on this principle, including emergers that are supposed to ride in the surface film, and bob back up after being pulled under.

Recently, a gentleman who works for the Johnson's Wax Company did some studies of CDC. He attached split shot to both natural and dyed feathers to observe their flotation qualities. I should mention that prior to these experiments, it was believed that once the feathers were subjected to dyeing, the floating properties were greatly diminished, since the duck's secretion doesn't survive the dyeing process.

The feathers were dropped into a glass tank full of water, where they promptly sank, thanks to the split shot. Photos were taken through the tank, using a micro-lens. These revealed a myriad of air bubbles, trapped by the thousands of tiny filaments along the barbs. This phenomenon imbues the feathers with buoyancy. When the split shot were cut loose, the feathers rose to the surface. The oil had little, if anything, to do with flotation! This news should make the suppliers happy, since they were reimpregnating the feathers with CDC secretion to compensate for the effect of dyeing.

My experiences with this material are a mixed bag. When it is fresh and properly applied, it does float. Astream, the problem I encountered was that after a fish or two, the cul de canard was no longer buoyant. When I cleaned and dried it thoroughly with a desiccant, it responded, but was never as good as when new.

Still, this is an intriguing material. Its propensity for trapping air bubbles in its fibers produces an effect similar to that which occurs in the wings of natural emergers and spent flies. I particularly like the looks of it on emerger patterns, because of its life-suggesting action in the water. You might give it a try.

Wool Head Material

This stuff is, simply, sheep's fur. It may be from a particular kind of sheep, but I'm not sure. It is sold in packages in the usual assortment of dyed colors.

The main application of this material is in making shaped heads on various types of flies, such as sculpins and baitfish imitations. It is tied onto the hook in a 360-degree deployment, packed, and then trimmed to the desired shape. It can be supplemented with eyes, which can be tied in beforehand (e.g., dumbbells) or added later (e.g., doll eyes).

Tying wool head material in place is just about the same as tying in Glo-Bug yarn. You have to envelop the hook with the material before applying thread wraps. Hold it in place, and make several very tight wraps, one atop the other. Pack the wool, bring the thread in front, and make some wraps tight to the front of the bunch, forming a thread dam.

Repeat if desired, using as many bunches as you want. Then tie off, trim to shape, and add eyes, as desired.

Interesting and attractive effects can be obtained by using more than one color. The wool can be stacked on one side of the hook only, so if you want to make a baitfish imitation with, say, a green top and a yellow bottom, you can do it. You can also layer it to replicate the mottling of a sculpin head. But be forewarned—this is time-consuming, and takes practice.

You may find variance among the wool products of different packagers, because of the specific type of sheep involved. For example, Icelandic sheep have a denser, more heavily matted wool that is a little harder to work with but yields a more compact effect. I notice that prices per package vary considerably, while quantities appear to be the same. I cannot account for this, but there may be some justification, relative to quality and characteristics.

Bob Popovics, whose saltwater flies are works of art, has a nice technique that involves wool head material. After trimming to shape, he coats the wool with a clear silicone adhesive (actually, it's the caulking material commonly used to seal bathtubs and such). The result is a soft yet tough texture that probably feels to a fish very much like the little squid and other delicacies on its menu. This technique should have other applications as well, when we get around to figuring them out.

Closed-Cell Foam

This is an interesting and versatile material. Its two most important attributes are that it floats well, and it's durable. The most common application is making bodies for dry flies. It is particularly valuable when imitating terrestrials, which tend to float lower in the water than most aquatic insects do.

There are a number of methods for making foam, and the characteristics of the finished product depend on the methodology employed in its fabrication. Some processes utilize chemical reactions to form bubbles, or cells. This is okay, but it tends to interrupt and weaken the linkage between the molecules. This may cause problems in tying.

An alternative method produces what is called nitrogen-blown foam. At the time the plastic, which is a form of polyethylene, is ready for processing, it contains nitrogen, but not in gaseous form. By melting and mixing it in a closed vessel under pressure, and pumping in more nitrogen, the nitrogen is forced to dissolve in the material, just as nitrogen dissolves in the blood of a deep-sea diver who comes up from the depths too quickly. In other words, the plastic is given a case of the bends! When the pressure is released, the nitrogen comes out of solution and returns to its gaseous state, which expands the plastic into closed-cell foam. Quite a remarkable transformation.

The advantage of this type of foam lies in its strength. It can be tied to a hook without the thread cutting it. I have found this to be a great advantage when making my beetles, for which I use Flycraft Ultra Beetle blocks, which are made from nitrogen-blown foam.

Foam is available in the fly shops, in sheets, and also preformed into shapes that facilitate making certain types of bodies. The Flycraft Company offers Super Ants and Ultra Beetles. Both come die-cut, for instant use. The Super Ant bodies consist of small cylinders, the Ultra Beetles of oblong blocks. Both are simple to work with, and can be made into realistic bodies with no trimming. The ant bodies come in white, as well as black, and can be colored with a waterproof marker very easily.

Other products from Flycraft include grasshopper bodies, inchworm bodies, blue damsel fly bodies, frog bodies and legs, popper bodies, and white emerger floats for making wings on emerging nymphs. A great bonus are the hopper bodies available in a shade of orange that very closely matches the color of the giant Pteronarcys stonefly known out West as the salmon fly.

At this time there are also several other companies offering closed-cell foam in various forms. Rainy's sells it in continuous cylindrical form, in four different diameters, and four colors. Ligas, famous for their innovative dubbing products, offers foam in sheets, which can easily be cut to whatever shape is desired.

Closed-cell foam is particularly useful for larger flies, because the bigger the piece of material used, the better it floats. It's a simple matter to cut the material into shapes that closely simulate grasshoppers, crickets, and those huge Western stoneflies mentioned earlier. When formed into extended bodies, foam allows the use of smaller hooks, which reduces weight, and makes the hook less conspicuous. Coloration is also no problem because waterproof markers work quite well on closed-cell foam.

The application of foam that has probably had the greatest impact on fly tying and fishing is in making bass bug bodies. Before foam, these were formed out of such materials as balsa wood, cork, and plastic. They all worked, but forming shapes was time consuming and tedious, especially when starting from scratch. They also mandated the use of some sort of aberrant hook, with a hump or zigzag in the shank, to hold the body in position.

With preshaped foam, making attractive and effective bass flies is much easier and quicker. You simply select the shape and size body desired, and mount it on the hook. Add some feathers, and perhaps some rubber legs, and you have a bass bug. Some bodies come precolored, with various markings; others are pure white, and can be colored with Magic Markers.

I should observe that many anglers who fly fish for bass still prefer hair bugs. When tied with skill, they are certainly marvels of craftsmanship, and very good fish-catchers. Hair-tying geniuses such as Tim England, Joe Messinger Jr., Billy Munn, and Jimmy Nix have taken this school of tying to art-form level. On the other hand, how many tyers want to put forth the time and effort required to tie such flies with competence? It's a demanding and time-consuming task. The foam bugs are much less time-and-technique intensive, which leaves more time for fishing.

Rubberlegs Material

This material consists of fine rubber strands. These come in several colors, including white, brown, and black. They are easy to use, and very fishy. I still remember my first trip west in 1968, and nailing trout on Bitch Creeks and Girdle Bugs, much to the consternation of my dry-fly-purist fishing partner.

Besides making wiggly legs on nymphs and attractor flies, rubberlegs material is widely used to make "skirts" and "teasers" on bass flies. I've also seen it employed as legs on hopper, cricket, and beetle patterns.

There's not much technique involved with tying this stuff on. Basically, you just figure-eight it into place on the hook shank. Sometimes you may want to tie knots in it, to simulate the leg joints. In the case of foam or cork poppers, the bass-bug guys either poke holes or make slits in the bodies, and insert the rubberlegs strands.

Swisstraw

This product is a form of synthetic raffia. Real raffia is a type of tough reed, or grass. Historically it was used to make dry-fly extended bodies, since it was very light and floated well. It was also quite delicate, and thus produced what I would classify as "one-fish" flies.

Glo-Bug Yarn

This stuff is a thick, soft yarn for tying—well—Glo-Bugs! Glo-Bugs are egg patterns, designed to stimulate the appetite of redds-raiding fish that don't have to worry about cholesterol! It comes in quite a few colors, some of which are intended to match the eggs of specific species, such as the Sockeye. Others are more whimsically conceived, and bear labels like Cream Delight and Oregon Cheese.

By varying the number of skeins used at one time, you can make larger or smaller Glo-Bugs. They are tied on little, short-shanked, curved hooks, which are available in various sizes. I prefer colored hooks, such as gold or red, in that they are closer to the color of the fly. I recall with faint embarrassment those long-ago days when I fished for spring-spawning rainbows in swollen streams with real eggs! I soon discovered that they worked better on gold hooks.

These flies are a real no-brainer to tie, once you've done a few, and get the hang of it. One thing though: use very strong thread, because you really have to lean on it. There's no subtlety here. The technique is to first apply a thread base centered on a short-shanked hook. Then, the desired number of pieces of yarn are laid in place, top and bottom. My method is to use one bottom strand for every two top strands.

Next, several very tight wraps of strong thread are made dead-center around the yarn, one atop the other, while holding it in place. Don't allow it to spin, as you would deer hair. Then, tie off, and trim with a sort of rocking motion, while holding the yarn firmly top and bottom. Curved scissors with serrated blades help shape the egg.

Biots

Biots are simply the short, stiff fibers from the leading edge of a bird's wing. In fly-tying, they most commonly come from geese and turkeys. Usually they have been stripped of fuzz, but I have seen them used in their natural state as well. They can be purchased for a modest sum in most fly shops and come in an array of dyed colors, as well as natural.

Biots are generally used for making tails on nymphs, but I've also seen them used for legs or antennae. There is an improbable-looking but very effective fly called the Prince Nymph that calls for biot tails and wings, if one can call them that.

Microfibbets

While we are on the subject, let's briefly examine a synthetic tailing material for dry flies. They are called Microfibbets. I have no clue to the derivation of that name. I'm also not exactly sure what they are, but they look and behave like nylon paintbrush bristles.

They make excellent individual tails on spent patterns. I see that some tyers use them for regular fiber-bunch tails on traditional dry flies. My experience is that flotation is questionable for this application.

Altering Colors

As surfers seek the perfect wave, fly tyers pursue that elusive, magical color. They're always looking for a hue that is irresistible to them, if not the fish. In today's world, it's hard to believe that there is any color *not* available from a fly tackle dealer, but it does happen. Salmon-fly tyers in particular are always complaining about not being able to get exactly what they want. The answer to this is simply—create it yourself!

William T. Roubal (known to his friends as Ted) lives in the Pacific Northwest. He holds a PhD in the science of altering colors, i.e., dyeing and bleaching. In fact, he has an international reputation as an expert in the field. He even grows exotic plants in order to extract natural colorants from them. He's also a superb salmon-fly tyer.

Dr. Roubal wrote a series of five articles for *American Angler Magazine*. They appeared sequentially in five consecutive issues, as follows: Part 1, *Introduction and Preparation*, May/June 1994; Part 2, *Acid Dyes*, July/August 1994; Part 3, *Natural Product Colorants*, September/October 1994; Part 4, *Fiber-Reactive Dyes*, November/December 1994; and finally, Part 5, *Bleaching*, January/February 1995. These can be obtained from *American Angler Magazine*, 126 North St., Box 4100, Bennington, VT, 05201-4100.

I should also mention that the publisher of the magazine plans to bring out a book by Dr. Roubal which will cover all of the above material, and much more. It should be very useful to tyers, and especially so to those shops and distributors in the business of supplying materials. I don't have a publication date yet, but it will probably be out some time in 1995.

I also want to mention a book currently in print: *Dyeing and Bleaching*, by A.K. Best. As most of you know, A.K. is a superb fly tyer who turned out countless thousands of excellent flies in the years during which he tied commercially. He offers us a wealth of experience in his book, especially about how to handle materials that are about to be, or have just been, dyed. These notes, along with the dyestuffs and chemicals specified by Dr. Roubal, will enable the reader to successfully alter the colors of many types of fly-tying materials.

I'm not going to go into too much detail about dyeing in this chapter, simply because such information has already been published, and it is someone else's hard work and diligent research that compiled it. I do have permission from Dr. Roubal to use excerpts and references, and this I will do.

Let's start by examining three substances: muriatic acid, acetic acid, and Synthrapol. In Ted Roubal's words, if there's a magic elixir in dyeing, Synthrapol is it. It is what is called a sulfactant, and it is used in both the preparatory processes and in the dye baths themselves. It takes the place of the various soaps, detergents, and similar products we've all been using, and infinitely improves the entire process.

The other essential ingredient in a dye bath is acid of one of the two types mentioned. Here, we encounter a small complication. There are two types of sulphonic acid-base dyes commonly used by laymen in dyeing fly-tying materials: leveling acid and milling acid. While the two additive acids mentioned above will work interchangeably to a degree, I strongly recommend that the particular type be used in the dye bath that is optimal for the kind of acid dye you're using.

Leveling-acid dyes work best with some type of hydrochloric acid, such as muriatic acid, which is found in swimming pool supply stores and many larger hardware stores. Milling acid dyes work best with acetic acid, in the form of plain white vinegar. The problem then becomes identifying which type of dye you're about to use.

If you're ordering from a commercial dyestuffs catalog, it should tell you. Failing that, you can call there and find someone who understands the question, and can provide an answer. However, the common dyes that are readily available to the average tyer or fly shop often don't specify. Further, some of them don't use any of the standard names included in Dr. Roubal's color charts, which appear in Part 2 of his series of articles in *American Angler* Magazine. This makes absolute identification tough for laymen like you and me.

Let me tell you how I proceeded while doing the dyeing exercises for this chapter. Ted Roubal sent me samples of six dyes that he had formulated himself. For two of them, he specified the use of acetic acid; for the others, muriatic. I followed his instructions, and got very satisfactory results.

Then I began playing with some other dyes. Arbitrarily, I decided to follow the leveling-acid process, using muriatic. I dyed materials such as bucktail, goose shoulder feathers, hen and rooster feathers, goat, and calf tail. I used Veniard and Fly Dye products, and also a couple of others in unmarked containers given to me by people who couldn't remember where they got them.

In each case, I got a very good result. In some cases, it is possible that I unknowingly broke the rule about which acid to use with which type of dye, but seeing that what I did worked, I'm not too concerned about that.

I noticed that the two dyes that came with instructions—Veniard and Fly Dye—both called for vinegar. I think there are reasons for this. Probably, those suppliers want to lead people in the direction of very safe, household-type products that are readily available. Also, acetic acid is more forgiving than muriatic. It is recommended for milling-acid dyes because they sometimes tend to produce blotchy effects, and acetic acid mitigates this. Probably, a more conservative approach would have been to start with vinegar, and see what happened. Certainly, if I knew what I was working with, I would use the appropriate acid, as recommended by Ted Roubal.

At this juncture, I will make one observation about the information in A.K.'s book. He mentions the use of Rit dyes, clearly stating that some colors work well, and others not so well at all. Personally, I would suggest that you avoid Rit altogether. Here's why: Rit, Tintex, and such products are formulated to dye *fabrics*. God only knows what kind of fabrics, there's such a variety out there, both synthetic and natural, and combinations of the two. In order for the dye to work with as many materials as possible, the manufacturer combines a number of different dyes in one package. Of these, at least one is suitable for natural materials, so that a person can dye wool, cotton, or whatever.

Having said that, I will offer this advice: if you still want to use Rit and those sorts of dyes, treat them as though they are milling-acid dyes, and use the process specified for such. Basically, this means you should use acetic acid (white vinegar) as a fixative, not muriatic acid, or some other form of hydrochloric acid. Also, if you are using the powdered rather than liquid form, be sure to shake and mix it thoroughly, since these dyes contain salts which tend to fall out of mixture, and end up in the bottom of the package.

Rit, *et al.*, represent a major compromise, and one we don't have to live with. As Dr. Roubal explains in Part 2 of his series, there are excellent dyes available for dyeing fur and feathers without all the extraneous, and often interfering, agents found in grocery-store dyestuffs. These are what we should be using. They will produce consistent, dependable results, and great colors. Also, they are inexpensive to use, because so little dye is required. In his articles, Dr. Roubal mentions a number of suppliers. I'll list two of them here: Veniard Products, which are available through better fly shops, and Fly Dye, Organic Dyestuffs Corporation, Box 4258, East Providence, Rhode Island. Each offers dyes in a wide array of colors, in small quantities.

You can also purchase dyes from commercial sources. There are plenty of them listed in the Yellow Pages of major city phone directories under Dyes and Dyeing. You might also look under Weaving Supplies, Art Supplies, and Spinning Supplies. These sources can also supply you with the most important ingredient in the dyeing/bleaching process: synthrapol.

The problem with dealing directly with commercial dyestuff suppliers is that they don't want to sell dyes by the ounce. They want to sell them by the pound—and who could blame them? Considering that fly tyers use these dyes in ¼ and ½ ounce quantities, a pound of dye is an enormous amount. If you are planning on doing a lot of dyeing, and know some others who will be doing likewise, you could buy as a group, and split up the large lots into small quantities. Organizations such as Federation of Fly Fishers clubs, United Fly Tyers, Trout Unlimited chapters, and so forth might find this feasible.

Dyeing

Now let's step through a simple dyeing process. First, you should make sure that what you're going to dye is as clean and oil-free as possible. Materials that have been bought from fly shops are usually quite satisfactory in this regard already, because certain processing was required before they could be put on the market. Most critical are materials that will be dyed skin and all. Anything that's been tanned is definitely grease-free.

Materials that are acquired from hunting or other fresh-kill activities will need more preparation. It is most important that all fats and greases be removed from them. In the case of materials on skins such as bucktails, initial preparation is done via the scraping, salting, and boraxing steps specified earlier in the book. Scraping is terribly important. It may require a little effort, but it's worth it. So please don't rely on the borax/salt mixes to remove large amounts of fat; scrape off as much as you can.

Yes, the bane of fly tyers everywhere is greasy materials, and when dyeing is contemplated, that goes double. Synthrapol works magic as a degreaser, but in the case of really nasty stuff, I like to give it some help.

For instance, if I'm going to dye a cape or saddle that wasn't well-scraped by the grower, I'll put it in warm water with one-half teaspoon of synthrapol, and gradually heat up the water, stopping well short of simmering. I let it set for perhaps fifteen minutes. Then I pour it into the sink and let it cool for a bit. When it's sufficiently cooled to allow comfortable handling, I inspect the skin. If I see any grease, I take a butter knife and try to scrape off as I can, without ripping the skin. Then I proceed with the dyeing process.

Once the materials are essentially grease-free, the next step is to condition them for dyeing. Simply place them in a solution of water and synthrapol that will actually become the dye bath. Let's say you want to dye one average-size bucktail, chicken pelt, or an equivalent amount of loose feathers. Here's the procedure:

1. Put on a kitchen apron and a pair of rubber or vinyl gloves. Spread some newspapers around, and put some clear plastic wrap over them. This will protect your kitchen countertops, and save your marriage.

2. Use only stainless steel or enamelware vessels. For stirring and extracting, you can use either stainless steel or plastic implements, provided the plastic is of a type that will withstand the heat of the dye bath.

3. Pour forty-eight ounces of lukewarm water into the dyeing vessel. Stir in one-fourth teaspoon of synthrapol and one-half teaspoon of muriatic acid. If you know that you are going to be using a milling-acid dye, use instead six tablespoons of white vinegar.

4. Add the materials, and gently but thoroughly stir them around, so that they become completely wetted. Let them sit for five minutes.

5. Place the vessel on a burner, and turn up the heat to around medium. Meanwhile, mix one-fourth teaspoon of dye in a plastic cup

with a tablespoon or two of hot water. Try to get all of the dye to dissolve.

6. Stir the dye into the bath, mixing quickly and thoroughly. Allow the heat to rise, stirring gently from time to time.

7. Observe what's taking place in the dye bath. Some materials will take the color quickly, and at lower temperatures. Others require more time, more stirring, and more heat. But under no circumstances should you allow the mixture to boil or even simmer; stop short of that.

8. Be patient. Typically, dyeing will complete in ten to fifteen minutes. However, some materials may take longer. Hard hairs, such as bucktail and calf tail, generally require more time.

9. Remember that materials when wet appear a shade or so darker than when dry. You can test as you go by extracting a small sample, rinsing it, and zapping it with a hair dryer.

10. If you feel that sufficient time has elapsed, and you still don't have the color saturation you want, there are several things you can do. First, observe the dye bath. If it looks weak, that means you've about used up the available pigmentation. At this point, you can add a bit more dye, mixing it in a cup with a little hot water like before, and stirring it in. If you do this, also add a touch more acid. Or you can pour out the dye bath, mix up a new batch, and start over. In this case, watch closely, because the materials may respond very quickly, and become too dark.

11. Once you have your color, the next step is to bring the dyeing process to a conclusion. This varies with materials. If there are no skins involved, just pour everything into the sink, and rinse with lukewarm water. In the case of skins, it is important to allow the materials to cool gradually, under wet conditions. If you are sure that your dye bath has fully exhausted, meaning that all pigmentation has been used up and no further dyeing will occur, just take the vessel off the burner and allow the contents to cool gradually. However, if you can see that there is a potential for further coloration to occur, place the materials in a pot of warm water and let them slowly cool to room temperature. Then rinse, squeeze out excess water, and set out to dry.

Having mentioned exhausting the dye bath, I will explain what that means. Ideally, if the amount of material relative to the amount of dye and the integrity of the process is calculated correctly, you'll end up with the color you want, and a dye bath that's virtually clear. However, you probably won't quite achieve this optimal result, especially with leveling-acid dyes, which don't exhaust quite as thoroughly as milling-acid dyes. This is not a problem unless it's extreme, that is, unless you still have a lot of unused dyestuffs in the bath. This can be a real problem, not so much because of the wasted dye, but because it may very well affect the result.

Dyes are a composite of colors, some more so than others. When a dye bath is only partially exhausted, it is quite possible that one of the color components will predominate, since they are prone to "take" at different rates. Thus, you don't get the color you had planned on, and you may get something quite bizarre. This is another reason to be patient and to allow the dyeing process to fully complete before doing whatever comes next.

Drying

There's more to drying than just allowing water to evaporate. You want the materials to come out in the best possible condition. In the case of feathered pelts, such as chicken capes and saddles, rinse them with the water flowing *with* the natural attitude of the feathers. To remove excess water, I like to put a pad of paper towels under and on top of the pelt, and roll with a rolling pin; this keeps everything flat. I gently shake out the pelt, holding it by the front end, and then lay it on a paper plate to dry. If you're concerned about curling, tack it to a piece of cardboard. Items such as bucktails, pieces of deer hair, and similar materials do have a tendency to curl when drying, but this can be reduced to negligible proportions by letting the stuff cool slowly, as outlined.

Loose feathers can be dried in several ways. Goose shoulders and feathers of similar type can be laid out to dry, but steps must be taken to ensure that the natural shape of the feather is restored. The rinsing-and-rolling-pin process will remove excess fluids, but the feather will probably not look like it did when it came off the bird; the fibers will be matted. This can be corrected by allowing the feather to dry partially, then gently shaking it, and stroking the barbs into alignment. You can accelerate this by using a hair dryer, but you must be careful. A little too much heat can frizz the barbs. Also, feathers that are rapidly blown-dry may take on unnatural shaping, influenced by the force of the blown air.

Here's a great trick for drying goose shoulders, and the like: Put them in an old pillowcase, seal with a strong rubber band, and throw them in a clothes dryer. Add an old sneaker or tennis shoe, and run a delicate cycle. Sounds really weird, doesn't it? But it works just beautifully! When the feathers are removed from the pillowcase, they are in perfect shape. I thank Nick Wilder, proprietor of Hunter's Angling Supplies, for showing me that one.

In his book, A.K. Best describes a neat way to dry loose feathers, such as teal and mallard flanks, and loose hackle. He takes a pair of panty hose, cuts off most of the legs, and sews the holes shut. He puts the feathers in a large sieve, and pulls the waist part of the panty hose around the top, allowing the elastic to seal the opening. Then he blow-drys through the mesh of the sieve. Very neat. But as stated earlier, be careful not to get the blow-dryer too close to the feathers.

Having mentioned flank feathers, a few further words about them. Veniard puts out a dye called Summer Duck, which is used to dye mallard and teal flanks to simulate wood-duck flanks. It can produce a really nice result, if properly used. The first thing you'll want to do is to ascertain that the feathers you're intending to dye are worth the trouble. Look the batch over carefully. If they have a lot of broken or distressed ends, forget them.

Assuming a suitable batch of feathers, proceed as follows: For a half-ounce bag (that's a lot!), use the same quantities as previously specified. Place the feathers in the water-synthrapol-acid mix and let them soak for ten minutes, stirring now and then.

Mix the dye, but be very conservative; I actually use less than the ¼ ounce called for. The reason is that once the flank feathers have been synthrapolized, the dye takes very quickly. The first batch I did was actually rendered a little too dark in just three minutes, and at moderate heat. I used less dye the next time, and hit it right on the money in about four minutes. Then I did another batch, using 6 tablespoons of white vinegar, and got another beautiful result but over a slightly longer time period, and with a bit higher temperature.

Bleaching

Removing color from fly-tying materials is both possible and feasible, but it is somewhat more time-consuming, costly, and labor-intensive than dyeing. Ted Roubal described two methods in Part 5 of his *American Angler Magazine* series: one for feathers and another for materials that required and could withstand harsher treament. These included such items as deer hair, squirrel tails, and bucktails.

In a few cases, materials can be bleached to very interesting shades, and used as they come from the process. More commonly, we bleach materials in order to prepare them for dyeing. This is particularly true with feathers, where often we are trying to emulate something that's no longer available.

Here's a prime example of the latter. When I first began corresponding with Ted Roubal, he sent me a sample of some feathers from a bird known as the Blue-Earred Pheasant, which he had bleached and then dyed. A Blue-Earred Pheasant is an exotic domestically-grown bird with long-barbed feathers similar to heron. It is very dark dusky blue, nearly indigo in color. Salmon-fly tyers use it for spey-fly hackle, in place of heron, which is a no-no because of current environmental regulations.

I was awestruck! The feathers were dyed a variety of pinks, yellows, greens, and reds. All were much lighter shades than the natural. How had he done this? He told me that he had simply bleached the pheasant feathers to white, or virtually white, and dyed them.

A couple of months later, after negotiating permission to get advance copies of his article, I sat down and read through the process several times, writing down the names of the various chemicals I would need. After a few wild-goose chases and some finger-walking through the Yellow Pages, I was able to locate all of them. I put on my plastic apron, rubber gloves and goggles, took a deep breath, and went to work.

My first attempt involved bleaching a cream rooster saddle, a mottled tan-and-cream hen saddle, and some cock ringneck pheasant rump feathers.

I worked my way methodically through the process. To my amazement, the chicken feathers came out almost pure white! However, the pheasant feathers retained some of their color, but Ted Roubal had warned me they'd be tougher. Probably, they would have lightened further if I'd left them in longer. I plan to give them another shot some time soon.

Then, after several more deep breaths, I dipped into my bag of Blue-Earred Pheasant feathers, and selected about fifteen for bleaching. I gulped a little, because this is a scarce and costly material. I was extra careful to adhere closely to the Roubal process. To my absolute astonishment, it worked again! After running the bleached feathers through a derusting solution to remove residual oxides left by one of the chemicals, I was staring at a bunch of white feathers that had been dark blue a few hours earlier. I felt like a true alchemist.

I set aside a few white feathers for photography, and dyed the rest, using light, bright dyes. That worked, also. All I can say is that it made a believer out of me. I would never in my wildest dreams have believed such a thing was possible, let alone that I could actually do it.

For this process, you will need the following:

- Lots of distilled water (supermarket)
- Synthrapol, per earlier description
- Ferrous sulphate (garden supply stores)
- Ascorbic acid in liquid form (Vitamin C, nutrition store)
- Hydrogen peroxide, 20-weight (meaning 10%, beauty supply store)
- Glass vessels
- IMPORTANT: bodily protection! Rubber or vinyl gloves, goggles, apron, painter's mask—these items are easy to find

A word about ferrous sulphate. Dr. Roubal stated in his series of articles that his favorite had been Greenol, an Ortho brand product, but it was no longer available. His recommended substitute was Lilly Miller's Iron-Plus Chelate. No one in my part of the world had ever heard of it. Frustrated, I called the guru. Ted told me to look for a chelated ferrous sulphate product. I found the stuff at an Agway store. It was labeled "iron sulphate" and a faint recollection from high-school chemistry enabled me to translate that as being what I wanted. It was granular rather than liquid, as Greenol had been. Ted's instructions were to use one and a half to two tablespoons.

Here is the process, step-by-step:

1. Rinse the material to be bleached under a warm-water tap. Then soak it in two quarts of *distilled water* and one tablespoon of synthrapol for one hour, rocking the vessel from time to time to facilitate mixing.

2. Pour one and a half tablespoons of the ferrous sulphate, one teaspoon synthrapol, and one and a half quarts distilled water into a glass or enamelware (not metal) vessel. Remove the material to be bleached from the water/synthrapol, squeeze to damp-dry, and put it in the new mixture. Soak for one and a half hours, stirring occasionally.

3. Remove and rinse well with distilled water. Then soak material in one and a half quarts distilled water in fresh mixture as above, but adding one teaspoon of ascorbic acid.

4. Pour one pint of the peroxide into a non-metal vessel. Add one-half teaspoon of synthrapol. Rinse the material in distilled water and put it into the solution. Gently rock the vessel while adding, drop-by-drop, some household ammonia.

5. When the mixture begins to foam, stop adding the ammonia, but continue to rock the vessel occasionally. Observe the materials closely; you don't want to bleach them more than is necessary. If you see floating particles, you've overdone it; stop the process immediately. Keep in mind that the materials will be slightly tannish—that's ferric residue. In my experiments, the Blue-Earred Pheasant bleached in about twenty minutes, as did the chicken feathers. The ringneck rump feathers still showed some coloration after forty-five minutes.

As I've mentioned, after bleaching, the feathers will be slightly tannish. Ted Roubal says this probably won't interfere with dyeing. However, if you want to get rid of it, soak the material in a dilute solution of fabric rust remover. Rit makes such a product. According to Ted, it may not be the best stuff for the job, because it contains sodiums that could harm the feathers. I couldn't find an alternative product that didn't contain sodium, so I went ahead and used the Rit, in dilute solution, leaving the feathers in just long enough for the rust to vanish. It worked, and from what I can tell, the feathers were not damaged.

You can now dye these materials to whatever color you please. Bleached materials dye best with leveling-acid dyes and natural colorants.

The second method for bleaching is much simpler and faster. It is also significantly more powerful, and should only be used with hairs, furs and tougher materials that can withstand the process. Even with them, you must be attentive, and not overbleach.

Here are the products you'll need:

- Lady Clairol Basic White Bleach (beauty supply store)

- Synthrapol, 20-volume peroxide, distilled water, vinegar

SERIOUSLY: Don't proceed without putting on the protective items listed previously. The painter's mask is particularly important here, as the Lady Clairol is a powder, and you don't want to inhale it. Here's the process:

1. Mix one-half cup Lady Clairol Basic White Bleach, three-fourths cup 20-volume peroxide, and one-fourth teaspoon synthrapol in a glass vessel until a paste is formed.

2. Rinse the material under tap water, then again in distilled water containing a little synthrapol. Work the paste into the materials, using a plastic spoon. It will soon begin to foam. Keep working it in. The more you do so, the shorter the time required, and the less chance you'll

run of overbleaching. When the desired results are achieved, remove the materials and rinse with tap water, then add in one quart of distilled water containing one-fourth cup of white vinegar, and rinse again under tap water.

Softer hairs, such as deer and caribou, bleach fast. For these types of materials about fifteen minutes will suffice. However, they are the most susceptible to overbleaching. Harder hairs, such as squirrel tail, are less easily damaged, but require more time, perhaps as much as an hour. It depends on just how much color you want to remove. Both gray and fox squirrel tails bleach to a very pretty amber shade quite quickly, and make great streamers and saltwater flies as is. If you want to render them light enough for subsequent dyeing, that takes longer.

Here's a suggestion that is helpful in either method of bleaching: include a small extra piece of the material being bleached. It can be removed periodically, rinsed, and blow-dried. Thus, you can track progress closely, and avoid overbleaching. It's also a good idea to keep a record of exactly how much time was required.

After rinsing and drying bleached materials, I noticed that they were rather dry in texture. I found that treating them with a common hair-conditioner, then rinsing it out thoroughly in cool water helped restore a more natural texture. If you're going to dye the material, wait until after dyeing to do this.

In summary, I hope that at some point I'll be able to find two items: a liquid ferrous sulphate chelate that is easier to work with than the granular stuff, and an alternative to the Rit derusting product that Ted Roubal warned me about. It has worked okay for me so far, but I'm nervous about it.

The Hair-Dye Method

Of all the helpful products and processes that have come along in recent years, the use of hair dyes on hackle feathers is near the top of the list. The guy who's done the most remarkable work with this is Ted Hebert, who raises those superb genetic chickens in Michigan. With advice and counsel from a local hairdresser, Ted has learned how to convert capes that are great in quality, but off the mark in color, into genuine treasures.

Several years ago, Ted handed me a rich, dark coachman brown cape. I gasped. The feathers were of magnificent quality, and up until then, no one had been able to produce both quality and color in this shade. I asked Ted how he had finally managed to pull it off. He just smiled, and told me to look the cape over carefully, which I proceeded to do. Except for its beauty, I saw nothing unusual about it.

After letting me dangle in puzzlement for a few minutes, Ted told me the secret; the cape was dyed! I couldn't believe this, since there was no dye on the skin. Then he told me that he had removed the cape from the bird, but hadn't skinned it out until after the dyeing process. What a wonderful, sneaky trick! I am not able to perceive any significant difference between these capes and Ted's naturals.

You can also do this at home. True, you won't be able to avoid coloring the skin on the back of a cape, because it will already have been skinned out by the time you get it. However, that won't affect the feathers. With Ted Hebert's permission and assistance, I'll describe the process, and give you a few recipes.

Actually, the process is a "no-brainer," because all you're going to do is follow the instructions in the dye kit, which you will buy across the counter in any store where such items are sold. In the package, you'll see a tube or plastic bag of conditioner. Get rid of that—it's for replacing the natural oils in one's hair that dyeing removes, and if you applied it to a rooster cape, you'd have a disaster on your hands.

A few important tips. Operate in a fairly warm room, with the temperature up around 78 to 80 degrees Fahrenheit. Use good-quality water. If your tap water is more than a little bit hard, you're going to get some strange colors. To be on the safe side it's best to buy some distilled water at the supermarket. When dyeing, keep the water as close to 98.6 degrees as possible, since that's body temperature, and that is what the dyes were designed to accommodate. Use pro-grade hydrogen peroxide, which is labeled 20-weight, or 10%.

I also must strongly emphasize the safety precautions that should be followed during this process. As both Ted Hebert and Ted Roubal point out, these dyes and the chemicals that go with them are among the more potent substances with which one might come in contact when altering colors. So please remember: use rubber or vinyl gloves, eye protection, and all that good stuff.

One dye kit will do up to five capes or saddles. You can vary the shades a bit by taking some of them out of the dye sooner than others. Remember that feathers are lighter when dry by a shade or so, but don't let them get more than one shade beyond what you want. Dyeing usually requires thirty to forty-five minutes, but keep a close watch. These catalytic dyes are very strong-bonding, and won't lose color while being rinsed. To maintain the overall size of the cape or saddle, tack it out while drying, to prevent the skin from shrinking.

Preparation is simple enough. A well-scraped genetic pelt needs only to be rinsed in a weak mixture of synthrapol and water. For this, see the instructions for the dyeing and bleaching methods covered earlier. If the pelts are greasy, follow that process. IMPORTANT! Put on your old clothes, plastic apron, rubber gloves, and goggles. This is not dangerous stuff, but it is very persistent.

Here are four favorite Hebert recipes:

- Coachman Brown. Start with feathers that are medium brown. Use Loreal Red Label, Natural Black Preference. Watch closely; it can get too dark rather quickly.
- Straw Cream. Start with a very pale-colored neck, such as off-white or creamy white. Here you'll be mixing two dyes: Wella Gold II and Very Light Blonde, the latter making up seventy-five percent of the com-

posite. Err on the light side—you can always correct to darker, but not the reverse.

- Hebert's Olive. Start with the same sort of color as for the straw, or a dirty cream. Use Loreal Blue Label, Excellence Bark Brown.
- Light/Medium Dun. Use pale feathers, as specified previously. The dye is Loreal Blue Label, Excellence Ash Blonde.

This will give you a light to medium dun. Darker duns are a problem with hair dyes; Ted informs me that often unanticipated and unwanted shades predominate. If you want medium gray dun, revert to the hot dye process described earlier. Veniard's dyes will work for this, and so will Fly Dye products. You should test with small amounts of the material to be dyed, to be sure the color will be what you're looking for. The important thing is to follow the Roubal method, and use his recommended chemicals. See the color pages for examples of Hebert hair-dyed colors.

Felt Markers

The use of felt marking pens is not all that recent a development in fly tying. My first encounter with them dates back approximately twenty-five years. Around that time, or shortly thereafter, they became all the rage. Someone discovered the Pantone brand, a high-quality line of waterproof markers with over a hundred colors. There were the inevitable magazine articles and soon many fly shops were stocking the product.

Markers do have some application in fly tying. For instance, you can take a piece of white closed-cell foam and daub it up to whatever color you want. Using this method, you can produce a nice Cinnamon Ant, or Black/Brown Ant, or Japanese Beetle.

I use markers to alter the color of the thread at the head of a fly, where I've tied off, because I often use pale-colored thread to blend with the body material, but I still want a more natural-looking head. This can be done in two ways: you can run the marker up and down the thread a couple of times, then make the whip-finish, or you can simply tint the finish knot. In any event, tint before applying head lacquer.

One cautionary note: Don't use a felt marker in conjunction with Zap-A-Gap, or any cyanoacrilate adhesive. The thinners will fight, and you'll see some rather startling colors as a result. I found this out the hard way. I was trying to darken up some stripped hackle quills in order to better simulate the body color of the male Hendrickson. The marker rendered the quills exactly the shade I wanted, so I proceeded to tie up a bunch of Red Quills. Then I tried to reinforce the bodies as I always do, with Zap-A-Gap. They turned a wild bright pink! Who knows, maybe I should have fished them anyway.

Innovate!

I hope that the information I've offered in this book proves to be helpful to all of you. Beyond that, I also hope that it ignites a spirit of innovation. I have always felt that thorough understanding and subsequent refinements of technique are the foundation of successful fly tying. I also feel that creativity is the next step, the new frontier.

We are seeing it all the time these days in the efforts of people like Bob Popovics, Jack Gartside, Toril Kolbu of Norway, John Goddard of England. I could name dozens more.

For example, there's Chuck Furimsky. I mentioned him elsewhere in the book. He's the Bugskin man. Within fly-fishing circles, Chuck is better known as the entrepreneur who puts on several excellent shows each year, notably the Fly Fishing Show, presently being held at the Garden State Exhibit Center in Somerset, New Jersey, and the International Fly-Tying Symposium, which last year was held at the South Jersey Expo in Pennsauken, New Jersey. To his closer friends, Chuck is known as a constant and persistent innovator who can spot a potential fly-tying material anywhere from a supermarket to a landfill.

Just as I was finishing up this book, Chuck sent me a box of stuff. He was taking a semi-vacation at his Jersey Shore place, and had happened onto a large crafts store nearby. Chuck is really dangerous in such an environment. It's like turning an ice cream addict loose in Ben & Jerry's.

The following are several examples of what Chuck came up with last summer. The items he picked up in the crafts store included various types of beads, some glittery stuff, and a most remarkable substance that carries the trade name Sculpey III. This last item is a clay-like material that can readily be formed around a hook shank into practically any shape one might wish. Then it is baked at 275 degrees Fahrenheit for ten to twelve minutes. This hardens the clay, and voila! You have an underbody that can be supplemented with tying materials, painted, or whatever you choose. The color pages show several different forms molded by Chuck, and the finished flies that resulted. Note the addition of beads and glitter, which were impressed into the clay before baking.

Chuck also purchased a type of bead called Indian beads. Perhaps these are the contemporary version of the ones that bought us Manhattan Island. These beads have holes in them large enough to pass over either the eye or barb of a pretty good-sized hook. Once mounted this way, a compatible sort of fly is tied and the front part, including the bead, is epoxied. A stick-on eye can be added prior to the epoxy, if desired. This facilitates the tying of a very serviceable, durable saltwater or freshwater fly, quickly and at very low cost. See the color section for examples.

The only way this book can be ended is that I declare it so—and I do, herewith. I hope that I've been able to create some order out of the chaos. And remember what I told you in the introduction about substitution: *if it eats grass, gives milk, and says moo, it's a cow!*

My very best wishes for tying success and pleasure.

Bibliography

Bates, Jr., Joseph D. *Streamer Fly Tying and Fishing*. Harrisburg; Stackpole Books, 1950.

Best, A.K. *Dyeing and Bleaching*. New York; Lyons & Burford, 1993.

Boyle, Robert H. and Whitlock, Dave. *The Fly Tyer's Almanac*. New York; Crown Publishers, Inc., 1975.

Camera, Phil. *Fly Tying with Synthetics*. Stillwater; Voyageur Press, 1992.

Gartside, Jack. *Fly Patterns for the Adventurous Tyer* and *Flies for the 21st Century*. Boston; privately printed.

Leisenring, James E. and Hidy, Vernon S. *The Art of Tying the Wet Fly and Fishing the Flymph*. New York; Crown Publishers, Inc., 1971.

Leonard, J. Edson. *Flies*. New York; Lyons & Burford, 1989.

Marinaro, Vincent C. *A Modern Dry Fly Code*. New York; Crown Publishers, Inc., 1970.

Stewart, Dick. *The Hook Book*. Intervale; Northland Press, Inc., 1986.

Talleur, Dick. *Mastering the Art of Fly Tying*. Harrisburg; Stackpole Books, 1979.

Talleur, Dick. *The Versatile Fly Tyer*. New York; Lyons & Burford, 1990.

Index